AF553524

POLITICAL IDEAS
AND
INSTITUTIONS

Compiled & Edited
by
Dr. R.K. Pruthi

First Published-2005

ISBN 81-8356-015-6

Published by

DISCOVERY PUBLISHING HOUSE
4831/24, Ansari Road, Prahlad Street,
Darya Ganj, New Delhi-110002 (India)
Phone: 23279245 • Fax: 91-11-23253475
E-mail:dphtemp@indiatimes.com

Printed at:
Arora Offset Press
Laxmi Nagar, Delhi 110 092.

Preface

Political ideas and institutions are the norms to guide human action. When an individual comes into contact with these norms a number of problems arise which need conceptual clarity. Why do they arise? What effect do they have on society? How have political scientists looked at these concepts?

Aim of this book is to deal with some of these questions relating to political ideas and institutions. Effort has been made to select material interesting and important for the use of students as well as teachers.

In preparing this book we have incurred gratitude of the authorities on the subject. We record our acknowledgements to them.

Librarians and their staff members have been kind and co-operative. We thank them all.

My publisher and his staff members have rendered every possible assistance. They deserve my readers love and patronage.

R.K. Pruthi

Contents

Functions of The State

Many political thinkers and philosophers have tried to answer the question about the end or purpose of the state. The question is in a way very simple and easy to be answered. But deep thinking about it shows that it is not so. In the light of their own ideas political thinkers have given different answers. Among the various schools of thought, the anarchists alone say that the state is an evil, which should be eliminated.

State to Serve Social Needs: The state was organised not for its own sake but for the purpose of meeting the needs of society. Most of the schools of political thought today regard the state as a means and not as an end in itself. We shall briefly review the evolution of thought on the ends and functions of the State.

1. Greek View

Partnership of Virtue and Goodness. The Ancient Greeks regarded the city-state as an end in itself, and the individual was supposed to enter a partnership with the city-state for a life of virtue and goodness. Conditions in ancient Greek city-states were quite different from those in modern states. Aristotle say that the state arose for the sake of life and continues for the sake of good life. (In modern times, writers like Hegel regarded the state as a super personality and looked upon it as an end in itself.)

No Rights against State. In modern times, most of the writers took into consideration the rights of the individual, while fixing the end or purpose of the state. But in ancient Greece the concept of the rights of the individual against the state as such did not prevail. Though the Greeks loved liberty of thought and action, they could never think of resisting the state, as they could not claim any personal freedom against the state. Even the great philosopher Socrates thought it was better to die by consuming hemlock than disobeying state order. Hence he died in prison as ordered by the state, though it was possible for him to escape death.

Slave-Owning States. All persons in a Geek city-state were not citizens. Women, manual labourers, slaves and foreigners were not citizens. Citizens, who formed a minority, needed leisure to discharge their responsibilities of citizenship. Therefore, they were served by slaves. It seems strange to the modern mind that liberty and slavery could co-exist in ancient Greece. In modern times, slavery is condemned and declared illegal. It can never go along with liberty in a modern state. Greek philosophers like Plato and Aristotle upheld and justified the institution of slavery.

Happy and Ethically Self-Sufficient Life. The great Greek philosophers considered the state as self-sufficient (no economically but ethically) and its end or purpose was a happy and self-sufficing life. Today we regard the state as a legal structure: but the Greeks considered it as an ethical society having a moral end. While political science to modern scholars is an inexact social science dealing with the problems of state and government, politics in the hand of the Greeks was an ethics of the whole society. In his *Republic* Plato fixed very high ideals for the rulers or philosopher-kings or guardians of the Republic. He underlined the importance of the superiority of virtue and the good and happiness of the community. The high aims of the state, according to Plato, could be realised through the rule of the philosopher-kings. Aristotle dealt with the true and false ends of the state. Normal forms of government worked for the true end, while the perverted ones for the false.

2. Roman View

State Not an End in Itself. The Romans, who were practical-minded conquerors, law-givers and statesmen, did not regard the state as self-sufficient, and never spoke in terms of entering into a life-partnership with the state. Though Rome was originally a city-state, she in course of time became the mistress of a mighty empire;

and hence had a wider scope to rule and evolve political principles than what Athens, the proudest city-state of Greece, could have.

3. Medieval View

State viewed through Religious Angle. In the middle ages, the Christian writers had implicit faith in the Church and could not think objectively about the true end of the state. Many medieval writers regarded the state as an instrument to safeguard the interests of the church. The ecclesiastical writers looked at the state through the religious angle.

4. Modern View

Society to be Distinguished from State. In understanding the purpose of the state in modern times, it has to be noted that society and state are not the same and a clear line of difference has to be drawn between the two. Society represents a large and complex network of human relationships whereas the state, the highest form of association, is a politically organised society in a given territory. In society, besides the state, there are many associations; but the state alone exercises sovereignty. In order to understand the proper sphere of functions of state, it should be realised that there is a basic difference between society and state. If the two are put on a par, there will arise an erroneous idea regarding the functions of state, and those who are in power in a state will try to bring under their control the entire range of human activity. This will sound the death knell of the individual's liberty.

State only a Means to an End. Modern writers (except those who advocate totalitarianism) do not regard the state as an end in itself. It is only a means to an end. The state exists for the sake of human beings and not *vice versa;* it is an agent or instrument of human beings living in society. Just as the individual's rights in a state are subject to reasonable restraints, the sovereignty of the state too is subject to limitations imposed by the basic and inalienable rights of the individual.

Totalitarianism. Only the advocates of totalitarianism and those why say that the state is an end in itself accept the view that the state can do whatever it like and there can be no restrictions on its authority. The Fascists in Mussolini's Italy and the Nazis in Hitlerite Germany stood for totalitarian control and regimentation of life. Their principle was: "Every thing for the state; nothing against the state; nothing outside the state." If the state is made omnipotent, it will also means that the men who form the government will exercise power without any restraints. A state acting through its government should not be allowed to control all aspects of a human being's life, but only some of them. If we make no distinction between state and society, and give unqualified powers to the state to deal with all human relationships and all human activates, the individual will lose all his liberty. It is of utmost importance, therefore, to draw a clear line of distinction between state and society.

Concept of Police State. Till the 19th century, most of the rulers who were absolute monarchs had a very narrow view of their duties and responsibilities. They thought they had unlimited powers and that people had very limited rights. Some of them even thought that the whole state was their private property, which they could use as they pleased. Very few were the kings who worked hard for the welfare of the people. People were expected to obey the laws implicitly even if the rulers neglected their duties. For a long time, states limited their functions to a narrow sphere, and did not do much beyond maintaining law and order and collecting taxes.

Concept of Welfare or Social Service State. In the 19th century, the concept of the police state was discredited and thrown overboard, and the concept of the welfare state or the social service state started gaining ground. The utilitarians spoke of the state promoting the greatest happiness of the greatest numbers. In the same century, individualists said that the aim of the state was only to maintain law and order. With the rise of socialism of various types the concept of the welfare state received further impetus. The state came to be regarded more and more as an agency of social service and not as an agency of power. Power should be employed for upholding law and order, maintaining justice and promoting the happiness of the people. It should not be forgotten that the state stands also for a fellowship of human beings for a happy and purposeful life. The state should discharge its functions in such a manner that it enriches common life. MacIver says on page 340 in *The Web of Government* (1959): "The great expansion in recent times of functions of general welfare is tending more than anything else to foster new conceptions of. the nature of the state. It puts government into more familiar and more co-operative relations with the ordinary man." If the state fails to promote the well-being of the people, its very existence becomes meaningless.

View of Burgess. The American political scientist, John W. Burgess, mentions three ends of state: (1) The primary end is the foundation and adjustment of government and liberty. (2) The secondary end is the perfection of the principle of nationality and the cultivation of national genius. (3) The ultimate end is the perfection of humanity.

View of Garner. In *Political Science and Government*, J.W. Garner points out three kinds of ends of state: (1) The primary and immediate end of the state of the maintenance of peace, order and justice among individuals. (2) The secondary end of the state is to meet the larger collective needs of society and promote welfare and national progress. (3) The ultimate and highest end is the promotion of the civilisation of mankind at large.

F.G. *Wilson's View:* In *The Elements of Modern Politics*, Francis Graham Wilson mentions the ends of the modern welfare state: (1) the satisfaction of wills; (2) the realisation of moral progress; (3) the achievement of the greatest happiness of the greatest number; (4) the development of the individual's personality; (5) the upholding of rights; and (6) the balancing and protection of interests.

Meaning and Aim of Functions of State

We may briefly examine the meaning and aim of functions of state.

Sense of Purpose and Realizing that Purpose. Ernest Barker says on page 340 in *The Web of Government* (1959) that the word *function* can be understood in two senses: (1) the sense of purpose or aim: and (2) the sense of a particular mode of action. In the first sense we speak of the state in general terms of the maintenance of a scheme of law or the service of rights or some other such aim." In the second sense, we speak of a special kind of activity, by means of which a government seeks to fulfil its general purpose and from this point of view we speak of the legislative, judicial or executive function."

Aristotle. Aristotle very briefly mentions the purpose of the state. The state exists for the sake of life and continues for the sake of good life.

John Locke. John Locke say that the purpose of the state is the "common good" or the "good of mankind".

Adam Smith. Adam Smith points out three purposes of the state: (1) protection from foreign aggression or internal violence; (2) protection of every individual from injustice and oppression; and (3) creation and maintenance of certain works and public institutions, which will not be possible by individuals or groups.

Aim of Realizing Human Happiness. Edward J. Urwick says on pages 10 and 14 in his book *The Social Good* (1927) that the realisation of human good or happiness is the ultimate aim of the state. He mentions five essentials of happiness: (10 "Work if possible, congenial work, but in any case work." (2) "Strong interests, and opportunity to develop such interests." (3) "The companionship of the people whom we like and who like us; and therefore, constant reciprocity of service." (4) "An ideal to live for in ourselves, if not outside." (5) "Immunity from severe physical hindrances."

Each one of these principles is of paramount significance to the development of individuals' personality and the promotion of his happiness. If the state enables the individual to realize his *good* or happiness, obedience to the state will be worth his while, and it is bound to be spontaneous and never reluctant.

Functions of State connected with the Rights of the Individual. The functions of state are intimately connected with the rights of the individual. The individual cannot have rights, if state fails to discharge its functions properly. Ernest Barker points out on page 262 in *Principles of Social and Political Theory* (1953): "Functions of government cannot be separated from rights of persons, except in the sense in which the reverse of a coin can be distinguished from the obverse." A state is supposed to render service to the community in upholding the rights of its members. "All authority and all functions of government, including the functions of immediate sovereignty are services owed to rights." (*Ibid,* p. 223).

Development of Personality. In upholding the rights of the individual, the state upholds the dignity of his personality and provides the widest scope for its development. R.M. MacIver says on page 150 in *The Modern State* (1950): "To establish order and to respect personality, these are the essential tasks positive and negative of the state and if we can follow out their implications we shall discover aright both its limits."

KINDS OF FUNCTIONS OF STATE

Broadly speaking, the functions of the state can be brought under two categories: (1) Protective or Police Functions; and (2) Welfare Functions.

1. Protective or Police Functions

Essential Functions. The most essential function of the state are called protective or police functions. The following police functions may be enumerated:

1. *Upholding Sovereignty and Protecting Life and Property.* The primary function of the state is to uphold its own sovereignty, that is, its own essence. The state should protect the individual's life and property, and save him from internal disorder and external aggression. This function is so essential that without it the state cannot survive.

2. *Making Laws.* The state has to make law for upholding sovereignty. It has to enforce obedience to law and maintain order and conditions of perfect security to life and property.

The state has to maintain in modern times well trained armies, navies, air forces and police forces to meet the requirements of law and order.

3. *Giving Impartial Justice.* The state has the very important function of punishing those who violate law and giving impartial justice. For this it has to organize a network of courts in which learned, experienced and impartial judges interpret law and mete out justice.

4. *Protecting Good and Useful Institutions.* The state should protect various types of good and useful political, social, economic, cultural and religious institutions and make laws for their proper protection and maintenance. For example, it has to protect the family and make laws pertaining to marriage, divorce, inheritance, adoption custody of children and other matters. The state should eradicate evil institutions like slavery, child marriage, human sacrifice, polygamy, polyandry and bonded labour.

5. *Organizing Means of Transport and Communications.* Another important function of the state is to organize efficiently means of transport and communication. Building of railways, roads, airports and harbours, maintaining them in good condition and running an orderly postal, telegraph and telephone system are among the essential functions in this connection. In modern times, when the world has shrunk owing to the elimination of time, and distance, the importance of highly developed means of transport and communications is indeed great.

6. *Regulating Markets.* The state should regulate markets, mint coin and money, inspect weights and measures, control prices and so on. Many such functions are put in charge of local self-government institutions over which government exercises only a distant supervision.

7. *Maintaining Foreign Relations.* A state has to maintain friendly relations with foreign states for trade and commerce, and political and diplomatic purposes.

Besides these, there are several other functions which may be regarded as protective. In ancient, medieval and early modern times, some states did not do full justice even to these primary functions. These states were keen only in collecting taxes and keeping the people in subjection with the help of the army and the police.

1. Welfare Functions

Need to Promote Social Welfare. It has been realised everywhere in the modern world that the state has to go far beyond the performance of the protective or police functions. No modern state regards itself as a mere tax-gathering and police organisation, and great emphasis is laid on the need to promote social welfare. While the principle of the welfare state has been accepted all over the world, all states have not progressed equally in discharging their social welfare obligations.

India a Welfare State. Under the Constitution of India (1950), the state has to reach the ideal of social welfare and justice. The Union and State Governments shall steadily move forward along the road leading to the welfare of all by following the guidelines given in the Directive Principles of State Policy. Since the commencement of the Constitution, much has been done, but much more yet to be done to reach the target.

Owing to many difficult problems and obstacles, India lags far behind the highly advanced countries of the West in providing social services. Many countries in the world had an unfortunate history, which put them on a lower level than that of the Western countries.

THE WELFARE STATE

Welfare State Concept a Guiding Star. The emergence of the concept of the welfare state has added new dimension to the discussion on the end and functions of the state. It has revolutionised the very concept of the state and its numerous obligations and services. The welfare or service concept has become guiding star to all states: the highly advanced Western

States and the developing states of the Afro-Asian countries and Latin America. In modern times, a state can be easily singled out, if it fails to promote the happiness and welfare of its citizens.

Meaning of Welfare State. The political scientist faces the same difficulty in giving an agreed definition of the welfare state as he finds in defining terms like nation, liberty and equality. A precise definition accepted by all is not available, as opinions differ on its connotation. However, it is possible to mention the features or qualities of a welfare state. The welfare state is one which is wedded to the principle of promoting the general happiness and welfare of the people. It regards itself more as an agency of social service than as an instrument of power. It draws up all types of plans according to its resources, the genius of the people and the ability and integrity of the administrators. The range of ministrant or service activity of the state for promoting human welfare and happiness is becoming wider and wider in recent times. G.D.H. Cole gives a fairly good definition of welfare state. "The welfare state is a society in which an assured minimum standard of living and opportunity becomes the possession of every citizen." [Quoted in Herbert L. Marx (Ed.), *The Welfare State* 1950, page 9.] Another good definition is of Arthur Schlesinger, who says that "the welfare state is a system wherein government agrees to underwrite certain levels of employment, income, education, medical aid, social security and housing for all its citizens." (*Ibid.*, p. 10) In the words of Herbert H. Leyman 'the welfare state is simply a state in which people are free to develop their individual capacities, to receive just awards for their talents, and to engage in the pursuit of happiness, unburdened by the fear of actual hunger, actual homelessness or oppression by reason of race, creed or colour." Certain writers are in favour of using the term "service state" instead of "welfare state," which they regard as boastful.

Importance of Welfare State. The concept of the welfare state is of tremendous significance all over the world. It has brought a great change in the relations between the state and the individual. Even backward or developing countries have fixed for themselves the goal of welfare. William Ebenstein say on page 679 in *Modern*

Political Thought (1960): "........It would be a tragic error to look upon this philosophy of the welfare state as a luxury, prerogative or monopoly of advanced Western nations. Arnold J. Toynbee, the most influential historian of our time, argues in *Not the Age of Atoms but the Welfare of All* (1951) that three centuries from now the twentieth century will be remembered not for its wars, horrors and crimes but for the fact that it is the first era in history in which people dared to think it practicable to make the benefits of civilisation available for the whole human race."

Origin and Implementation of the Concept. The term Welfare State originally came into usage to describe the labour government formed in Britain by Clement Attlee in 1945 at the end of the Second World War 1939-45 (See the essay of Asa Briggs in *Perspectives on the Welfare State,* 1966, page 3, Edited by S.P. Aiyar.) Political leaders, scholars and journalists began to use the term, and gradually it gained currency in the European countries and the rest of the world. Efforts were not made to explain the precise definition and meaning of the term, though its usage was becoming very common. It is very difficult to say when exactly the concept of promoting the welfare of the community took birth, though it is true that in the various countries of the world even in the remote past benevolent kings worked hard for public welfare. For example, in India Emperor Ashoka (c.272-232 B.C.) had very high ideal of kinship and tried to make his subjects happy. He regarded the happiness of his subjects as his own happiness. Scores of kings all over the world to a lesser or greater extent worked for the welfare of the people.

In Victorian England legislation was passed to provide relief to workers, women and children in factories. In 1909 Lloyd George's budget was meant "to wage implacable warfare against poverty and squalidness." Old-age pension and unemployment insurance in England moved towards what we may cal today as the ideals of a welfare state. In Prussia, Bismarck made provision for old-age pension.

In the USA, the Federal and State governments passed legislation for promoting social welfare.

Functions of Welfare State

Not a Mere Tax-Collecting Agency. A welfare state goes far beyond the basic obligation of collecting taxes and maintaining peace and order. It undertakes the responsibility of promoting the material welfare of the people. It upholds the rights of all and respects the dignity of the individuals' personality. It enthusiastically and vigorously strives to raise the standard of living of the people.

The following are the functions of the welfare state:

1. *Protection of Health.* The welfare state takes preventive and curative steps to protect the health of the people. Health ministries in advanced countries spend large sums of money on hospitals, and much is being spent on medical research. Adequate steps are taken to safeguard the health of the people and to prevent the outbreak of epidemics. Legislation is passed to prevent the exploitation of workers, to regulate their hours of work, to provide them with leisure and recreation, and to improve their health and general conditions. The state is aware that only healthy people can work hard with pleasure in making the nation great.

2. *Creation of Conditions for Personality Development.* The state creates conditions favourable for the development of the individual's personality to the highest possible level. It treats all individuals in the same manner and provides adequate opportunities to all for education and employment. All individuals are provided with the same rights, and there is equality before the law. No class or caste is given any special rights or privileges at the expense of the rest of the community. The state particularly protects the weaker sections of the community, which badly need protection. The people are made to feel that they are cared for and that the state has a big stake in their well being and progress. They feel a sense of pride that those in power are interested in making them happy. This creates a bond between the state and the people, who are ready to obey it and co-operate with it.

3. *Spreads Education.* The state provides adequate facilities for education, which is put within the reach of all. While the state may not be able to provide higher education to all, it provides at least free and compulsory primary education. Unfortunately, there are several states, whose resources are so poor that even compulsory primary education is like a luxury to them.

4. *Improves Economic Conditions.* The state takes adequate steps for improving the economic conditions of the people. It takes full responsibility for improving agriculture and industry, trade and commerce and for providing full employment to the people. "Full employment does not mean literally no unemployment—full employment means that unemployment is reduced to short intervals of standing by with the certainty that very soon one will be wanted in a new job that is within one's powers." (William Beveridge, quoted in William Ebenstein, *Modern Political Thought*, 1960, pp. 681-82.) The state may draw long-term plans for economic development.

5. *Renders Social Services.* The welfare state renders various kinds of social services. Western countries have set a good example in providing such social service. France and Prussia took the lead in Europe in providing state-controlled education. In England, a national compulsory unemployment insurance scheme was introduced in 1911, and similar schemes were adopted in most of the other European countries.

A great landmark in the history of social service in the world was the Beveridge Plan, which was prepared by Lord William Beveridge in England and released in 1942. "The Beveridge Report on Social Insurance issued in 1942 is one of the great social documents of our time." The Plan envisaged the following: (1) Unemployment and disability (sickness) benefits; (2) retirement pension; (3) maternity benefit; (4) dependent allowance; (5) industrial pension; (6) marriage dowry; and (7) adult funeral grant.

The total cost of implementing the plan was on the basis of the 1942 price level approximately 700 million pounds. The British

Government prompted by the Tories rejected the Plan as too expensive, and had its own plan of social services.

In France also the importance of social welfare has been stressed. The Preamble to the Constitution (1946) says: "The nation shall guarantee to all, and particularly, to the child, the mother, and the aged worker protection of health, material security, rest and leisure."

In Italy too the government is charged with the duty of promoting social welfare. Article 38 of the Italian Constitution (1947) says that "every citizen unable to work and deprived of the means necessary to live has the right to support and to social assistance."

The administration of President F. D. Roosevelt in the USA, which introduced the *New Deal,* accepted the responsibility of the federal government to promote human welfare all over the country.

The USSR also has done much to promote social welfare, Ogg and Zink say on page 893 in *Modern Foreign Governments* (1957): "The Soviet Union has prided itself on vigorous interest in public welfare enterprises of one kind or another. The outside world has heard more of the OGPU ....than of efforts to improve health, of housing, educational facilities, charitable assistance, and similar enterprises, and is inclined to judge the Soviet regime by the reputation of the former rather than by the achievements in the latter fields........"

In the Scandinavian countries too, there are social welfare schemes.

India as a Welfare State

Objective of Welfare State. The Constitution of India (1950) aims at the establishment of a welfare state. The Union and State Governments are expected to direct their efforts to achieve this objective.

Directive Principle. The realisation of welfare state as the goal of India has been specifically mentioned in the Directive

Principles of State Policy. Article 38 of the Constitution, which is one of the Directive Principles, says: "The State shall strive to promote the welfare of the people by securing and protecting as effectively as it may a social order in which justice social, economic and political, shall pervade all institutions of national life." The state shall exert itself to bring about social, economic and political justice. It is also refreshing to note that the Constitution speaks in terms of the abolition of forced labour, untouchability and communalism. It also lays emphasis on the spread of education, equality of opportunity, equality before the law, toleration and brotherhood.

Preamble. The Preamble to the Constitution of India bears testimony to the grand aims of the Constitution "to secure to all citizens: Justice, social, economic and political; Liberty of thought, expression, belief, faith and worship; Equality of status and of opportunity; and to promote Fraternity assuring the dignity of the individual and unity of the nation."

Socialism with Democracy. Since independence (1947) and particularly after the commencement of the Constitution (1950), Parliament and the various State Legislatures passed many laws for promoting the welfare and happiness of the people. The government is guided by the principles of a socialistic pattern of society and socialism is to march hand in hand with democracy.

Five Year Plans. Very ambitious Five Year Plans have been implemented and the standard of living has been raised. Steps have been taken to increase the production of wealth by encouraging various types of industries; so also concerted efforts have been made to step up agricultural production. Panchayati Raj has been organised almost everywhere in India, and democracy has been taken to the grass-root level. Steps have been taken to increase opportunities of employment. The real income of the people in India today is more than the real income three decades ago.

Welfare State and Democracy

Concept of Welfare State against Democracy. Political scientists have provoked a hot controversy on the question whether the concept of the welfare state will annihilate the concept of democracy and whether the vast powers conferred on the officials of the welfare state will undermine the foundations of democracy. (This question is discussed under caption: Planning in the Modern State in the next Section). It is argued that the citizen will be robbed of all his rights in the name of the welfare state, which can never be democratic, when its government dictates to the citizen as to what he should do and what he should refrain from doing.

Concept of Welfare State Indispensable for Democracy. On the other hand, it is argued with equal vehemence that the concept of the welfare state is indispensable for the very survival of democracy. Whether a state which accepts the principle of the welfare state will cease to be democratic or not will depend upon the manner in which power is wielded by the officials of the state, who are called upon to implement the various welfare schemes. If they do not care for democratic values and depend only on the big stick and ruthless regimentation of the lives of the citizens, democracy will perish. But, if they are able to evoke public co-operation and support, cherish democratic values and cleverly bring about a reconciliation between the concept of the welfare state and the principles of democracy, democracy will not only survive, but even become stronger and healthier. Mark M. Herald says on page 144 in the *Perspectives of the Welfare State*—1966 (Edited by S. P. Aiyar): "The Virtues of the concept of the welfare state are definable in terms of those *guarantees* it can give for *individual liberties* and *opportunities*. Its dangers are measurable in terms of the extent and manner in which it imposes *regimentation,* curbs personal *freedom of thought, freedom of choice,* and *freedom of action,* and the extent to which it destroys *individual initiative* and *individual responsibility.*"

Planning in Modern State

Failure of Capitalism and Planning for Social Justice. Planning is undertaken on a large scale in modern state. In many states ambitious plans are drawn up for promoting the welfare of the people. Enlightened governments have given up obsolete economic ideas and are now following new economic principles to give social and economic justice. The capitalist system which arose with the Industrial Revolution brought much suffering and frustration to the people. H. N. Brailsford in his *Property or Peace* (1934) points out the inherent defect in the capitalist system, which did not work in the interest of the people. To save people from selfish, grabbing and exploiting industrial capitalism and to do justice to the individual, the state had to undertake planning on a large scale. Brailsford says: "We must seek order through conscious organisation and deliberate planning.... It (capitalist civilisation) has, however, solved none of its major problems, economic or political, and the expedients to which it has resorted to—national self-sufficiency, the limitation of social expenditure, and the artificial restriction of the supply of the primary materials and foods—can only reduce the general standard of life." *Perspectives of the Welfare State*—1966, Edited by S.P. Aiyar.) Another eminent thinker G.D.H. Cole has explained why planning is necessary. "Because, as matters stand, our physical power to produced goods has outrun our ability to provide for their consumption and the result is seen in widespread unemployment, suffering, and bodily and mental deterioration of our people. Because it is ludicrous that man should starve in the midst of the potential, or even of actual abundance, if they are not left actually to starve, we should prefer keeping them alive on doles to setting them to useful work."

State Regulation and Control for Improving Standard of Living. The modern state has to meet the various ever-increasing needs of the people. It should not leave the people to their fate, but should undertake various kinds of economic and regulatory functions on an large scale. The challenge of modern times cannot be met by the individual, if he is left alone. Planning has a purpose behind it; it is a means to an end and not an end in itself. Planning in democratic countries like England reveals that it is capable of bettering the standard of the living of the people without destroying the freedom of the individual. Almost every modern state has understood the significance or indispensability of planning on a large scale. We find in certain countries, the masses of people are steeped in abject penury, degradation, illiteracy and ignorance. The means of production that really count are in the hands of a few who exploit the poor ruthlessly and vulgarly without the least compunction. The state, therefore, has to exercise some control and regulate economic and other activities. In every country in the 20th century, there is a strong desire to raise the standard of living. The two World Wars (1914-18 and 1939-45) created awful problems and millions of people suffered from terrible misery and want. Planning was absolutely essential for tackling the problems which arose in the wake of the two global war.

Definition and Meaning of Planning

Planning by Government. Planning is made by government with the advice of experts in the field. The resources to be allotted, the distribution of resources between agriculture and industry, and between the private sector and the public sector, the various targets, methods of control and several other matter are decided by government S.S. Ghosh says in *International Political Science Round Table,* Bombay (Jan. 1964): "Planning in practice means drawing up of preferences by experts and their imposition on the people who do not actively participate in plan activities at any stage. Moreover, plans are carried out through social legislation which necessarily implies coercion."

Central Control on Decision-Making and Allocation of Resources. Planning involves central control on decision-making and allocation of resources. Dasgupta, Sen and Sengupta say on page 1 in *Planning and the Plans* (1961): "In common parlance planning means and form of behaviour governed by conscious expectation.... Planning sometimes denotes and programme of action according to a pre-arranged pattern, such as Colombo Plan or Marshall Plan. In economics the word planning has, however, acquired a special connotation, namely, that of substituting the spontaneous market forces by deliberate action and central control over the process of decision-making in the creation and allocation of resources."

Rationalised Central Control of Economy. Planning can be found in almost all states, though the principles of planning may vary from state to state. Planning implies large-scale activities and controls of government in the economic field. Ferdynand Zweig says on page 17 in *The Planning of the Free Societies* (1962): "Economic planning consists in the extension of the functions of public authorities to the organisation and utilisation of the economic resources.... Planning is often defined as *rational* centralised control of the economy; other writers define it as *social* or *political* control. These definitions do not exclude each other, but are to a certain extent complementary."

Objectives of Planning. We may enumerate the following objectives of planning: (1) to improve the general welfare of the people; (2) to provide full and adequate employment to people; the objective may be fully realised, though full employment is fixed as the target; (3) to provide economic security and do economic justice to the people; (4) to bring about social and other types of equality; and (5) to bring about the backward areas in a country on a level with other areas.

It is not enough if plans are made; they should be actually implemented, and this is not an easy task. V. Vithal Babu says on page 19 in *Towards Planning:* "Planning is a continuous process which necessitates incessant review of scientific application and constant re-examination of economic, financial social and other polices and programmes of the Government."

Essential Conditions of Success. Certain conditions are necessary, if plans are to be successful. (1) Proper study of the resources of the country should be made on a scientific basis. (2) The targets of plans must be realistic and not utopian. (3) The personnel in-charge of the plans should be highly competent and dynamic. (4) The government should be honest in its efforts, and it should take people in its confidence. (5) People who should be kept informed about the plans should be involved in planning and made aware that plans are for them. (6) The implementation of plans should be properly supervised. (7) Government should be vigilant. It should see that corrupt and incompetent men are detected and punished.

State Interference but not Totalitarian, Control Necessary. While *laissez faire* (free trade) encouraged production up to a certain stage, ultimately it failed and was rejected. No state today is prepared to stand fully in support of *laissez faire* principles. Most of the writers think that state interference is necessary for the common good, though they are against totalitarian control.

Nationalisation. Several writers are of the opinion that the best antidote to the ills of production is nationalisation of important means of production. The advocates of nationalisation point out that in the capitalist system the production and distribution of wealth are in the hands of a few, and obviously production never caters to the needs of the people. Under capitalism, production is haphazard and unplanned; there is excessive competition with all its evil corollaries. Capitalists are guided by the profit motive, which is upheld even at the cost of the community. What needs to be produced is either never produced at all or not produced in adequate quantities, and there is an enormous wastage of resources and talents. What is not required by society may be produced to cater to the needs of the minority. Under nationalisation, the state not only brings under its control public utility like the railways, motor transport, and posts and telegraphs, but also important means of production. The principle of nationalisation has been accepted in many countries, though all the means of production are not nationalised in every state.

Types of Planning. Planning which is of different types can be brought under four categories [See D.V.P. Gupta in *Towards Planning* (1950) by V. Vithal Babu]: (1) Central Planning under socialism (Russia and China); (2) Guided Capitalism and dynamic competition (Post-war America and Germany since the War); (3) Planned Capitalism (France and Britain); (4) Mixed Economy or the synthetic approach as adopted by India.

There have been plans in totalitarian states and so too in democratic states. The totalitarian state of Nazi Germany had Four Year Plans and Stalin's Russia had Five Year Plans; India a democratic country, has Five Year Plans.

Whether Planning is Anti-Democratic

View that Planning Results in Despotism. Several thinkers

are against planning, state control and regulation. They are in favour of free enterprise. Friedrich A. Hayek, the author of *The Road to Serfdom* (1964) and Walter Lippmann, the author of *The Good Society,* can be cited as conspicuous examples. Lippmann says: "Not only is it impossible for the people to control the plan, but what is more, the planners must control the people. They must be despots who tolerate no effective challenge to their authority." (Quoted by William Ebenstein on page 655 in *Modern Political Thought*—1960.)

F.A. Hayek is of the opinion that planning and democracy cannot live together, as one is against the other. Planning, it is argued, weakens democracy by increasing state control. Hayek observes on page 178 in *The Road to Serfdom* (1964): "Our point, however, is not that dictatorship must inevitably extirpate freedom but rather that planning leads to dictatorship, because dictatorship is the most effective instrument of coercion and the enforcement of ideals and as such essential if central planning on a large scale is to be possible. The clash between planning and democracy arises simply from the fact that the latter is an obstacle to the suppression of freedom which the direction of economic activity requires.

Planning Easy in Totalitarian State. It is true that planning in a totalitarian state becomes easy, and plans there can be implemented quicker than in democratic states, as the individual has no right to criticize the state. The individual is never consulted or taken into confidence by the totalitarian state. He has to subject himself to the coercion of the state without resisting or questioning it. While full employment is difficult to be realised in a democratic state, matters are comparatively easy in a totalitarian state. William Ebenstein says on page 676 in *Modern Political Thought* (1960): "Full employment in a totalitarian state is relatively simple, because the state forces people to work for low wages and under oppressive working conditions. What Beveridge seeks to achieve with his proposals is full employment in a free society."

Planning Not Necessarily against Freedom. The shining examples of countries like Britain show that planning need not necessarily imply loss of freedom. Barbara Wootton does not agree with Prof. Hayek who says that planning leads to serfdom. Planning need not and has not led to destruction of liberty everywhere. Democracies have planned successfully without destroying liberty. Wootton says on page 139 in *Freedom under Planning* (1945): "Planning need not even be the death warrant of all private enterprises; and it is certainly not the passport of political dictatorship. A happy and fruitful marriage between freedom and planning can be arranged........Success or failure turns on the behaviour of the actual men and who have the responsibility of planning."

Planning Conducive to Growth of Liberty and Equality. Planning no doubt implies some coercion, control and regulation; but it does not lead to the destruction of liberty. Planning is in the best interests of all, and it is conducive to the growth of liberty and equality. S.K. Saha says at the International Science Association Round Table, Bombay (Jan. 1964): "Hayek's contention that planning leads to dictatorship is not tenable. Planning would lead to economic betterment and even distribution of wealth and income. Thus planning is not only compatible with democracy but essential for the very survival of democracy."

Planning in India. India has been planning on a large scale for a better standard of living through her Five Year Plans since 1952. Even the worst critic of planning in India cannot deny that much improvement has taken place since the commencement of planning.

Limits of State Control

Opinions of Different Schools. As F.W. Coker says on page 381 in *Recent Political Thought*, marking out the sphere of state activity "is the most difficult of all problems of political theory." To what extent a state can control the life of an individual and whether any limits can be imposed in state control cannot be answered easily. These are highly controversial questions and different schools of thought have given different answers. Each school looks at the problem of limits to be set to set control through its own angle and in the light of its own ideology. For instance, the Individualists, who put forward the *Laissez Faire* (Free trade)

Theory desire the state to exercise the maximum control over the individual's activities. The Idealists, particularly those of extreme views, are prepared to give unlimited power to the state which they regard as a march of God on earth. On the other hand, the Anarchists regard the state, as an evil, and desire to abolish it unceremoniously. The views of the various schools are explained in the forthcoming chapters.

Matters Outside State Control

Democratic Government to uphold Human Dignity. Many political thinkers favour a democratic type of government, as it respects the dignity of the human personality and does not interfere in certain clear-cut fields. We have already observed that a clear line of difference should be drawn between society and state. It must be emphasised that the functions of the state do not embrace the whole range of human activity.

The following are the matters over which a democratic government does not exercise control. These are left entirely to the freedom of the individual:

1. *Wholesome Customs and Usages.* The state does not try to exercise control over wholesome customs and usages, as people will lose their freedom if this is done. Long-standing customs have great significance, as they restrain and regulate the behaviour of the people. In fact, such customs are useful to the state in governing people with comparative ease and in enforcing law. R. M MacIver says on page 161 in *The Modern State* (1960): "Custom when attacked, attacks law in turn, attackes not only the particular law, which opposes it, but what is more vital, the spirit of law-abidingness the unity of the general will.........the main body of social customs beyond the range of law and is neither made nor unmade by the state."

   However, the state should take steps to abolish obnoxious customs and pass the necessary legislation. Customs like offering human sacrifice, trial by ordeal, female infanticide, *sati,* Child marriage and the *Devadasi* system should be eradiated by the state. Suppressing bad customs is as essential as upholding good customs in the larger interests of society.

2. *Religion.* A good democratic government does not interfere with the religious beliefs of the people. In the past, all over the world, rulers tried to meddle with religious affairs in some way or the other. Some of them showed rabid fanaticism and persecuted their subjects in every possible manner. In the recent times most of the governments have been giving complete religious toleration and allowing the various religious communities to live in peace and freedom. A wise government regards religion as a personal affair, and, therefore, leaves the individual entirely free to practice his own faith. It neither encourages nor discourages any religion and does not promote the cause of any religion. Under the Constitution of India (1950), secularism is upheld. India is not a Hindu or Muslim or Christian or Sikh or Zoroastrian state. It holds in even balance all religions, and does not permit its policies to be influenced by any religion. Right to religious freedom is a justiciable Fundamental Right in India.

   It is unfortunate that narrow-minded and superstitious people encourage the growth of obnoxious religious beliefs, which spell harm on society. The state should not hesitate to crush religious practices which are cruel, barbarous and unjust. Religious practices, which lead to breach of the peace and promote social conflict and disharmony, should be ruthlessly suppressed.

3. *Culture.* Culture or the way of life of the people is placed beyond the control of a democratic government. Food habits, mode of dress, social customs, religious and spiritual ideas, art, literature and learning, and a general attitude toward life constitute the culture of people. The cultures of the majority and of the minorities are life untouched by a liberal, wise and far-sighted government. All people enjoy full cultural freedom and the cultural rights of minorities are fully protected. No cultural regimentation is attempted by the state. In India people enjoy complete cultural freedom. Cultural and Educational Rights are guaranteed by the Constitution of India (1950).

4. *Ethical and Moral Values.* A good government also does not interfere with the ethical and moral values of the people and their sense of right and wrong. These are closely connected with the culture and religious beliefs of the people. The state keeps out of the field of morals and does not try to impose morality on the people through legislation. The state, however, tries to create conditions, which are conducive to the moral growth of the community. R. M. MacIver, who says that the state should not try to pass law on morals, points out on page 154 in *The Modern State* (1950): "The inner sanction of morality should never confused with that of political law. We obey the law not necessarily because we think it right to obey the law.... Morality is always individual and always in relation to the whole presented situation of which the political fact is never more than an aspect."

5. *Public Opinion.* In the matter of public opinion, too, a good government does not interfere. It does not try to control or suppress public opinion provided the expression of such opinion is peaceful and constitutional and not injurious to civilised norms and morality. A government, which works for the good of the people, would welcome the free expression of public opinion, because it would be in a position the know the reaction of the people to its various laws and policies. Government will be able to know the grievances of the people only when people speak freely. In the light of public opinion, government has scope to reconsider and reorient its policies. In totalitarian state, people do not have rights as in democratic states, and public opinion is not respected. In fact, public opinion has no proper channels of expression in the face of ruthless suppression. On the other hand, in a democracy, government is responsive to public opinion. In democracies, freedom of thought, expression and writing form one of the basic rights, because without this, democracy has no substance. Democracy is sometimes regarded as government by public opinion. R.M. MacIver says on page 140 in *The Modern State* (1950) that

the state "should not seek to control opinion no matter what the opinion may be," except incitement to break law and to develop defamatory opinion. A state, which tries to suppress public opinion, stands against truth, and in the ultimate analysis, it attempts to crush the human mind.

6. *Art and Literature.* A democratic government does not try to influence, regulate and control art and literature, as long as they do not violate norms of law and morality. While governments are justified in regulating the activities of educational institutions, they should refrain from exercising control over the minds of artists and writers. Any effort to make artists and writers government minded will spell the doom of true and creative art and literature. Immoral and unwholesome trends in art and literature may be watched and proper action taken by government; but merely controlling or suppressing them because they are not pro-government will be fatal to art and literature.

Theories of Sphere of State Activity

While discussing the functions and sphere of state activity, various theories have to be examined.

Idealism, Individualism, Utilitarianism, Socialism, Communism, Nazism, Fascism and Anarchism. The theories explaining the sphere of state activity are: (1) the Idealist theory, (2) the theory of Individualism, (3) the Utilitarian theory, (4) the theories of Democratic Socialism and Revolutionary Socialism or Communism, (5) the Fascist Doctrine, (6) the Nazi theory, and (7) the Anarchist theory.

Each theory explains the area over which the state can conduct its activities. The exponents of these theories give their idcas according to their own mental attitude, conditioned by the forces of history or environmental influences.

In certain cases, there is a world of difference between two theories. For instance, the idealist theory of Hegel is prepared to give unlimited power to the state, and the individual is a negligible quantity. But the theory of individualism gives much freedom to the individual, and provides a limited area for the activities of the state. The anarchists do not want the state at all.

In modern times, it is being increasingly admitted that the state cannot be a mere passive onlooker, but has to regulate human activity for the good of the community.

Each theory tries in its own way to explain the position of the individual in relation to the state. (These theories are discussed in the forthcoming chapters.)

Books for Further Study

1. Aiyar, S. P., *Perspectives of Welfare State—1966,* Manaktalas, Bombay.
2. Babu, V.V., *Towards Panning*—1950.
3. Barker, Ernest, *Principles, of Social and Political Theory*—1953.
4. Coker, F. W., *Recent Thought*—1966, The World Press, Calcutta.
5. Cole, G.D.H., *Principles of Economic Planning*—1935.
6. Dasgupta, Sen and Sengupta, *Planning and the Plans*—1961,
7. Ebenstein, William, *Political Thought in Perspective*—1957.
8. Ebenstein, William, *Modern Political Thought*—1960.
9. Garner, J.W., *Political Science and Government*—1995, The World Press, Calcutta.
10. Gupta, Bharat Bhushan, *The Welfare State in India*—1966, Central Book Depot, Allahabad.
11. Hayek, F.A., *The Road to Serfdom*—1964.
12. Hobhouse, L.T., *The Metaphysical Theory of the State*—1918, Allen & Unwin.
13. Hobman, D.L., *The Welfare State*—1950.
14. Laski, H. J., *A Grammar of Politics*—1957.
15. Lippmann, Walter, *An Inquiry into the Principles of the Good Society*—1950.
16. MacIver, R. M., *Modern State*—1950.
17. MacIver, R. M., *The Web of Government*—1959.

18. Marx, Harbert, L., *The Welfare State*—1950.

19. Ogg and Zink., *Modern Foreign Governments*—1957.

20. Paul, W., *The State in Origin and Function.*

21. Plamenatz, John P., *The English Utilitarians*—1958, Basil Blackwell.

22. Soltau, R. H., *The Economic Functions of the State.*

23. Titmuss, Richard M., *Essays on the Welfare State.*

24. Urwick, Edward, *The Social Good*—1927.

25. Wilson, Francis Graham, *The Elements of Modern Politics.*

26. Wilson, R. K., *The Province of the State*—1911.

27. Wootton, Barbara, *Freedom under Planning*—1945.

28. Zweig, Ferdynand, *The Planning of the Free Societies*—1962.

2

The City-State and Nation-State

Mr. Bernard Bosanquet, in his, *Philosophical Theory of the State,* makes some interesting remarks on the City-States of the old (European) world and the Nation-States—Professor Seeley's Country-States—of modern days.

He considers the Greek City-State as differing from associations in the non-Greek World "above all things by its individuality". It had youth, maturity and decadence, and was self-conscious, had a recognizable tone and spirit, and "expresses its mind in the various regions of human action and endurance much as an artist expresses his individuality in the creations of his genius". This, he thinks, existed in the Greek City-State, and in that alone.

> The demand for "autonomy"—government by one's own law —and for "isonomy"—government according to equal law—though far from being always satisfied, was inherent in the Greek nature. . . The very instrument of all political action was invented, so far as we can see, by the Creeks. The simple device by which an orderly vote is taken, and the minority acquiesce in the will of the majority was if it had been their own—an invention no less definite that that of the lever and the wheel—is found for the first time as an everyday method of decision in Greek political (*Loc. cit.*, Chap. i, pp. 3-5. 2nd Ed. Macmillan & Co., London.)

City States

The treatise of Aristotle on *Politics*—or on *Government*—is devoted to the City State, and we have already seen (Lecture, ii, p. 35), that whole he considers the family and the village as necessarily antecedent to the City, he does not trouble himself about them. He alleges that:

> Every City must be allowed to be the work of Nature... for to this, as their end, all subordinate societies tend, and the end of everything is the nature of it. For what every being is in its most perfect state, that certainly is the nature of that being, whether it be a man, a horse, or a house; besides whatsoever produces the final cause and the end which we desire must be best; but a government complete in itself is that final cause and what is best. Hence it is evident that a city is a natural production, and that man himself is a political (*Loc. cit.,* Book I, Chap. ii, p. 12.)

Mr. Bosanquet gives a very a very admirable exposition of this passage of Aristotle, on the meaning of the City being "a natural production". He writes:

> The fundamental idea of Greek political philosophy, as we find it in Plato and Aristotle, is that the human mind can only attain its full and proper life in a community of minds, or more strictly in a community pervaded by a single mind, uttering itself consistently though differently in the life and action of every member of the community. This conception is otherwise expressed by such phrases as "the State is natural," *i.e.,* is a growth or evolution, apart from which the end implied in man's origin cannot be attained; "the State is prior to the individual," *i.e,* there is a principle or condition underlying the life of the human individual, which will not admit of that life becoming what it has in it to be, unless the full sphere or arena which is constituted by the life of the State is realised in fact. The whole is summed up in the famous expression of Aristotle, "man is a creature formed for the life of the City-state." ...The central idea is this: that every class of persons in the community—the statesman, the soldier, the workman—has a certain distinctive type of mind which fits its members for their functions, and that the community essentially consists in the working of these types of mind in their connection with one another, which connection constitutes their sub-ordination to the common good. This working or adjustment obviously depends in the last resort on the qualities present in the innermost souls of the members of the community; and thus the outward organisation of society is really, as it were, a body, which at every point and in every movement expresses the characteristics of a mind. (*Ibid.,* pp. 6,7.)

This is the philosophic idea which underlay the ancient Hindu system of caste, the place of the man in society being according to his qualities; the rigidity of the later caste system, its reliance wholly on birth instead of qualities, and the impossibility of changing from the caste into which a man was born, have transformed it from a most beneficent social order into an obstacle to freedom and therefore to evolution.

Aristotle defines a City, after defining a citizen:

> He who has a right to a share in the judicial and executive part of government in any city, him we call a citizen of that place, and a city, in one word, is a collective body of such persons, sufficient in themselves to all the purposes of life. (*Loc. cit.*, Book III, Chap. I, p. 81.)

If one wanted to be very critical, one might remark that if Aristotle is to be strictly interpreted there were no citizens, for men were not sufficient in themselves for all the purposes of life, since they could not reproduce themselves, and women were not sufficient because they had no right to share in any part of the government, and therefore were not citizens, by Aristotle's definition ! Let us, however take Aristotle's City as Aristotle made it, of citizens who were masters, husbands and father, exercising in their households herile, nuptial and paternal forms of government, and being in the outer world free men, composing a government. Some men, he considers, are by nature superior, and some are by nature inferior. The former are masters, the latter slaves; the superiority consists in the mind:

> A being who is endowed with a mind capable of reflection and forethought is by nature the superior and governor, whereas he whose excellence is merely corporeal is formed to be a slave; whence it follows that the different state of master and slave is equally advantageous to both. (*Loc. cit.*, Book I, Chap. ii, p.10.)

He maintains that a slave is an instrument, possession, and he:

> who by nature is nothing of himself, but totally another's and is a man, is a slave by nature; and that man who is the property of

> another is his mere chattel, though he continues a man: but a chattel is an instrument for use, separate from the body. (*Ibid.*, Chap. iv, p. 15.)

Men,

> who are as much inferior to others as the body is to the soul, are to be thus disposed of, as the proper use of them is their bodies, in which their excellence consists; and if what I have said be true, they are slaves by nature, and it is advantageous to them to be always under government. (*Ibid.*, Chap. v, p. 17)

It will be seen how far inferior in this matter was the Greek to the Indian civilisation of the same period. Aristotle, however, excepts from his definition of "a slave" men who are made slaves by law or by war, and he acknowledges that there are men whom no situation could make slaves (*Ibid.*, Chap. vi, p. 19)

We will defer the consideration of Aristotle views on forms of government, occupying Books III to VI, till we come to that subject.

Aristotle's "City State" is an ideal. Practically, in early Greek history, there was the association of families into "gentes" or "clans," or "houses," and these ultimately into a Confederacy, or a City, for defensive purposes under a chief or King, hereditary and with a council of Elders. Each gens had its own deities, its own rules and customs, and these were maintained within the centre of the Confederation, the City. The gentes united into phratries, brotherhoods of a religious type, with a common object of worship; these united again into a tribe, the tribes into a City.

> The City State grew up by successive amalgamations: patriarchal families grew into village communities, village communities into phratries or brotherhoods, phratries into tribes, and tribes into the City State. The bond that held the family together was chiefly that of blood relationship. The village community depended upon economic interests as well as the blood tie; the phratries upon religious ties, the tribe upon the communal ownership of land. So, too, the City State, in its beginnings as a union of tribes, was held together by this descent from the old families and the possession

of land. (*History of Education.* Paul Monroe, Ph.D. chap. iii, pp. 67, 68. The Macmillan Company, New York.)

Thus, Coulanges, in his book, *The Ancient City* (pp. 169, 179), points out that an Athenian belonged to four groups, a family, a phratry, a tribe, a city, and entered each through a religious ceremony; at 16 or 18 years of age he was initiated into the public worship of the City, and thus become a citizen. (Quoted by Wilson, *loc. cit.,* Chap ii. § 51.). Long before Athens however, Cities, of the Hellenic type were dotted along the Mediterranean coasts; Wilson speaks of Ægean seamen in the 13th century, B. C. and gives a vivid account of the way in which "towns begat towns in prolific generation" between 750 B. C. and 550 B. C. each colony becoming a Mother City, until Sicily and Italy, and France, and even Spain, bore the Hellenic Cities. They were "completely independent, self-governing institutions," taking the sacred fire from the Mother City, but each becoming at once "a sovereignty separate State, no less its own mistress in all things than the City from which it had come out" (*Ibid.*, §§ 62-70).

The Athenian conception of life is one of the noblest in the world, especially in its view of the intimate relation of the Citizen and the City, or, as we should say, of the Individual and the State. The education which prepared the young Athenian to fill his place in the body politic was carefully planned. For the first seven years of life he lived in the family, and his parents were responsible for his training, which was oral and chiefly physical; if his father neglected this education, the son was free from the obligation to support his father in old age. From 7 to 16, the boy was at school, in the personal charge of a tutor-servant who attended on him, and he went to a teacher, learning literature, music, and physical exercise, including dancing. At 16 he passed under the instruction of a State official, though his father or guardian remained responsible for his home life, learned the use of arms, and was instructed in his moral duties and civic responsibilities for two years. At 18, if he proved his fitness, he was enrolled in the list of free citizens, took the civic oath and received his shield and spear.

The oath ran as follows, and was repeated in the presence of the free citizens of Athens; it was called the oath of the Ephebi, or cabet corps:

> I will not dishonour may sacred arms; I will not desert my fellow-soldier, by whose side I shall be set; I will do battle for my religion and my country whether aided or unaided; I will leave may country not less, but greater and more powerful, than when she is committed to me; I will reverently obey the citizens who shall act as judges; I will obey the ordinances which have been established, and which, in time to come shall be established, by the National will; and whosoever would destroy or disobey those ordinances, I will not suffer him, but I will do battle for them whether aided or unaided; and I will honour the temples where my fathers worshipped. Of these things the Gods are my witnesses. (*The Education of the Young in the Republic of Plato.* Bernard Bosanquet, M. A., LL.D. Introduction, p. 9 University Press, Cambridge.)

Another two years intervened before the full duties of citizenship were assumed; the first of these was spent in a camp near the city, and he was subjected to severe military training and taught practical administration of the State. The second year was spent as a soldier in more distant places, that he might become acquainted with the frontiers and general topography of the country. Taking part in religious and social festivals formed an important part in the training of the four years, and "in these festivals training in religious devotion and patriotism is combined with the cultivation of the graces of life and of harmonious physical development. The end of the first year [of the second period from 18 to 20] was signalised by a public examination in the use of arms; that of the second, by a similar examination upon the duties of citizenship which were then assumed." (These details are summarised from Monroe's *History of Education*, before quoted, Chap. iii, pp. 82-86.)

The author gives the following fine description of the Athenian life:

> Even here [at the end of the Ephebi period] the process of education did not cease, for life of the Athenian citizen was one neither of private enterprise nor of private indulgence. On the contrary, the

> State demanded such services of the citizen that a life of economic activity for personal ends was hardly possible, certainly not to be extent common in modern times. The pleasures of private life, whether amusements in sports and games, attendance upon the theatre, or social gatherings for eating and drinking, were controlled by the Athenians, though somewhat less directly than by the Spartans, for ends that were social. The State and the entire social life became a school, in which, although effort for physical perfection was not neglected, yet greater emphasis was laid upon intellectual and moral growth. Thus was obtained the highest conception of the elements of nobility and virtue that constituted the ever developing "worth" of the Athenian citizen. (*Ibid.*, p. 86.)

"Worth" is described as originally indicating "Worth to the State," but as cities were formed:

> the worth of a citizen to the State takes on an entirely new character. Supremacy is now to be maintained more largely by a superiority in intelligence, in moral judgment, and in such an appreciation of the finer aspects of life as would distinguish him from the base-born multitude. Thus it happened that in the Greek City States especially among the Ionian race, there was evolved for the leisured class an ideal of worth, or nobility, more largely spiritual than had previously been attained. According to this ideal, service to the State and superiority to the barbarians and the low-born can be shown only by attainment in those interests in life which the Greeks considered under the peculiar protection of the Muses—the fine arts, the sciences, and philosophy. Nobility, now becomes worth, or virtue, in the spiritual sense as well as in the more practical sense. Ancient wealth and worth in the sense of property and birth are now considered not so much the essential elements of nobility as presuppositions to the more spiritualize forms of wealth and worth. As Aristotle expresses thecontrast, the aim of tribal and village organisation is mere living, that of the City State is the *good* life. Worth in this sense can be attained and it can be lost; and at all times is to be maintained by a striving, that not only is of service to the State, but produces with it, as the essential feature of the process, the development of free and clearly defined personality. This conception of nobility, or worth, is the bond with holds the City State together, gives it its superiority, and, at the same time, becomes the ideal attainable in the life of every individual. To produce this worth becomes the aim of

education, whether viewed by the State after its interests or by the individual according to his interests, though to the Greek, in the "old" period, these were indistinguishable. (*Ibid.*, pp. 69, 70.)

Pericles (Thucydides, Book II, para 40) describes the Athenian life in vivid terms; it is translated by Monroe (*Ibid*., p. 80).

> If then we prefer to meet danger with a light heart, but without laborious training, and with a courage which is gained by habit and not enforced by law, are we not greatly the gainers? Since we do not anticipate the pain although, when the hour comes, we can be as brave as those who never allow themselves to rest; and thus, too, our city is equally admirable in peace and in war. For we are lovers of the beautiful, yet simple in our tastes, and we cultivate the mind without loss of manliness. Wealth we employ, not for talk and ostentation, but when there is a real use for it. To avow poverty with us is no disgrace; the true disgrace is in doing nothing to avoid it. An Athenian citizen does not neglect the State because he takes care of his own household; and even those of us who are engaged in business have a very fair idea of politics. We alone regard a man takes no interest in public affairs, not as a harmless, but as a useless character; and if few of us are originators, we are all sound judges of a policy. The great impediment to action is, in our opinion, not discussion, but the want of that knowledge which is gained by discussion preparatory to action. For we have a peculiar power of thinking before we act, and of acting too, whereas other men are courageous from ignorance but hesitate upon reflection. And they are surely to be esteemed the bravest spirits who, having the clearest sense both of the pains and pleasures of life, do not on that account shrink from danger.

It will be noticed that religion was interwoven with patriotism in the City State, that religious ceremonies marked the stages of training, that he taking part in religious festivals was a civic duty. Furthermore, freedom was held to imply freedom from subjection to the body, spiritual freedom, not the mere freedom from physical bondage. The body was to be trained into beauty and strength, but it was to be the slave of the Spirit. Hence the "free citizen" had his moral obligations and his civic duties, and in the perfect discharge of these lay the demonstration of his freedom. His will was Self-determined to the beautifully, the Good and the True.

This is well put by the Waynflete Professor of Mental and Moral Philosophy at Oxford, Mr. J.A. Smith, in a lecture on "The Contribution of Greece and Rome," delivered at a Summer School at the Woodbroke Settlement, near Birmingham, in August, 1915, and published with others in a volume entitled, *The Unity of Western Civilisation.* He pointed out that the Greek contribution was the thought of Civilisation-through-Knowledge, a thought which was not a thought only, but a patent and effective instrument of action, not a mere ideal, but an ideal governing, directing, and realised in action and life.

We have also to recognize another most powerful influence of which they were the vehicles—closely related to the other. The Greeks first articulately conceived and deliberately pursued the ideal of Freedom. It was, I say, closely related to the other, for they meant by it not merely freedom from physical or political constraint, but also inward freedom prejudice and passion, and they held that knowledge and freedom rendered one another possible. We may amend our formula and restate their contribution as the idea and fact of civilisation, regarded as a process in and to Freedom under the control of knowledge or Reason, each inspiring, guiding and fertilizing the other. (*Loc. cit.,* p. 76. Humphrey Milford, University Press, Oxford.)

I wrote in the first number of *The Young Citizen,* January, 1913—where, by the way, appears the short version of the Citizen Oath of Athens—the following passage on the State, embodying the teaching thereon of the great Greek philosopher, Pythagoras, and it may fitly close our brief study of the Greek City-State, the ideals of which, I believe, will be largely embodied in the New Civilisation of the reconstructed Nations, when the Great War is over:

The Ideal of the State among the Greeks was a very lofty one. It comes out strongly in the following:

> Organised Society exists for the happiness and welfare of its members, and where it fails to secure these, it stands *ipso facto* condemned. "Government exists only for the good of the Governed." So said Pythagoras, preaching on the hill of

Tauromenion, and the phrase has echoed down the centuries, and has became the watch-word of those who are seeking the betterment of social conditions. Only when the good of the governed is sought and secured does the State deserve the eloquent description with which the great Greek Teacher closed one of his lectures to the Greek Colony of Naxos, whose citizens were gathered round him on the hill:

"Listen, my children, to what the State should be to the good citizen. It is more than father or mother, it is more than child or friend. The State is the father and mother of all, is the wife of the husband, and the husband of the wife. The family is good, and good is the joy of the man in wife and in son. But greater is the state, which is the Protector of all, without which the home would be ravage and destroyed. Dear to the good man is the honour of the woman who bore him, dear the honour of the wife whose children cling to his knees: but dearer should be the honour of the State, that keeps safe the wife and the child. It is the State from which comes all that makes your life prosperous, and gives you beauty and safety. Within the State are built up the Arts, which make the difference between the barbarian and the Man. If the brave man dies gladly for the hearthstone, far more gladly should he die for the State."

And I then wrote:

Such is the Ideal of the State that we would urge on our young citizens. The State should not be to them a cold abstraction, but a pulsing, throbbing Life, to be loved and served with enthusiasm, with passion, with uttermost self-sacrifice. When this spirit is embodied in the coming generation, the future of the Aryan Empire will be secured.

In a pamphlet, entitled *Theosophy,* I had described the above as "the Theosophical Ideal of the State—the father-mother of its citizens, the Protector of all".

So far as the City of Rome is concerned, its genesis closely resembled that of the Greek City State from the gens to the City, with its King and Council of Elders, but the King in Rome was elected, not hereditary as in early Greece. The City became a Republic in 509 B. C. the Roman finding Kings troublesome, and extended its power in a somewhat casual fashion, that being the Roman, as now the British, way. Rome conquered, made terms with each conquered tribe or province, and grew continually, spread outside and decayed within, until she slid into an Empire, and paved the way for modern Nation States.

But Rome has also made her great contribution to western civilisation, and Mr. J.A. Smith has stated it with a terseness and a clearness which I have not met before, though the general ideas are familiar. He points out, and this, I think, is new:

> We are accustomed to think of her empire as a gigantic military power, but in reality it was in aim and result essentially pacific, and so appeared to those who lived under her sway. To them the name of her empire was the "Roman peace". It was as such that the memory of it haunted the minds of men when it too broke down from internal economic disorders and external pressure, and a distracted and divided Europe back to it as the pattern for a restored civilisation.

The aim and result of the Roman Empire was Peace, a world-wide Peace. (*Loc. cit.*, pp. 84-85.)

Mr. Smith then points out that Rome regarded "a supreme sovereignty, one and indivisible" as "the absolutely indispensable condition of a world peace"—a conception which seems to have been revived by Germany in our own days, for Rome was to dominate and impose her will on the world, as Germany has sought to do. But her lasting contribution was Peace through System and Order, Justice, and "a Legal System, based upon a known body of legal rights and duties" (*Loc.* cit., p. 85). He concludes:

> The Roman ideal must be transformed, must be reborn, if it is not to lead our anticipations and our actions wholly astray... Yet the spirit which gave it life and efficacy is immortal and the study of the secret of its vitality and power is a necessity for us. In the work of reconstruction, we must learn from the Romans the value of System and Order, of Justice and Law, as from Greece we have ever afresh to learn the love of Freedom and Truth. (*Ibid.*, p. 88.)

Italy showed, through Middle Age Europe, types of the old City State, as in Florence, Milan, Pisa, Venice, The Free Cities of

Germany are sometimes assimilated with these, but it seems to me that they are fundamentally different. They grew out of Teutonic independence and self-government, out of democracy; the others out of aristocracy and slavery.

THE VILLAGE AND THE TOWN IN THE WEST

It is noteworthy that the investigations into village life in the West have been made mostly by German writers, even when the subject of study was Great Britain. Little is know, I believe, of the social conditions of the early inhabitants of Britain, beyond what may be found in the writings of Caesar, and we must be content to begin our review with the villages of the Angles and Saxons, invading and settling in Britain in the fifth century of the Christian era. This matters the less, as the state of the country during the preceding centuries would only show the conditions under Roman domination, and the results of the breaking up of the Roman power, when the Roman's "law relaxed its hold upon us".

Dr. Wilson points out that the Romans had left Britain nearly forty years before the Teutens made their first permanent settlement (A.D. 449), and that they brought their own institutions with them:

> Local tribal government always precedes national government. Men governed themselves as families and small communities before they were governed as nations. For the Germans of that early time the village was the centre of political life; national organisation they at first scarcely knew except for purpose of war; kinship among them was honorary and typical rather than real. The freemen of each little community in times of peace directed their own affairs with quite absolute freedom in village meeting. Even in war each freeman had a vote in the distribution of booty, and could set his own imperative individuality as a more or less effectual check upon the willfulness of his commander. A very democratic temper seems to have ruled in the politics of that rough primitive time. (*Loc.*, cit., Chap. § 833.)

> Kingship easily arose in war and conquest, and small kingdoms were formed. But the internal organisation of the tribe was probably not deeply affected by he fact that a throne had been set up. The

> people gathered, as was their long time wont, into more or less, compact but always small communities, round about the homesteads and villages the Romans had built; enjoying their lands according to some system of ownership which left the chief pastures and the principal water-supply open to use by all, and reserved only the arable land to separate use by individuals. Justice and government still proceeded, as of old, at first hand, from the meeting of village freemen. (*Ibid.*, § 834.)

Sir Henry Maine in his *Village-Communities,* already referred to, summarizes German writers for the most part, and relies on Von Maurer and Nasse; he refers us to a paper by Mr. Morier, English Charge d'Affaires at Darmstadt, published in *Systems of Land Tenure in various Countries,* and states that Mr. Morier had sent him some territorial maps of backward parts of Germany, in which could be traced vestiges of collective property in land.

As we have seen that the aryan race in Central Asia sent out successive streams of emigrants westwards to the Caucasus and beyond, before finally transplanting itself bodily southwards into India, after many invasions of, and settlements in, its future home, there is nothing surprising in the similarity between Slavonic, Teutonic, Scandinavian and Indian Village Communities. And this similarity comes out strongly in the general arrangements of the village as well as in its holding of land, and in the need of aggregation for purposes of defence. Sir Henry Maine quotes from Mr. Willian Marshall's *Elementary and Practical Treatise on Landed Property,* published in London in 1804, and the descriptions are good, though the writer's words are sometimes a little misleading, as he treats the collective property in land from the modern standpoint as a "common farm cultivated by the tenantry of a single landlord" (Maine, *Loc. cit.,* Lecture iii, p. 90).

Marshall describes the village, with the residences surrounded by small enclosures or grass yards, for calves and other farm-stock. Then came the ring of arable fields for corn, pulse and fodder; then meadows for hay, and pasture grounds for cattle; the; lands furthest from the village were left wild for timber and fuel, rough pastures, each villager having the right to pasture there in summer as much live stock as he maintained in winter. Each villager had his share of the arable and better pasture and meadow lands, while the poorer pasture was held in common; the arable lands were further divided into three equal areas, one to lie fallow, one for wheat or rye, one for spring crops (barley, oats, beans, peas), thus sècuring alternation of crops. The inhabitants, being thus concentrated in villages—called also parishes and townships—were "not only best situated to defend each other from predatory attacks, but were called out by their lord with greater readiness in causes of emergency" (Marshall, *loc. cit.,* pp. 111-113, quoted by Maine, *loc. cit.*, Lecture iii, pp. 90-94). It will be noted that Marshall takes "their lord" for granted, knowing the feudal system, but not the earlier village communities, to which we turn.

The Teutonic Village Community, as reproduced in England by the Angles and Saxons, "consisted of a number of families, standing in a proprietary relation to a district divided into three parts These three portions were the Mark of the Township, or Village, the Common Mark, or waste, and the Arable Mark, or cultivated area. The community inhabited the village, held the Common Mark in mixed ownership, and cultivated the Arable Mark in losts appropriated to the several families" (Maine, *ibid.*, p. 78). It will be noted that Marshall, describing the methods of cultivation in England from 1770 to 1820, had figured out the same three areas or Marks: the Village in the centre, the Arable, or cultivated, Mark, with its appropriation, and the Common Mark or waste, held collectively. Maine remarks:

> The picture of the ancient state of England which follows was formed in his mind from simple observation of the phenomena of custom, tillage, and territorial arrangement which he saw before his eyes. You will perceive that he had not the true key in his possession, and that he figured to himself the collective form of property as a sort of common farm, cultivated by the tenantry of a single landlord. (*Ibid*., p. 90.)

The absence of "the true key" in one way makes Marshall's picture the more valuable. He drew it from the facts he observed, and had no theory into which he sought to fit facts. He formed his theory by induction from observations. Later writers have been able to test it by new observations, and have thus risen to a clearer knowledge in the regular scientific way.

The word "Mark" is from the Anglo-Saxon "Mearc," a boundary. It was used in mediaeval Germany to denote a tract of land held in common by a Village Community. Hence it is used by modern scholars for the tract of land similarly held by one of the Village communities of primitive Teutonic times. (See *Oxford Dictionary,* sub-voce.) The custom among villagers of "beating the boundaries" on old Lammas Day still survives in some parts of England, as a testimony to the ancient common rights, and it is noteworthy that the Act which changed the English Calendar provides that the old calendar shall be followed for the dates of the period during which common rights are enjoyed.

It may be noted that the allocation of areas within the Arable Mark to heads of households was transformed later into individual ownership of land, just as here in India the raiyatwari system was created by the British, following their own then long-established custom of private ownership of land.

The father, the head of a household, was supreme within the family tenement, and none outside the family, not even the officers of the law, might enter the house, save with his permission (*Ibid.*, p. 78). Hence the proverb: "The Englishmen's house is his castle". Maine recurs to this (*Loc. cit.* Lecture iv, p. 113):

> The description given by Maurer of the Teutonic Mark of the Township, as his researches have shown it to him, might here again pass for an account, so far as it goes, of an Indian village. The separate household, each despotically governed by its family chief, and never trespassed upon by the footstep of any person of different blood, are all to be found there in practice.

These heads of families shared the used of the Common Mark:

> It is a strict ownership in common, both in theory and in practice. When cattle grazed on the common pasture, or when the householder felled wood in the common forest, an elected or

> hereditary officer watched to see that the common domain was equitably enjoyed. (*Loc. cit.* Lecture iii, p. 79.)

We recall the Shepherd or Cowkeeper, of the Indian village.

The Arable Mark was divide into three great fields or areas, as observed by Marshall, each lying fallow once in there years, and a rotation of crops being observed in the others. The Arable Mark was not cultivated in common, as already said:

> Each householder has his own family lot in each of the three fields, and this he tills by his own labour, and that of his son and his slaves. But he cannot cultivate as he pleases. He must sow the same crop as the rest of the community, and allow his lot in the uncultivated field to lie fallow with the others. Nothing he does must interfere with the right of other households to have pasture for sheep and oxen in the fallow and among the stubbles of the fields under tillage. (*Ibid.*, p. 80).

Maine thinks there is evidence that the family lots were periodically re-distributed, but that this system came to an end,

> and each family was confirmed for a perpetuity in the enjoyment of its several lots of land. But there appears to be no country inhabited by an aryan race in which traces do not remain of the ancient periodical redistribution. It has continued to our own day in the Russian villages. Among the Hindu villagers there are widely extending traditions of the practice; and it was doubtless the source of certain usages, to be hereafter described, which have survived to our day in England and Germany. (*Ibid.*, 81, 82.)

Maine quotes from Morier a useful observation:

> These two distinct aspects of the early Teutonic freeman as a "lord" and a "commoner" united in the same person—one when within the pale of his homestead, the other when standing outside that pale in the economy of the Mark—should not be lost sight of. In them are reflected the two salient characteristics of the Teutonic race, the spirit of individuality and its spirit of association; and as the action and reaction of these two laws have determined the social and political history of the race, so they have in an especial manner affected its agricultural history. (*Ibid.*, p. 82.)

The traces of this type, the Teutonic Village Community, are to be found all over Britain, Maine contends, and are woven into it common law and land-laws. The process by which the Arable Mark and the Common Mark have been brought under cultivation is not yet wholly deciphered; the "Lord of the Manor"—a name to be explained in a moment—or the Lord in co-operation with the "Commoners," is a central figure in the changes, and the Enclosure Acts mark out many of the stages. But I think—with all deference to so great an authority—that Sir Henry Maine lays insufficient stress on the break caused by the Norman Conquest and its results. The resistance offered to the Normans by the sturdy Village Communities led to an antagonism to them which brought about the passing of law which sapped their independence, and huge grants of lands to Norman nobles, ensuring the triumph of feudalism in England, established the power of the great Barons, who wrenched Magna Carta—based on Saxon laws—from King John, and who formed a band which held the monarchy in check, until Edward IV finally destroyed their rival authority, and paved the way for the tyranny of the Tudors and the Stuarts, to be overthrown by the Great Revolution confirmed by the minor one which drove out James II and established the monarchy of William III and of Anne, followed by the Guelphs—now renamed the House of Windsor.

Nasse, the German writer who so carefully studied the English problem, is quoted by Maine (*Ibid.*, pp. 88, 89) as saying:

> In almost all parts of the country, in the Midland and Eastern countries particularly, but also in the West—in Wiltshire, for example—in the South as in Surrey, in the North as a Yorkshire, there are extensive open and common fields. Out of 316 parishes in Northamptonshire, 89 are in this condition; more than 100 in Oxfordshire; about 50,000 acres in Warwickshire; in Berkshire half the country; more than half of Wiltshire; in Huntingdonshire, out of a total area of 240,000 acres, 130,000 were commonable meadows, commons and common fields. (*Ueber die Mittelalterliche Feldgemeinschaft in England,* p. 4.)

Charles Bradlaugh, in his *House of Brunswick,* dealt trenchantly with the robbery of these rights of the villagers. The turning of arable land into pasture under the Tudors, and, later, the confiscation of common village lands were the two main causes of the decay of agriculture in England, the lessening of food-production and the multiplication of landless men, the proletariat, with only their labour to sell; hence the wage-slavery of masses of the people, now partially broken by Labour Unions. Bradlaugh quotes a popular song, which, referring to the punishment of the thief who stole the goose from the common, asks as to the punishment of the men who stole the common from the goose.

In Scotland, similar traces were found by Sir Walter Scott, and Maine refers us to his novel, *The Pirate,* and his diary, quoted in Lockhart's *Life of Scott,* vol. iii, p. 145. In a *Return of Boroughs or Cities in the United Kingdom, possessing Commmon Land,* Appendix I, House of Commons, August 10, 1870, quoted by Maine (*Ibid.*, pp. 95, 96), interesting details are given, as of Lauder Common, 1,700 acres in extent, part of which, about 130 acres, is periodically broken up and ploughed, and then later again laid down in grass and grazed, when another portion is similarly treated; each own of "burgess acres," was allotted one share of this cultivated land for each burgess acre, the particular share being decided by lot. Each burgess may also graze two cows or their equivalent, and a certain number of sheep on the common.

American Colonies

It was natural that in the American Colonies, Village Communities should spring up much in the old way. Maine has drawn attention to this, and says:

> It is a very remarkable fact that the earliest English emigrants to North America—who, you know, belonged principally to the class of yeomanry—organised themselves at first in village communities for purposes of cultivation. When a town was organised the process was that "the general court granted a tract of land to a company of persons. The land was first held by the company as property in common." (*Loc. cit.*, Lecture vi, p. 201. The words in inverted commas are quoted from Palfrey,'s *History of New England,* ii, 13.)

Here we see in America the formation of villages artificially, as in India.

Maine proceeds:

> An American commentator on this passage adds; "The company of proprietors proceeded to divide the land by assigning first house-lots (in Marlborough from fifteen to twenty acres), then tracts of meadow land, and in some cases mineral land, *i.e.*, where bog-iron ore was found. Pasture and woodland remained in common as the property of the company, but a law of the General Court in 1660 provided that "hereafter no cottage or dwelling-house be admitted to the privilege of commonage for wood, timber, or herbage but such as are already in being, or shall be erected with the consent of the town'. From that time the commoners appears as a kind of aristocracy, and the commons were gradually divided up." This is not only tolerably exact account of the ancient European and existing Indian village-community, but it is also a history of its natural development, where the causes which turn it into a manorial group are absent, and of its ultimate dissolution. (*Ibid.*, p. 201.)

Dr. Wilson speaks of the early Colonies as "small isolated settlements, and these settlements grew in their own way to be States. The slow process was from local, through State, to National organisation" (*Loc. cit.*, Chapter xi, §§ 1034). The settlements varied in type, and formed independent towns; these became loosely united for convenience. The townsmen met and elected their officers, who were responsible to their electors, and the grouped towns sent delegates to a central assembly (*Ibid.*, §§ 1038, 1039).

VILLAGE COUNCILS

The Teutonic, or the English, Village, as we have seen, had its meeting of elders or freemen; when the Villages were grouped into Hundreds—we recall Manu's groups of 10,100, etc.—there was the "Hundred-moot, or meeting, to which the villages sent representatives, and which was chiefly judicial, and above this the Folk-moot, or popular assembly, in which all freemen gathered. As the small States merged together, a National Council arose, the Assembly of the Wise, or the Witenagemot, which had the right of electing and deposing the King, and was also the highest judicial court and the legislature.

FEUDALISM

Gradually a change spread over Europe, as a new system, the feudal, emerged, and in England, this was sharply marked off by the Norman Conquest in A.D. 1066. The free and sturdy Saxon Villages resisted the new rule, and the Conqueror, to break down this resistance, made large grants of land to his barons, they holding it under conditions from himself. The old Villages continued to exist, but no longer as free communities; they were attached to a Lord. As Maine puts it:

> I will call the new group the Manorial group, and though my words must not be taken as strictly correct, I will say that a group of tenants autocratically organised and governed, has succeeded a group of households, of which the organisation and government were democratic. (*Loc. cit.* Lecture v, pp. 133, 134.)

Some of the lands were held by "free tenants"—"tenement land"—from the "Lord of the Manor"; others by tenures servile in origin—the "Lord's domain". The two together formed a "Manorial Group". The waste, or common land, became "the Lord's waste," but the old freeholders, or "commoners" kept their rights of pasture and of cutting fuel, and quarreled for centuries over enclosures with their Lord (*Cf. Ibid.,* pp. 135-147). Thus was created, throughout Western Europe, the great landlord class, and the freeholders—the yeomen—gradually sank in the social scale, and almost disappeared their place being taken by tenants who rented their farms from the Lord, and held them at his will, generally for a term of years by lease, at the end of which the rent might be raised, the tenant turned out, his improvements confiscated. The immense disproportion between incomes was gradually produced—before the advent of power-machinery—by this absolute vesting of the land, as private property, in the hands of a privileged class, and the accompanying dispossession of the people, changing the "Merrie England" of the older days to the discontented and restless England of the later eighteenth and nineteenth century. Out of these conditions, aided by the aggregation of people in towns, the springing up of huge centers of population round factories, and the creation of large stores of capital by the introduction of power-machinery and the increase of the labourer's productiveness, while he was excluded from sharing the results, all these led to the struggles between capital and labour, the formation of Trade Unions to equalise the conflicts between the capitalist and the skilled wage-slaves, and the crushing down of the unskilled into brutalizing conditions, and finally to the birth of Socialism, and the demand for the reconstruction of Society on a better foundation than competition.

GERMANY

We have reviewed the Teutonic Village Communities as planted in Britain by the Teutonic invaders, and need therefore only glance briefly at them here. Wilson truly says that their system combined

> with singular completeness, though in somewhat crude form, tribal unity and individual independence amongst them, as amongst other Aryan peoples; kinship constituted the basis of association and the primal sanction of authority, and the family was the unit of government. Kinsmen, fellow-tribesmen, were grouped in villages, and each village maintained without question its privileges of self-government, legislating upon its common affairs, and administering its common property in village meeting. Its lands were the property not of individuals, but of the community; but they were allotted in separate parcels to the freemen of the community, upon would-be equitable principles, to be cultivated for private, not for communal, profit. Chiefs there were who exercised magisterial powers, but these chiefs were elected in village meeting. They did not determine the weightier questions of custom in the administration of justice: that was the province of the village meeting itself; and such judicial authority as they did exercise was shown by "assessors" chosen from the whole body of their free fellow-villagers. (*Loc. cit.,* Chapter v. 287.)

The Village comprised freemen, serfs, and slaves, and political power was vested in the freemen alone. The chief peculiarity of the German Teutons, in their own land, seems to have been their habit of association as a host of armed emigrants, under an elected chief—King, from *könig,* the "man who can," as Carlyle puts it—and who invaded some more desirable land than their own and occupied it, then the King parcelled it out, as William the

Conqueror did in England, on military tenures, so that it was held from himself. These tenants, military chiefs, made similar grants of land from their own fiefs, on conditions of military service, so that the final outcome of these emigrant hosts was the establishment of feudalism over Europe, while the traditions and remnants of the Roman Empire reappeared in the powerful Roman Catholic Church, and the so-called Holy Roman Empire, founded by Charlemagne, King of the Franks, at the beginning of the 9th century, A.D 800. A good example of these armed emigrant hosts is afforded by the Franks—"freemen" a combination of north-western German tribes—and their King, who invaded and settled in France, in the 5th century, creating in northern France "Francia Teutonica."

Annie Besant

3

Political Obligations

The term 'obligation' is a term derived from Roman Law. Obligation is defined in the *Institutes* of Justinian as 'a legal bond (*Juris vinculum*) in virtue of which we are tied by necessity to some performance'. Such an obligation may be either civil or political.

When it is civil, and takes the form of a bond between private persons, I am tied as a private person to perform some act for another such person, and the necessity by which I am tied is that of enforced law. When the obligation is political, and takes the form of a bond between me as a citizen and the governing authority as such, I am tied as a citizen to perform an act, or rather a number of acts, for the governing authority; but what is here the necessity by which I am tied to performance? Above me as a private person and any other private person there stands the necessity of enforced law, as something apart from us both

What is the nature of the necessity which stands above me as a citizen and the governing authority as such, and which is something apart from us both? It cannot be enforced law; that is simply a mode or aspect of governing authority, and not something above, it and separate from it. Some other answer has to be found. We may begin by considering three different theories which have been propounded by way of answer.

(a) *The Theory of Divine Right*. Upon this theory the necessity which stands above and apart from the citizen and the governing authority is that of the Divine Will and ordinance. I am obliged to obey the government authoiity because I am

obliged to obey God, and because and governing authority is essentially an emanation and delegation of divine authority. This theory goes back to the East and the ancient Eastern monarchies; but in its European form it is based on the teaching of St. Paul. 'Omnis anima potestatibus sublimioribus subdita sit: non est enim potestas nisi a Deo: quae autem sunt a Deo, ordinate sunt.' St. Thomas Aquinas, as has already been noted, followed the teaching of St. Paul, and accordingly ascribed to God the *principium* of all authority. But knowing also the doctrine of the Roman lawyers, that the *princeps* derives his authority and power from an act of the people in delegating and transferring to him *omne suum imperium et potestatem,* and knowing too the doctrine of Aristotle that the assembled people should have the right of electing its magistrates initially and calling them afterwards to account, St. Thomas adds a rider to the teaching of St. Paul. If God Himself gives the *principium* of authority, the people determines its *modus,* or permanent constitutional form, and it also confers the *exercitium,* or actual enjoyment and employment of power by the persons or body of persons possessing it for the time being. (St. Thomas also suggest that the people may criticize, and in the event of misuse withdraw, the *exercitium* which they have conferred: indeed in one passage of the *De Regimine Principum* he even says that 'a ruler who fails to act faithfully, as the office of kingship demands, in the government of a community, deserves to suffer the consequence that his subjects should refuse to keep their *pact* with him', thus appearing to combine a theory of social contract with the theory of divine right.)

The theory of St. Thomas, which was the generally accepted theory of the Middle Ages, was thus a theory that the king, as the head of a body politic, had a claim to the necessary obedience of each member of that body in virtue of an authority coming *from* God, but coming, in its course, *through* the body politic of which he was head. The thought of the sixteenth century, departing from that of the Middle Ages, amputated as it were the body from the head: it rejected the notion that authority came to the head through the body: it left the head with a solitary authority unqualified by any act of the people. It is in that century, but not before, that we find a new theory of divine right as the right of a bodiless head. This bodiless head may either be regarded as receiving authority directly from God, or he may be held, as he is Sir Robert Filmer, to have received it indirectly through a patriarchal succession from Adam who received it originally and directly from the hands of his Maker. The result of the latter view is a theory of divine hereditary right, with the emphasis on the word 'hereditary'; but both views alike involve a theory of divine right which leaves no room or place for the body of the people. The medieval theory had been monarchico-democratic: the theory which emerges in the sixteenth century is purely a monarchical theory, and it is especially so in the seventeenth-century version which makes the line of heredity the line of the transmission of right.

It is not necessary here to accept or reject the theory of divine right. There is a sense in which, at any rate to the theist, it is eternally true that all power is of God, and that every holder of power is responsible to God; and if it is also eternally true that the holders of power are responsible to the community, we have seen that the medieval version of the theory, if not in the later versions of the sixteenth and seventeenth centuries, recognised and proclaimed this truth. But the form and vesture of the theory belong to a vanished age, in which kings governed as well as reigned; and while we may recognize a permanent core of truth in its essential doctrine, we must also recognize that the setting of the core is now an antiquity. Indeed in the sixteenth century thought was already moving away from the idea that kings derived authority from God, and was seeking to give them a different title.

(b) *The theory of prescriptive possession.* Upon this theory, which began to be advanced in France, and which may be termed the theory of legitimism, the monarch rules by customary right: not *jure divino* (though that right might also be alleged as an additional support), but *jure consuetudinario.* Long possession, ripening into property, is the title of kings to governing authority; and from this title, upon the assumption that men are tied by necessity to respect all property-rights, the conclusion is drawn (though, as we shall see, it is not a logical conclusion) that subjects are tied by necessity to respect the property-right of kings to the exercise of governing authority. Bodin, in his *de Republica* of 1576, connected a theory of this order with a theory of patriarchy, though he did so without bringing into his argument, as Filmer afterwards did in his *Patriarcha* of 1680, the idea of a divine commission of authority to the original patriarch Adam. The theory of Bodin may be resumed in three propositions. The first is that the family is a given natural fact, which you must simply accept, and that it naturally involves for its head a right both of property in possessions and of authority over persons, which you must also simply accept. The second is that the family is the source and origin of the State. The third, which follows logically on the second, is that the authority of the head of the State is the same authority, with the same natural title, as that of the head of a family, inasmuch as the State is only a derivative and extension of the family. The theory of Bodin is in one way superior to the theory of divine right current in his day. He makes the king not a bodiless head, but the head of a family; and by thus introducing the idea of the family he gives to governing authority not only the title of prescriptive possession, but also a natural title grounded in human feeling. The objection to his theory is that the State has long ceased to be, if indeed it ever was, an extension of the family, and that the position of the head of a State is therefore not the position of the head of a family—still less (as he seems to assume) the position of the head of a family vested with that peculiar degree of *patria potestas* which was practised among the early Romans.

Another French jurist, Loyseau, in his *Traité des Offices* of 1614, is more thoroughgoing than Bodin, and puts his trust in the simple theory of prescriptive possession, which is the essence of legitimist ideas. He does not seek to justify the claims of governing authority to impose obligation on subjects by basing such authority upon something exterior to itself, as even Bodin does when he invokes the name and sanction of the family: he is content to base it upon itself, if only it includes within itself the element of duration. Kings, he holds, have *arisen* in different ways, some by popular concession, others by simple force and 'ancient usurpation'; but as they now exist, after the process and passage of time, 'they have all acquired by prescription the property in sovereign power'. In other words, continuous use has given them something more than the exercise of authority: it has given them *ownership* of authority; and their subjects are thus tied to them, and to the authority which they own, by the necessity of respecting ownership and all the rights which it carries. This mere legitimism could, and did, ally itself with ideas of the divine right of kings, on the plea that a long-time warrant was also the warrant of God. It might carry weight in that conjunction; but in itself, and taken by itself, it fails to explain why the subject is tired and obliged to governing authority. It degrades authority over persons to the level of property in things; and it brings the problem of political obligation down into the area of civil obligation, to which it does not belong and in which it cannot be solved. Moreover it is a theory which has a sole application to monarchy, and to monarchy which is a governing as well as a reigning monarchy.

(c) *The Theory of Contract.* Upon this theory in its simpler form the citizen is tied to the governing authority, first, because he, in common with all other citizens, has made a contract with a person or body of persons, under which that person or body receives authority in return for the protection and service of declaring and enforcing a system of legal rules, and secondly, because he and his fellows are bound by natural law to respect and perform the terms of that contract. But reflection soon suggests to the mind that this simpler form, taken by itself and in itself, is inadequate and incomplete. How could men bargain collectively with the person or body of persons to be vested with governing authority, unless they were already of the nature of a collective body, and how are we to explain their being already of that nature? In order to answer that question thinkers of the school of contract were ultimately forced to the conclusion that there was a double contract, or more exactly, two stages of contract: first the contract of society, the *pacte d'association,* as it is termed by Rousseau, or the *Gesellschaftsvertrag,* as it is termed by Gierke, or 'the social contract proper', as it may also be termed; and secondly, the contract of government, or the *pacte de governement*, or the *Herrschaftvertrag,* or the social contract loosely (and even improperly) so-called. Under the 'contract of society' all persons in a given area, an area supposed somehow to be definite agree with one another to form and to be a collective body of the nature of a *societas* or partnership. Under the 'contract of government', or the social contract loosely so-called, this *societas* or partnership, once it is formed, agrees with a person or body of persons, supposed somehow to be separate from it, to institute a *potestas* and to confer it upon that person or body on certain conditions. The first contract thus creates *societas,* and the second *potestas;* or, as we also say, in the specific terms of Roman law, the first contract is the result of an act of simple consent expressing itself in the form of partnership or *societas,* and the second the result of a similar act expressing itself in the form of agency, or, as it was called by the Roman lawyers, *mandatum.*

Is there any element of truth in the first of the two contracts thus distinguished: the contract of society? If the nation a of a social contract is meant to explain the nature and the existence of national Society, as the use of the word 'social' implies, it fails to achieve its object, not only because a national Society is never actually the product of contract, but also because it is totally unlike anything that could possibly be produced by contract. A national Society, as we have seen, knows no limits to its purposes, as contractual partnership always do: it cannot be dissolved by agreement, as partnerships can be: it has, as a national Society, no organisation or administration, as partnerships always have. If, however, the idea of a social contract is meant to explain the nature and existence not of national Society, but of the national State—the State as distinguished from national Society, the State as a legal association super-imposed on such a Society—then it may be said to achieve its object. Though we cannot apply the idea of contract to national Society, and though the adjective 'social' is a misnomer, we can apply the idea of contract to the national State, and we may not improperly speak of a political contract. But the 'political contract' of which we may thus speak is something entirely different, as the course of the argument will show, from the 'contract of government' assumed by the old thinkers of the school of contract. If it has to be distinguished from the contract of Society, it has equally to be distinguished from the contract of government as that contract used to be conceived.

How, then, are we to conceive the nature of this political contract? We must begin by admitting, or rather contending, that it does not serve to explain, and is not for a moment meant to explain, the chronological antecedents of the State in general, the State at all times and places in all its manifestations. It serves only to explain, and is meant only to explain, the logical presuppositions of the State in particular: the State as it exists at the present time, and as it exists at the present time in the Western world—the world of Western Europe, the British Commonwealth, and the Americans. If we look at the State in general, as it arose and grew in the course of past time, we are bound to recognize that it did not arise and has not grown in the climate of contract. It was formed and developed by a variety of factors; the bond of kinship uniting, or supposed to unite, a people or group of peoples; military force and diplomatic policy welding different peoples into some sort of union; the bond of neighbourhood joining the residents of some definite area in a common system of economic and social relations, apart from, or over and above, any bond of kinship or any employment of force and policy. But if we look at the State in particular, as it exists in our own time and in the area of the Western world, we are equally bound to recognize that it lives and has its being in a climate of contract, and of all the concomitants of contract: mutual concession, mutual toleration, mutual discussion, and general give and take. The modern State of the Western world is a legal association. As such it depends upon, and it constituted by, a memorandum of association, or a set of articles of association, or in other words a 'constitution', which states the contractual terms on which the association is made and under which is henceforth acts. The constitution of a State may thus be regarded as the contract on which its action, and the action of its members in their capacity of members, is ultimately dependent; and from this point of view political obligation may be regarded as contractual obligation. This is especially plain where there is a written constitution, as there is in the great majority of the States of the Western world, but it does not cease to be plain where the constitution is partly or even largely unwritten: there is, after all, no difference of kind between the 'written' and 'unwritten' constitution, and indeed the sense of obligation may be felt as much to the 'unwritten as to the 'written' constitution. The contractual nature of the constitution, and the contractual nature of the obligation incumbent under it on each citizen, becomes even more plain when the constitution contains not only a 'frame of government', or a statement of means and methods, but also a 'declaration of rights', or a statement of ends and purposes; for such a statement of ends and purposes is even more obviously a formulation of contractual terms than is a statement of means and methods.

We may now turn from our examination of the truth of the first form of contract, the contract of Society, to an examination of the truth of the second, the contract of government. Here we may say at once that the logic of the previous argument necessarily involves us in rejection of any idea of a separate contract of government. If we accepted that idea, we should be committed to the view that the citizen is tied or obliged to the governing authority by the necessity of a contract separately and specifically made with that authority: a contract other than, and additional to, the political contract expressed in the constitution. There is no need for any such view; and if it were adopted, it would unduly exalt the governing authority by making its members a body separate from the general civic body, and independent enough to negotiate on equal terms with that body. The one political contract expressed in the constitution is sufficient for every purpose, and adequate in itself to explain the basis of governing authority. That one contract, so expressed determines all positions in and under the constitution: it determines governing position as well as, and along with, the general civic position of the ordinary citizen. A person who is a member of the governing authority simply adds to his general civic position, in which he is already placed and obliged by the terms of the political contract, a further and particular governing position, in which he is also placed and obliged by the terms of the very same contract. If he differs from the ordinary citizen in having two positions, and not one only, he owes both of the positions which he holds to the same origin in the same contract, the one and only contract expressed in the constitution. When once we grasp the idea that the constitution of the State is the one and only contract, we can see that, fundamentally, the citizen and the holder of governing authority stand on the same footing by virtue of an identical title. The idea of a separate contract of government, giving a separate title to the holder of governing authority, could only arise in the absence of a constitution: it was a rudimentary attempt to provide the rudiments of a constitution, in the form of a bilateral contract regarded as simply determining the position of governing authority in its relation to the general body of citizens, and determining nothing more. Actually the constitution, as men saw in the light of further experience (beginning with the American Revolution of 1776, and continued in the French Revolution of 1789), determines much more than that: it determines *all* positions: it regulates equally, and in the same way, the position of governing authority and the position of ordinary citizens. When once men grasped the breadth of the contract of the constitution, the rudimentary idea of a contract of government had served its turn, and faded away.

Political Obligation and the Idea of Justice

Is it a final solution of the problem of political obligation to argue that we are bound by our own contractual act in forming and continuing to accept the constitution of our State? That argument certainly provides us with a legal bond in virtue of which we are tied to performance by a necessity: not the necessity of enforced law, which is what holds us to our civil obligation; but the necessity of the constitution, which is what holds us to our political obligation. But the question may be raised, Why is the constitution itself necessary, or in what sense is it a necessity which we are bound to accept? We may reply to that question by saying, or repeating, that the constitution, after all, is our act (though the communist or the revolutionary might rejoin that it was not *his),* and that our acts, when they are once established as objective facts in the external environment of our lives—when once they have gone out of us as promises made to others, on which others rely and on the performance of which they count—oblige us necessarily as things now beyond recall. *Fides est servanda.* But our minds crave something more even than the sanctity of promise and pledge. We want to know not only that we *are* now bound and tied, but also that we *ought* to be: we want to know not only that there has been an act, of our own, but also that the act has value, or is directed towards a value, so that we are bound not only by the act as an act, but also by something valuable in it or above it. We are thus led to ask ourselves where, and in what, we can find the final and ultimate ground of political obligation. The answer to that question in suggested by the argument of the previous Book. The ultimate reason why we are obliged is not that the State is our act and deed: it is because the State represents and realizes, and in so far as it represents and realizes, that system of political values, and that general idea of justice controlling and coordinating the system, which finally claim our obedience. If the State does *this,* and to the extent that it does *this,* our obligation is perfect.

It is not, therefore, the fact that the State has a basis of contract which finally commands our allegiance. It is the fact that the State is the expression and organ of justice. We are obliged to the governing authority of the State, and we obey and perform its commands, because the State as a whole is, on the whole, such an expression and organ. If the State fails to be that, or in so far as it fails to be that, we are left with an obligation which hangs, as it were, in the air, and has no final support. Then there arises the problem, 'Which is the true obligation: our obligation to the State, or our obligation to justice?' It is the problem which confronts the communist in a non-communist State: it is equally the problem which confronts the liberal and the democrat in a State which is neither liberal nor democratic: it is, in a word, the problem whether the major obligation is simply to the State-expression of justice, or to a demand of justice which the State either fails to express or falls short of expressing fully.

To that problem we shall return at the end of the argument of this Book. Meanwhile we are left with the proposition that the State as a whole is, on the whole, the expression and organ of justice, and that this is the final source of political obligation. The proposition involves both a positive and a negative implication. Neither of these implication will justify any and every act of the governing authority of the State: both of them justify only the action of the State *in general* (or in other words the State as a whole), and that only in respect of the *general trend* of such action. The positive implication is that when the State is declaratory—when it declares, in the form of law, the body of deductions which flow from the idea of a right order of human relations, as that idea now stands at this given stage of common conviction—we are actively obliged to accept and to carry into effect the law so declared, because it is ultimately a declaration of the dictates of an order which we ourselves acknowledge to be obligatory. In fulfilling the law which the State declares, we obey, and we are obliged to obey, our own idea of what a right order of human relations should be. The negative implication is that when the State is compulsory—when it compels us by the use of force to recognize in a particular case, and that our own case, the general rule which we recognize as binding for all cases—we are passively obliged to accept and suffer the compulsion so applied, because, once more, it is ultimately the compulsion of an order which we ourselves acknowledge and acknowledge to be obligatory. In undergoing compulsion we are being made to obey, not the State as a will or a power impinging on our own will or power, but the something behind the State which is not a will or a power, but a system of right order which we believe to be right as a system, even though we may have infringed it at a particular point.

Political Obligation and the 'General Will'

Two lines of thought have been followed in the argument hitherto advanced. Along the first line an attempt has been made to explain political obligation in terms of contract, and as the result of the political contract embodied in the constitution. Along the second the attempt has been made to explain it in terms of justice, and as being a logical consequence of the idea of a right order of relations which is at once demanded and supplied by our own reason and thought. We have now to draw the two lines together and to combine the two explanations. If they are left unconnected, difficulties ensue: explanation ceases to be valid, and obligation does not oblige. If obligation be regarded as simply a matter of contract, we are faced by the possibility of two opposite consequences, both of them disastrous, if diametrically different. On the one hand some of the parties to the contract may stickle and cavil about the State's action, and arguing, 'This was not in the bond', they may refuse accordingly to be obliged. On the other hand, the contractual association, acting as a whole, or at any rate by a majority decision, may hold that its own will and deed is final, whatever that will and deed may be, provided only that the form of the constitution is duly observed: indeed, since an act of the association, or that of a defined and prescribed majority within it, can alter the form of the constitution, the will and deed of the association may even be held to be unconditionally final, without proviso or qualification. In that case the members of the association will be obliged by the necessity of obeying mere will, as such and apart from its content. These are the difficulties which ensue from a simple reliance on the notion of contract. But there are also difficulties which ensue from a simple reliance on the notion of justice. If obligation be regarded as simply a matter of justice and of obedience to the dictates of justice, then it will follow that a governing authority which wills and enforces those dictates will necessarily oblige us, even if it is a pure autocracy, in no way based on consent, and therefore destitute of any contractual element. This may seem an abstraction, or even a fantasy. In effect it *is* a fantasy; for if justice is a *common* conviction, then it and autocracy can never be yoke-fellows. But it is a fantasy which haunted the benevolent despots of the eighteenth century, and has haunted in our time the leaders and dictators of the twentieth century. Nor has it haunted them only. It has also been accepted by many thinkers, who have believed that the cause of impartial justice is best served by the mind of the 'one best man' who is lifted above all passion.

The problem before us is that of reconciling the principle of a common will, expressed in the notion of contract, with the principle of a common rule, expressed in the notion of justice. In other words we have to combine democratic might with sovereign right: to unite the volume and dynamic power of a common will with the stability and control of a common rule of reason. It is an easy escape from this problem, illustrated in the writings of Rousseau, to proclaim the sovereign right of democratic might. But it is an escape, and not a solution: not a reconciliation of both of the terms, but an elimination of one at the expense of the other; not the joint dominion of a common will and a common rule, but the single dominion of a will which, because it is merely will, is ultimately nothing but might. Is it also an escape, or is it a solution, if we start at the other end: if instead of attaching sovereign right to democratic might, we seek to attach democratic might to sovereign right? Does that too eliminate one of the terms at the expense of the other, or does it succeed in reconciling both? At any rate there is a case for inquiry. We may therefore inquire where the argument leads if instead of beginning—and ending—in will, we begin with the 'rule of right' or common rule of reason. On this basis we take our start from the idea of a right order of relations postulated and given by reason and therefore prior to will; and we seek to discover how this sovereign right proceeding from reason can acquire democratic might, by becoming the common conviction of the whole of a community, and by inspiring and enlisting in support of itself the common will of the members of that community.

The inquiry involves three stages. In the first of these stages we are confronted by the idea of a sovereign right, as the ultimate source of obligation—the idea of justice the orderer, 'joining' and 'fitting together' both the positions of persons and the principles on which those positions are assigned, and thus producing what we have called a right order of human relations. This was the fundamental meaning of the theory of Natural Law, as that idea was expressed by the Stoics and the Roman lawyers in antiquity, by the Fathers and the schoolmen of early and medieval Christianity, and by thinkers of the secular school of Natural Law in the seventeenth and eighteenth centuries. But there was an imperfection and an abstraction in the theory of Natural law, particularly in the last of its phases. We cannot assume, as the thinkers of the seventeenth and eighteenth centuries did, that there are truths of a 'natural', or ideally rational, justice to be discovered and deduced by the reason of the solitary jurist, as there are truths of geometry to be discovered and deduced by the reason of the solitary geometrician. Still less can we assume that, even if they could be discovered and deduced by such a process, they would remain thenceforth unchangeably true. There are differences between geometry and justice. For one thing, geometry is concerned with impersonal space, which does not think; justice is a matter of a personal system of human relations, and therefore of living persons who themselves think about those relations, whose thought constitutes that system, and who, in a word, think justice into existence. It is not the solitary jurist who discovers the truths of justice: it is the whole body of persons who stand in relation with one another and think out together the problems of the right order of their relations. For another thing, geometry is concerned with a space which is constant and invariable, and it remains accordingly constant itself; justice is a matter of human relations which change and grow in the process of time with changes of social thought, and it adjusts itself and changes accordingly. There is, indeed, a constancy of justice; but justice has also life and growth, and therefore mutability. It is an 'ever-fixed mark'; but it is also an ever-flowing stream.

This brings us to the next and second stage of our inquiry. If justice, as a matter of human relations, involves a society of persons thinking about their relations and thinking into existence a right order of those relations; if again, as such a matter, it also involves the possibility of a change of relations, and therefore of thought about relations, and therefore of the scheme of right order created for them by thought; it follows that we can add to the idea of sovereign right, which confronted us in the first stage, the idea of creative general thought, busy in a constant process of disengaging this sovereign right from the multitude of relations and the constant flux of their change. Justice is made by the general thought of all the member of a community engaged in relations with one another; or, more exactly, it is always in process of being made by that general thought, and it is therefore always in a state of 'becoming' or development. The general thought of the community is the maker of sovereign right, and it is always making it afresh. We can see an example of its making and remaking if we take the instance of marriage, or the relation of husband and wife. Thought has created and sustains the idea that permanent monogamy is the justice or right order of that relation. It has been a long work: it is a work which is still being changed and modified. Greater equality has been introduced into the relation by the reduction of the power of the husband: greater liberty is being sought (sometimes with too little regard to the principle of co-operation, in the rearing and training of children, which is also a principle of marriage) by the extension of facilities for divorce in the event of grave disagreement. At point after point, and in stage after stage, the general thought of the community, which originally applied the idea of justice to the relation of the sexes, is constantly applying it afresh, and therefore constantly changing the general opinion about the right order of that relation and, with it, the law which reflects and declares that opinion.

The third and last stage of our inquiry confronts us with the question, 'What is the product that issues from this general thought of the community, and what is the form and shape in which it is distilled and expressed?' Gierke, as we have noticed, seeks to express the product in the term 'common conviction' (*Gesammtüberzeugung)*. Rousseau sought to express it in the term 'general will' (*volonté générale*). Both of these terms are shorthand, and either of them is the half rather than the whole of the matter. Perhaps we shall answer our question best if we put the two terms together, and if, in the course of doing so, we also seek to indicate, more precisely than has yet been done, both the area in which the general thought of the community acts and the time-span of its action. On that basis we may say that, as the result of a *long-time* process of thought, moving in the area of Society and being therefore a process of *social* thought, there emerges a *common conviction which is also, a general will* about a right order of human relation and the obligatory nature of that order.

The *long-time* character of the process of thought is a fact of primary important. Burke stated this fact in memorable words, 'Man is a most unwise, and a most wise being. The individual is foolish. The multitude, for the moment, is foolish, when they act without deliberation. But the species is wise, and when time is given to it, as a species, it almost always acts right.' If we substitute 'Society' for 'species' the statement of Burke is the expression of an indubitable truth. The benefit of time is needed for the production of the common conviction which is also a general will. It was the error of Rousseau to ascribe to the meeting of the multitude for the moment a *volonté générale* which can only be the fruit of slow time and of something more than the multitude.

That something more (and here we come to another fact of primary importance) is Society, national Society, as defined and explained in the beginning of the whole argument; and it is accordingly *social thought,* in the strict sense of the word, which produces, by its working in time, a common conviction and will. The area in which the general thought of the community acts is essentially and primarily the area of Society, and not the area of the State. This is not to say that such thought is not operative in the are a of the State: it is only to say that it operates there, as it were, at a remove, and by a translation or transference from its original area. The State, as such, is the area of electoral votes. parliamentary statutes, executive order and regulations, judicial decisions, and all the formal declarations which constitute, in one way or another, the scheme of positive law. All these declarations register social thought. But that thought is prior to the registration; and it acts, in its original motion, elsewhere than in the area of registration. It acts in and through the social organs which precipitate social thought and conduct with one another the discussion of what they precipitate: it acts in and through the churches, the clubs and societies and parties (not in themselves a part of the State but rather a part of Society, however much they impinge on the State), the professional and occupational groupings, the newspaper and pamphlet and book, and all the other organs for the ventilation and the comparison of different social ideas. We can thus see social thought in all its forms and with all its organs, which correspond to the multiplicity of Society, proceeding by the way of discussion, which is its great and sovereign way; and we may even begin to see in advance the emergence of the idea of democracy, which is a system of 'government by discussion', and therefore a transference of the method of social thought into the area of the State and government.

Proceeding thus by way of discussion, social thought produces a mental output (and here we come to still another fact of primary importance) which is partly a conviction of the value, and partly a will for the establishment, of a general order of social relations and the general rules of that order. It would be an error to concentrate attention exclusively on the element of will in this output: it would also be an error, and a still greater error, if, having so concentrated our attention and isolated the element of will, we ascribed that element exclusively to the State. The will is conviction as well as will, and conviction before it is will; and the primary area of its residence is Society, even if its effects are transferred and translated into the State and the State's legal system.

But the term 'general will' has come to be used in political theory as a shorthand term for that common conviction-and-will which, arising in the area of Society, transmits its action and operation into the area of the State. There is some reason for the use of the term; but there are also reasons for using the term with caution, and with reservations and qualifications. In favour of its use we may argue that a national Society, as such, and as distinct from the State, develops in the course of its common life a growing general conviction about the just and proper order of the relations between its members, and a growing general will for the establishment and maintenance of that order as its own way of life and type of civilisation. This has been the line of development of French national society; it has equally been the line of development of British national society.

Upon this basis we may go on to argue that the national State, as the legal incorporation of a national Society, should acknowledge this general will at each stage, in the form and expression which it has attained at that stage, as the ultimate standard of its action. Thus conceived, the general will, as a contemporary thinker has said, is 'the standard by which political willing should be guided': in other words it is the ultimate and permanent will (if we can rightly use the word 'will') by which the immediate and day-to-day will of the governing authority ought to be determined, as it also is the ultimate will (if again we can rightly use that word) by which the will of the citizen ought to be obliged.

But though we may thus speak of the general will as the standard by which political willing should be guided, alike in the governing authority and in the citizen, we must also remember the qualifications to which any use of that term is subject. The first qualification is a matter of the *mental character* of this will. The will is a conviction as well as a will, and a conviction before it becomes a will. The essential and primary thing about it, as Gierke has said, is a conviction that something already is, and that a standard exists and is there, rather than a will that something shall be. From this point of view we may also say, as Rousseau strove to say, that the essence of the general will is not the persons or 'subjects' willing, but the things or 'objects of their will: the things or 'objects' which are primarily a content of common conviction, and which only become a content of common or general will because they are already a content of common or general conviction. The second qualification, which ensues upon the first, is a matter of the factor of *time*. So far as the general will is will, it is not an act of willing at a given moment of time: it is a permanent trend of will, which is growing as well as permanent, and which, we may even say in a paradox, shows its permanence most clearly in its capacity of growth. The third and last qualification, which ensues in turn on the second, is a matter of the *area* or residence of this general will, thus operative through time as a permanent and yet growing trend of the mind in the members of a community. The area or place of residence is not the legally organised State. The 'general will' is not political willing, and its home is not the political sphere. It belongs to the social area; it is a function of Society.

The qualifications are so numerous that we may well come to the conclusion that the general will is almost of the nature of a will-o'-the-wisp. The truth which that term is designed to express may be stated more simply in other terms. Instead of committing ourselves to the notion of the primary or supreme sovereignty of the general will, we may prefer to speak of the primacy of a socially created and socially developed conception of justice—that last and most majestic sovereign which stands behind and above the 'sovereign' constitution, as that, in its turn, stands behind and above the 'sovereignty' of the parliament of the State. Upon this basis we may proceed to enumerate a series of propositions.

1. The supreme sovereign which stands in the background of any political organised community is justice: justice in the sense of that right order of human relations which gives to the greatest possible number of persons the greatest possible opportunity for the highest possible development of all the capacities of their personality.

2. Justice is mediated by, or comes through the medium of, a process of social thought, which in the course of its operation produces a body of common conviction about the dictates of justice, backed by a common will or purpose of acting in the strength and under the guidance of that conviction.

3. This product of social thought is mediated in turn by the State, in the sense that it undergoes a process of being declared and enforced by a legal association contractually formed for that object by the creation of a constitution, and acting henceforth in virtue and under the rules of that constitution.

4. The citizen is obliged, at the end of the whole process, to obey the law so declared and enforced by the State, for the immediate reason that the State is based on his own contractual act, but for the ultimate reason that the State expresses the product of social thought which itself is the expression of justice.

A number of problem are raised by, or involved in, these propositions. (a) The third of them raises the problem of the proper method of the mediation of social thought by the State; it leads us to inquire whether the democratic form of constitution and the democratic method of government are the most correspondent, in their own nature, to the form and method of social thought, and the most likely, in their results, to translate the product of such thought into a clear and effective expression. (b) The first proposition, and especially its first clause, confronts us once more with the problem of sovereignty: it leads us beyond what has already been said about that problem at an earlier stage, and involves us in an inquiry into the ultimate nature and final residence of sovereign authority. (c) The fourth proposition, in its final clause, suggests, or implies, one of the gravest (if not the gravest) of all political problems. Granted that the citizen is obliged to obey the law of the State because the State expresses in its law the product of social thought, which itself is the expression of justice, does it follow that he is obliged to obey when that reason is not present? If and so far as the State does *not* express in its law the product of social thought, but expresses something different from, or even contrary to, that product, does obligation then to that extent cease; is disobedience then justified; and, if it is, may it even be carried to the length of resistance? This is the problem of the limits of political obligation: it is also, at its furthest reach, the problem of the right, or duty, of resistance. It is a problem as old as the *Antigone* of Sophocles, and indeed as old as the State itself; but it is always assuming new shapes, and if in the past a Creon or a Caesar was challenged in the name of religious conviction, today democracy itself is challenged in the name of the economic creed of communism.

Political Obligation and the Democratic System

If the State can be regarded as mediating social thought about justice to its members, and as expressing in its law the product of such thought, we may draw from that premises the conclusion that the State should itself correspond, in its own nature and operation, to the process of social thought which it mediates, and should thus be a broad open channel for the flow of the product which it expresses. The process of social thought is a process in which all the member of Society can freely share, and to which they can all contribute freely. It follows that, if there is to be correspondence and a broad open flow, the process of the activity of the State should also be a process in which all its members can freely share and to which they can all freely contribute. We may argue that this demand is satisfied, and satisfied only, by the democratic State. Indeed we may argue that it is satisfied doubly by the democratic State; first in the form of its constitution and the way of its coming into being, and next in its method of government and the way of its operation.

In their actual coming into being, as has already been noted, States are historical products of very various patterns, due to a variety of historical causes. But the question before us here is not a question of the far-off origins, back in the mists of time, of the States we know today in their changed and developed form as the modern States of our Western world. It is a question of the basis and *raison d'être* of the modern State *as we know it now,* in the form which it has now assumed in the world in which we now live. What set of ideas, and what motions of the mind, have formed and brought into being the State we now know in the form it now has? Some answer to that question has already been given; and it is only necessary to summarize briefly the head of the answer. A national Society, in the course of a process of social thought, creates and sustains and idea an ideal of a right of order relations between its members: an idea and ideal of justice. But it cannot attain its ends, or turn the idea into fact and the ideal into reality, without an organised system for the declaration and enforcement of the dictates of justice. We must therefore conceive the society as making itself, or 'constituting' itself, an organised system *for this purpose,* or, in other words, as forming itself into a *legal* association or State, while still continuing to exist and act as a Society, and still continuing, as such, to maintain and develop that process of social thought which is continually fertilizing the idea and ideal of justice. This act of the 'Constitution' of a State by the members of a national Society results, and expresses itself, in a 'constitution' in another and further sense of the word: the Constitution with a capital C; the articles of association (both written and unwritten) which warrant, authorize, and control the actions and the organs of the legal association. We may say that this Constitution or set of articles of association, is of the nature of a contract, which we may call the political contract; and in that sense, as has already been noted, we may say that the State has a contractual basis. We may also say that the constitution of a State by a national Society and by all the members of that Society, or in other words by the people, is the first stage and the foundation of the democratic method of government. In it, and by it, the people have given themselves the basis of political action by a first democratic act of creation. Will they not then go on, still following the same path, and give themselves a method of government and a way of permanent operation in which they are equally active?

To find a firm basis for a theory of the democratic method of government in the modern State, we must go back to the process of social though from which the State issues and to which it always remains attached. The process of social thought is naturally and necessarily a process of discussion. Ideas emerge here and there: each emergent idea becomes a magnet which attracts a clustering group of adherents: the various ideas, and the various groups they attract, must either engage in a war of competition with one another to achieve a victory, or attempt a method of composition which fuses and blends them together in peacc. The military idea of a war of competition between ideas is prominent in the philosophy of Hegel. His dialectical ldealism (which Marx turned upside down, or as he preferred to say 'right side up again', in his dialectical materialism) assumes a war of ideas, in which 'one shrewd thought devours another': a battle of thesis and antithesis, in which each side fights for itself. But even Hegel's military conception of the war of ideas ends in a sort of composition between thesis and antithesis; or, more exactly, it ends by producing the synthesis of a higher truth in which the partial truths of the thesis and the antithesis are abolished and transcended. It has thus, after all, some approach to the principle of discussion; but Hegel's theory of discussion is rather that of a logical process inside a solitary mind (even if that mind be conceived as the 'objective' mind of a whole Society) than that of a social process among and between a number of minds. The theory which is implied in Aristotle's *Politics* is much nearer to the idea of such a social process. Instead of assuming a war of two conflicting ideas, to be ended by a transcendent and triumphant synthesis, he assumes a plurality of social ideas, to be fused and blended together in a 'scheme of composition'. Just as it takes all sorts of men to make a world, so it takes all sorts of ideas to produce a 'catholic' and all-round view. Aristotle applies this conception to the field of culture and the province of artistic judgment: here, he says, 'some appreciate one aspect, and some another, but all together appreciate all'. But he also applies it generally to the whole field of social thought; and he applies it, in particular, to matters of political judgment. The Many, he holds, 'when they meet together', and put their minds fairly to one another, can achieve a composition of ideas which gives their judgment a general validity.

If we follow the guidance of Aristotle, we shall say that social thought proceeds by the way of a plurality of ideas, by the way of debate and discussion between the different ideas, 'when they meet together' and come into contact with one another, and by the way of a composition of ideas attained through such debate and discussion. We shall also say that this social way must also be, and also is, the political way: in other words it must also be, and also is, the method of the State's government and the way of the State's operation. This is not only because the State should be true to the Society from which it comes, and on which it continues to rest: it is also because the way of Society (the way of plurality of ideas, debate among them, and composition of them) is right in itself and universally right—right for Society, right for the State, and right wherever men are gathered together and have to act together. The one way to get at practical truth, the right thing to do, the straight line of action, is, in any form of group, the way of thinking things over together and talking them over together, with a view to finding some composition of the different threads of thought. It is the way of the Friends, when they seek what they call 'the sense of the meeting'. It is the way of democracy, which is not a solution, but a way of seeking solutions—not a form of State devoted to this or that particular end (whether private enterprise or public management), but a form of State devoted, whatever its end may be, to a single means and method of determining that end. The core of democracy is choice, and not something chosen; choice among a number of ideas, and choice, too, of the scheme on which those ideas are eventually composed. Democracy is incompatible with any form of one-idea State, because its essence is hospitality to a plurality of ideas, and because its method (which is also its essence) consists in holding together a number of different ideas with a view to comparison and composition of their difference. The democratic criticism of the one-idea State is not a criticism of its object (which may also be the object of the democratic State, or at any rate part of its object): it is a criticism of its whole process of life.

This last phrase, 'process of life', suggests a further consideration which is of vital importance in the theory of democracy. One of the archbishops of Canterbury, Frederic Temple, once said that there were two schools of political thought: one which held that politics existed for the production of a result, or the *ergon* school; an another which held that politics was valuable in itself as a process of activity, or the *energeia,* school. The school of production judged political by the results which it produced: the school of process preferred to judge on a different basis, and it was content, and more than content, if the process of the political life of a community elicited and enlisted for its operation the minds and wills of its members, thus aiding, and indeed in its measure constituting, the development of their capacities as persons. The distinction here suggested, which goes back to Aristotle, is a just pregnant distinction. We are naturally apt to think of politics in terms of making, rather than of doing, as if our political activity were directed wholly to achieving an object outside itself (and not immanent in itself), such as a scheme of legal order, or an adjustment of economic relations, or some other similar structure. But this is not the whole of the matter, or even the greater part. It is certainly true, and indeed it has already been urged in the course of our argument, that the State as a legal association must necessarily produce a result: it must produce a scheme of declared and enforced law which gives expression to the idea of justice. But there are two other things which must also be borne in mind. First, the ultimate purpose behind justice, and therefore behind law, is the development of the capacities of human personality in as many persons as possible to the greatest possible extent. That is the final result which the State must produce—or rather help to produce; for the result produces itself in each person through his own internal activity, even if it needs help, in the way of removal of hindrances and the offering of opportunities, in order to produce itself fully. This first reflection naturally leads to the second. If we hold that behind and beyond the *production* of law by the State there is a *process* of personal activity and personal development in its members, we may go on to say that the production should itself be drawn into the process. In other words we may argue that the productive effort of the State, the effort of declaring and enforcing a system of law, should also be a process in which, and through which, each member of the State is spurred into personal development, because he is drawn into free participation in one of the greatest of all our secular human activities.

These reflections suggest a second main justification of the democratic system. Not only is it justified, as we saw at the beginning of this section, by the fact that it makes the State true to the method of general discussion and composition of ideas which is the method of Society; it is also justified, as we now see, by the fact that it makes the State, in the very process of its own operation, true to the fundamental purpose which lies behind its operation, the purpose of the development in action of the capacities of personality. This is the justification urged by John Stuart Mill in his *Considerations on Representative Government.* Arguing, in his second chapter, that "government is at once a great influence acting on the human mind [according as it elicits, or fails to elicits, its energy] and a set of organised arrangements for public business' [that is to say, for producing the result of a scheme of legal order], he lays stress on the sovereign importance of the first of these two aspects. He has a strong sense of the 'practical discipline which the character obtains' from the demand made upon the citizen to exercise some function; he has an equally strong sense of the intellectual discipline which is also obtained by the mind, when the citizen is required to rise above private partialities, and to apply principles and maxims which are based on the idea of the common good.

If we accept the democratic system as justified, we must also accept the party-system. Party is a great and necessary factor in any method of general discussion; and that is its permanent justification. A party begins as a set of connected and coherent ideas (an 'ism', as when we talk of socialism or liberalism or conservatism), emerging and acting in the area of social discussion. It becomes, in the process of its development, a body of persons united in entertaining such a set of connected and coherent ideas: a body of persons, forming a social group in the area of Society, who discuss their common ideas among themselves, formulate them in a policy or programme, and vindicate that programme in discussion against other similar groups in the same social area. Finally, and in the culmination of its development, a party becomes an organisation, with its own accredited leaders, for the purpose of carrying a programme into effect by securing for it a majority of the votes of the political electorate, and by then proceeding to turn its leaders into the political government. In all these stages, but particularly in the last, party serves as a mediator between social thought and political action; and this is a reason why it is a great and necessary factor in the democratic system. We may accordingly say that a party may be defined as a social formation which (1) serves as a social reservoir for the collection of a set of connected ideas from the area of voluntary society, and also (2) serves as a political conduit or channel by which the ideas collected from that area flow from their social reservoir into the system of the State and turn the wheels of political machinery in that system. So conceived, party performs the service of enabling society to run into the State, and thus of keeping the action of the State constantly and wholesomely responsive to the play of social thought. This is a reason why we may deprecate any legal regulation of party, unless such regulation is made imperative by serious flaws and defects in the working of the party system. The effect of legal regulation is a transmutation of party, which ceases, when such regulation is applied, to be an informal organ of society freely expressing a trend of social thought, and freely seeking to transmit that trend into the area of political action, and tends to become instead a formal and legal organ of the legal association. To regulate by law the meetings of party organisations, and to prescribe their methods of nominating candidates, may be, on occasion, a 'cruel necessity'; but it is, in itself, a grave alteration of the proper relation between the State and party. Regulation should only enter, as a desperate remedy, when the general system of parties, in the act of carrying over a current of social thought into the are a of the State, becomes clogged by the manipulation of party managers, and when the State, as a liberating agency, is thus called on to clear the channel of transmission by providing that the meetings and actions of parties shall be free from any such clog.

But there are other and larger conditions which party must also satisfy if it is to perform its proper function in a system of democracy. In the first place, there must necessarily be a plurality of parties. A one-party State is a one-idea State: it is a falsification, and not a mediation, of social thought and of that general process of social discussion which must in its nature include a number of different ideas. On the ground of principle, and looking at party as a set of ideas held by a body of persons within the process and for the purpose of social discussion, we must demand at least two parties as the necessary condition of any discussion, and we may demand even more than two, or in other words a multiple system of parties, if that is the proper expression of the varieties actually present in the process of social thought and discussion. On the ground of practice, and looking at party, in its other aspect, as an organisation for the purpose of creating and supporting a government—and also an opposition which will criticize the government and keep it effective—we may welcome a two-party system; but equally we may deprecate a multiple-party system, on the ground that it turns the creation of a government into a matter of temporary and interested coalitions, as it also makes the support of a government uncertain and incoherent. Considerations of principle and considerations of practice are thus agreed in postulating more than *one* party; but they are not agreed when the issue is one of more than *two,* for then considerations of principle may be in favour of more than two, and considerations

of practice will be in favour of two and two only. We can only say that, in such a case, considerations of principle may have to overbear considerations of practice, and that when social thought develops more than two trends of opinion it will be necessary to have more than two parties, even though the presence of more than two parties may involve coalitions and shortlived governments. It would be a pity if *raison de government* were allowed to have the last world, and if the whole rational process of social thought and social discussion were subordinated to the *raison.*

A second condition which party must satisfy if it is to perform in proper function in a system of democracy in that each party should be a set of *general* ideas, backed by *general* body of persons. A party must not be a set of particular ideas about a single interest, backed by a particular body of persons connected with that interest. This is what Burke had in mind when he defined a party as a body of men united for promoting the *national* interest upon some particular principle: he meant that all parties alike should be concerned with the same general object, and that each should be partial or partisan only in its particular angle of approach. It is true, indeed, that a one-interest party may sometimes express a trend of social thought which is broad enough, and unselfish enough, to warrant such a form of expression; an abolitionist party, or even a prohibitionist party, may be held to be of this order. On the other hand, a one-interest party, composed of a one-interested body of persons, cannot be in its nature an organisation for the purpose of creating and supporting a government, or even for the purpose of helping to create and support a government; and a party cannot perform its full function, as a channel of mediation between Society and the State, unless it is able, at the very least, to *help* in the creation and the support of a government.

Political Obligation and its Relation to sovereignty

When we survey the whole process which begins with the formation of social thought and ends in its translation into terms of political action, we find ourselves confronted by a problem which has already arisen in other connexions, but which arises more particularly here, in connexion with the theme of political obligation. This is the problem of sovereignty. Where, and at what point of the process, is the last word said to the citizen—the word of words which carries a final and conclusive authority—about what he is bound and obliged to do as a member of the State? And who, or what, says that last word? We may begin our answer by seeking to recapitulate the preliminary conclusions already attained in previous stages of the argument.

At the first of these stages, when our view was still confined within the limits and the four walls of the legal association, and did not, as yet, embrace the wide area of Society and social thought those limits and outside those walls, we attempted a preliminary view of sovereignty in purely political terms. On that view sovereignty was regarded as being, in its nature, the power of final adjustment within the association; the authority of last resort in the State, which said the last word within the State. Sovereignty upon this view, is not public power, or State-authority, as a whole, in the whole of its range: it is the summit, and not the mountain; it is the topmost rung of public power or State-authority, where the final word is pronounced on legal issues which get so far as to rise to that rung. It that is the nature of sovereignty, conceived in purely political terms and viewed purely as an attribute of the State, the place of its residence must be regarded as being the summit of the structure of public power and State-authority. That summit, at its highest peak, is the constitution itself, and the constitution is thus the ultimate or normative sovereign; but under the constitution, and subject to the constitution, we may ascribe the possession of immediate or active sovereignty to the legislature, and we may accordingly say that the legislature is the immediate sovereign when, and in so far as, it acts by the norm of the constitution.

At a second stage of the argument, though our views was still confined within the limits of the State, we made a fresh step, and added a new consideration, which affected further our view of the nature of the immediate sovereignty of the law-making body. The gist of this new consideration was that 'law-making', as it is called, is not the creating of law in the sense of issuing a command to the community, in the imperative mood, about what *shall* or *shall not* henceforth be done, but is rather the declaring of law in the sense of issuing a statement to the community, in the indicative mood, about what already *is* the standard of will and action accepted by common conviction. It follows from this view that the immediate sovereignty of the legislature, acting within the limits and the four walls of the State, is not only subject to the ultimate normative sovereignty of the constitution: it is also subject, in itself and by its own very nature, to the limit imposed by the fact that it is an organ for the expression and declaration of common conviction. This common conviction, resident in the members of the legal association, is a conviction about the idea of justice: a conviction about the dictates or deductions which issue from that idea: a conviction that justice is the value of values, and that standards of will and action flow from this supreme value. We may accordingly say that the immediate sovereignty of the law-making body is inherently and by its own nature subject to common conviction and thereby to the content of common conviction, and thereby to the idea of justice, and thereby to the standards of common life that issue from that idea.

Finally, at a third stage of the argument, we went still farther, and going beyond the limits and the four walls of the State we took into our view the area of Society and social thought which lies outside those limits. Here we arrived at the conclusion that the idea of justice had its ultimate origin in Society, and originally sprang from a process of social thought proceeding by way of social discussion. We thus advanced be yond the conclusion of the previous argument. We moved from the view that a common conviction about the dictates of justice, resident in and entertained by the members of the legal association of the State, was the basis of law and the inspiration of the law-making body; and we rose to the higher and broader view that social thought about the nature of a just order of human relations, moving in the area of Society and developed by social discussion, was the basis of the existence and the inspiration of the activity of the whole legal association. We thus gave justice, as it were, a new bodily habitation, by arguing that it resided not only in the common conviction of the legal association as such, but also, over above that, in the social thought of national Society as such, standing behind and rising above the walls of the legal association. We also gave this justice, with its new bodily habitation, a new and final authority as the ultimate sovereign of sovereigns: we made it the extra-legal or supra-legal sovereign, sovereign even over the constitution, which is an instrument it has created, and sovereign therefore over the legislative, which is an instrument of that instrument.

We may now seek to draw together the conclusions attained at these different stages. When they are thus drawn together, they maybe enunciated in two propositions, which have already been implied in the previous course of the argument.

(a) Prior in order of thought to the State and to the form (or forms) of its sovereignty, though the State in its early condition of a power-organisation may itself have been prior in order of time, there is the idea of justice and of the sovereignty of justice, resident in the social thought of the members of a national society about the right order of their relations. There are those who would seek to separate the idea thus resident in thought from the thought in which it resides; who would argue that the idea of justice is one mater, and the seat of its residence another; and who, having made that distinction, would proceed to conten that it is social thought, under the name and style of 'the general will', which ought to be deemed to be sovereign, rather than the

idea of justice. But we cannot make a distinction between the sovereignty of the idea of justice and the sovereignty of social thought. The two are inseparable. There is no justice but social thinking makes it so; and conversely there is no social thinking about the order of human relations but issues in the idea of justice. We may therefore speak of the supreme sovereignty of a socially crated idea of justice, which is brought into being by social thought and the process of social discussion. Upon that basis we may make an admission, which is also, at the same time, a contention. There was, after all, a great measure of truth in the ideas of the votaries of natural law. When they urged the cause of the supreme sovereignty of natural law, and even went to the length of making null and void all laws and acts of government which were contrary to such law, they were groping after the idea, of the sovereignty of the idea of justice. The one thing they failed to grasp was the fact of the social creation of the sovereign they sought to enthrone.

(b) When the State has emerged into action as a legal association, for the purpose of realizing the idea of justice by translating it into a system of declared and enforced law, it is, in the last resort, subject to the supreme sovereignty of the idea of justice by which it was created and by which it is sustained. But considered in itself and by itself it develops within its own limits two other sovereigns or forms of sovereignty. They are both of them legal sovereigns or forms of sovereignty; and as such they are both distinct, and different in kind, from the social sovereignty, as it may be called, of the idea of justice. The first of these legal forms of sovereignty is the ultimate sovereignty of the constitution which is the creative act, as the idea of justice is the creative spirit, that brings the State into being and controls its subsequent action. The second legal form of sovereignty is the immediate sovereignty of the law-making body; the body of persons, legally subject to the constitution, and inherently limited by its own nature as an organ appointed for the purpose of declaring common conviction, which is concerned

with the issue, and has a general control of the enforcement, of the rules of positive law. Within the State, and looking only at the State, we see only these two sovereigns. If we go beyond the State, and take into account the play of Society and social thought outside the State, we see a third sovereign beyond these two; a sovereign idea of justice, moving and finding expression in the play of social thought, which is not a sovereign in any legal sense, and yet is the standard and final control of all legal action and legal sovereignty.

It is tempting to reduce the three sovereigns to one, and instead of being content with a hierarchy to seek a single and simple unity. It is particularly tempting to seek such unity in a personal source of will, whether the source be a single person or same one body of person. We are naturally apt to think in terms of a Sovereign Will or a Sovereign Sanhedrim of Wills. But we cannot thus deify will, whosesoever the will may be; whether the will of a decreeing person or a body of such persons, on the ground that they are creators of the rules by which we live, or the will of the People itself, on the ground that it is the super-creator which limits, and may even control, the decreeing person or body. If we make will final, we really make force final, for a will which prevails just because it is will, without regard to the object it wills or the standard by which it wills, is a force. We may allow, indeed, as we have already done, that a law which has issued from the will and action of a law-making body, acting as the organ of common conviction, is legally valid and finally conclusive within the area of the state, provided that it is duly enacted according to the rules of the constitution which are the final arbiter of legal validity; and in that sense, and to that extent, we may admit the sovereignty of legislative will and action. But we must also allow that a law which has issued from that source, even if it possesses legal validity and imposes legal obligation, will not possess moral value or impose moral obligation unless it squares with the idea of justice, as formed in and expressed by the movement of social thought. That still leaves us with a hierarchy rather than the simple unity of a single personal factor. In the sphere of social and political theory, which is bound to embrace both Society and the State, there is no one and only sovereignty of which we can say 'Its will is our peace.' The peace of acquiescence in such a will is denied us by our own nature.

The Limits of Political Obligation and the Problem of Resistance

The very fact that this problem is presented to us is itself a proof that we cannot enjoy the peace of acquiescence in a final will. It is, in effect, a double problem. The first of the problems is whether there is a sphere of life and conduct in which there is no political obligation. The second is whether political obligation, in the sphere in which it exists (whatever that sphere may be) is absolute, or conditional.

Mill, in his *Essay on Liberty,* assumed the existence of two different spheres of conduct. One sphere or part of the conduct of anyone, he argued, is that which concerns others; and for that he is 'amendable to society'. The other part is that which merely concerns himself; and here 'his independence is, of right, absolute…and the individual is sovereign'. The assumption made by Mill is open to a double criticism. In the first place, as his critics have urged, he separates the inseparable. The conduct of any man is a single whole: there can be nothing in it that concerns himself only, and does not concern other men: whatever he is, and whatever he does, affects others and therefore concerns them. In the second place, it would also appear that Mill fails to separate the separable. He lumps together, as the phrase 'amenable to society' suggests, both the social and the political: he vindicates the liberty of the individual, in one breath, both against the Mrs. Grundy of social convention and the St. Stephen's political enactment. We cannot separate two different compartments of individual conduct; but we *can* separate the sphere of Society from that of the State. Because we cannot separate our individual conduct into two different compartments, and because we are bound to regard the whole of our conduct as concerning others no less than ourselves, we have to admit that the whole of our conduct is controllable—*so far as the criterion of its concerning others is the criterion of judgment.* But because we *can* separate the sphere of Society from that of the State; because we are able, and even bound, to regard the one as the sphere of voluntary action, proceeding by the method of free co-operation, and the other as the sphere of uniform and regulated action, based, in the last resort, on the method of compulsory enforcement; we are free to contend that there are some things which are best left to the first of these methods, and others which are best left, and indeed must be left to the second.

How are we to decide which things belong to the sphere of Society, and which to that of the State? That question has already confronted us, and an answer to it has already been attempted, at an earlier stage of the argument. In general terms, the answer is that since the State acts by the method of compulsory enforcement, the things that belong to it are the things which had better be done under compulsion that not be done at all; and since Society acts by the method of free cooperation, the things that belong to it are the things which, in their nature, must be done freely if they are to be done well and to have any value. If we seek to translate these general terms into detail, we may say that the things (if they may be called things) which are best left to the sphere of Society are the expression of thought and opinion, in matters of the mind; the exercise of the moral virtues, such, as, for example, the virtue of temperance; the practice of religion, not only in private profession, but also in public worship and the public propagation of belief; the development of culture, in the sense of a general way of life or type of civilisation, and (along with that, and as part of it) the making and changing of social customs, habits, and fashions. But it cannot be said that any of these things belong to Society so wholly and so absolutely that no factor or element in them can ever belong to the State. On the contrary, there may well be factors or elements in each (for instance, even in the expression of thought) which had better belong to the State, and be brought under State-regulation, because they involve the method of compulsory enforcement. There is no fixed category of things which must always and in all cases be left to Society; there is only a fixed principle about the sort of things which it is better *generally* to leave to Society—*exceptis excipiendis.*

This notion of 'exceptions' may appear to be dangerous, and particularly dangerous when it is applied to the expression of thought. We all assume it as an axiom that the expression of thought, opinion, and belief is a matter for free social action, limited only by the decencies of courtesy and consideration for others. So it is, in the main: but it cannot always be left there. There are elements or factors in the expression of thought which enter the area of the State and are amenable to State-regulation. If an author's expression and publication of his thought and opinion is adjudged by the common conviction of the members of the political community to be a nuisance—that is to say an injury to the health of their minds, as being unclean and obscene, in the same way as an open sewer is an injury to the health of the body—it will be the duty of the State, in the course of declaring and enforcing common conviction, to deal with the nuisance by its own method of compulsory enforcement, and to vindicate the community's claim that it should not be made to suffer injury against the writer's claim that he should be free to express his thought. The issue, if we probe the matter, is not in the last resort an issue between the writer and the State. It is an issue between two parts or sections of the community; between two trends of opinion; between the claim of one part or section to a right of expressing its opinion, and the claim of the other to a right of keeping its own opinion uninjured and undamaged. There is a danger of shock or collision between the two opposite sides; and the State has to act, as it were, in the office of a buffer for the purpose of absorbing the shock. It must diminish the collision by adjusting the conflicting claims; but in doing so it will act as an arbiter, and not as party in the case.

The issue, however, is far from simple. How can we be sure of the fact that there is a common conviction? And even if we are sure of the fact, a further question arises. Why should the writer be required to obey a conviction which in his view, and possibly also in the view of his profession generally, is mistaken; and why should the claim of others, however numerous, to be free from suffering the supposed nuisance of the expression of his thought overbear his claim to express his thought for what he believes to be the benefit of the public? An answer may be made to these question which is cogent enough so far as it goes. Within the political community a claim of the members, endorsed by a common conviction formally expressed in law and thereby registered as a fact, has the validity of a right, and a writer is thereby *politically obliged* to respect that right in his expression of his thought. But there is an answer to this answer. The writer whose works are challenged on this ground may plead that there is something higher than political obligation: that his final obedience is due to the demand of that something higher, the cause of beauty or the cause of truth; and that political obligation accordingly ceases when it is contrary to that demand. This plea, in effect, is a plea that political obligation is conditional, and not absolute; due under certain conditions, when it does not clash with a higher demand, but not due under all.

We are thus confronted with the second of the problems raised at the beginning of this inquiry. Is political obligation, within its sphere, an absolute obligation, which is due under all conditions, or are there occasions and conjunctures in which a member of the community, or a group of members, are justified in refusing obedience, or in offering resistance? Various grounds have been taken, in the course of the history of political thought, by those who have sought to find an answer. First (and this is the oldest ground) there is the ground of natural law. Here the contention advanced is that all positive enactments and administrative acts contrary to natural law are null and void. They may therefore be disobeyed; they may even be resisted, if an attempt is made to apply them by force. The paradox of this contention, if the term 'natural law' be interpreted strictly, is that it results in the proposition that law may be legally disobeyed. But the real gist of the contention is something less, or more, than that. It is that law may be disobeyed *justly,* and that it is possible, in the name of justice, to disobey a law which does not express, as all law should, the idea of justice. This was the ground adopted in the American

Declaration of Independence of 1776, with its appeal to the laws of nature and of nature's God; and with some modifications it is a ground which, as well shall see, may still be defended. There is less to be said for a second ground, which is that adopted by the Utilitarians at the end of the eighteenth century. On his ground the issue between the acceptance and the rejection of political obligation was reduced to a calculus of material utility. According to Bentham it was 'allowable to, if not incumbent on, every man... to enter into measures of resistance... when ... *the probable mischiefs of resistance* (speaking with respect to the community in general) *appear less to him than the probable mischiefs of obedience'*. By virtue of this calculus, as Paley frankly admitted, 'the justice of every particular case of resistance is reduced to a computation', with danger and grievance on one side and the probability and expense of redress on the other. There is little satisfaction to the mind in a computation of this order, which weighs the consequence but omits the cause. More may be said in favour of the ground which is taken by the French jurist Duguit, when he argues for the limited and conditional nature of all political obligation. His contention is that all laws or other acts of the persons styled 'governors' may be resisted passively, defensively, and even aggressively, if they conflict with the Rule of Right (*régle de droit*) deduced from the basic fact of economic solidarity. The ground thus taken enthrones Right above law, and makes the obligation of obedience to law conditional on the conformity of law to Right; but the Right thus enthroned by Duguit is only a derivative or expression of economic fact and process, or rather of a part of such fact and process.

Is there anything to add to these answers, or any way of drawing them together in a comprehensive view which does justice to the elements of truth they contain? We may begin by drawing a distinction which has already been implied in the previous course of the argument. (1) Within the State, and so far as concerns the State and its operation, there is an absolute and unconditional obligation, incumbent upon its members as such, to obey a law duly passed by the legislature in conformity with the constitution, or an act of government duly done under a law so passed. Even here, however, and even within the limits of the State, obligation to a law is conditional upon its being in conformity with the constitution; and it may thus be contended that, in a strict sense, the only unconditional obligation is the obligation due to the constitution. The proviso is just; but it need not prevent us from laying it down that just as a law is unconditionally and absolutely valid when once it is duly passed in conformity with the constitution, so obligation to a law so passed is unconditional and absolute, *within the State and in terms of the State.* (2) If we transcend the terms of the State, and take into view the play of Society and the activity of social thought in creating and developing the idea of a just order of relations, we have to amplify, or rather to qualify, our view of the nature of political obligation. Upon the assumption, previously made, that the socially created and socially developed idea of justice is the supreme sovereign, we are bound to admit that obligation, even to a law duly passed in conformity with the constitution, is after all in *some sense* conditional upon its squaring with the idea of justice. The distinction which has just been drawn would appear, prima facie, to involve a contradiction. We seem to be saying in a breath that political obligation is unconditional and that it is, 'in some sense', conditional. What exactly is meant by the latter of these sayings? It is not meant for a moment that political obligation ceases, for a man or a group of men, when once they conceive that a law, or a set of laws, fails to square with the idea of justice entertained in their minds. The view suggested is entirely different. Political obligation, *as such,* remains: indeed we may even say that, *as such, and within the State,* it remains an unconditional obligation. But a new and super-political obligation enters as soon as we take into our view the socially created and socially developed idea of justice: an obligation which we may call 'social', in the sense that it springs from Society and from the product of social thought. This super-political or social obligation may conflict with, and be pitted against, the political obligation which exists in the area of the State. A dilemma then arises. What is to be done in this dilemma? What is the weight of political obligation, and what is the weight of the super-political, when the two are opposed to one another? How is the State to act to the 'protestant' who pleads against it the cause of justice, and how is the 'protestant' pleading that cause to act to the State?

Because political obligation, as such, remains, and because it remains, as such, absolute and unconditional, we may lay it down that in any case of disobedience or resistance to law, based on the idea of social justice and social obligation, it is the clear duty of the judge, in his capacity of judge, and of all the organs of government, in their capacity of organs, to enforce the established law (it is not their business to recognize, far less to enforce, any idea of justice other than that expressed in such law); and it is equally the clear duty of the disobeying or resisting citizen to obey, as a citizen, the established law, by accepting the legal consequences involved in this disobedience or resistance. But because social obligation is also a fact, and because, to the 'protestant' penetrated by a conviction of its sovereign nature, it is the highest fact, it is also his duty to accept its demands and to offer his testimony to its sovereignty.

Here, however, a problem arises, which must always vex the mind of every serious and reflective 'protestant'. If the higher obligation is *social,* how can a mere individual, relying on his own idea of justice, or even a group, relying on an idea entertained only by its members, defy the general run of opinion? Must not any challenge to established law be based upon, and be backed by, some measure of general *social* support? This difficulty disappears if we reflect on the nature of social thought and the process of its formation. The process is one of the initial production, the subsequent discussion, and the eventual composition, of a number of different ideas. Each individual, and each group, has something to throw into the pool of discussion in order to stir the waters. Sometimes the contribution must be made in pain if it is to achieve that stirring. A group which feels its idea to be a vital element in any just order of relations will then feel bound to stake itself upon that idea: it will disobey, or even resist, any law to the contrary: it will seek, by the visible testimony of its disobedience and its acceptance of the legal consequences, to impress the value of its idea on others, to get in incorporated in social thought, to make it part of common conviction, and ultimately to secure its adoption as part of the law of the State. Many causes have followed this way in the course of the centuries: the cause of the abolition of slavery, for instance, in the United States, and the cause of the enfranchisement of women in the United Kingdom. It is not, in itself, a way of revolution, though it may sometimes seem to approach the verge. It is at once a rejection and an acceptance of political obligation: a rejection, so far as it denies that obligation on a particular issue: an acceptance, so far as it affirms it in general and on the whole, and so far as it attests its affirmation by facing and accepting the legal consequences of the partial denial. Indeed we may almost say that resistance of this order is still in the area of debate, and is a method of persuasion rather than a recourse to force. The resister puts his plea into the arena of debate, and stakes himself upon it: and if he invites the application of force to his own person, he does not seek to apply it to the persons of others.

But the resister who thus courts martyrdom (which in the original Greek from which it is derived meant the simple giving of witness, but with us has come to mean the giving of witness in and by the suffering of pain) can never escape the dilemma in which he is necessarily involved. In following to the utter-most some idea which is part of himself he is also breaking, at some point, the scheme of political obligation which is also part of himself. Nor is that all. There is more in question than the breach of political obligation at a *particular* point. The resister who defies a law is also disturbing (and incidentally encouraging others—less scrupulous than himself and more intent on private ends—to disturb) the *general* scheme of law and order, and the *general* validity of obligation. He has therefore to ask himself whether the contribution which he may make to social thought about justice, by staking himself on the particular idea he wishes to add, is worth the possible cost of disturbance of the whole scheme of existing law and order, itself based upon and itself expressing the idea of justice. This is to make a calculation, and as such it is something like—and yet also very unlike—the calculation of which Bentham and Paley wrote. It is like, in so far as in either case mischief has to be measured against mischief: it is very unlike, in so far as the mischiefs to be measured differ greatly in the two cases—the mischief's weighed in the one case being mischiefs to the cause of utility, and those weighed in the other being mischiefs to the cause of justice.

There is no simple rule for the weighing of the mischief's of obedience against the mischiefs of resistance. There is only the general rule that weighing is need in every case in which a conflict arises between political obligation and the obligation which is super-political. The weighing itself will differ according to time and place; and the decision will depend on the degree of stability of law and order existing in a given country at a given period. The common love of use and wont, the strength of convention, the habit of tradition, are sometimes a sufficient guarantee of the stability of law and order; and where and when that guarantee is present, the electric disturbance of a new idea, pressed to the point of resistance, may serve to correct men's tendency to settle down on the lees of custom. On the other hand, it may well be said that the age in which we live is already sufficiently electric; and it may also be said that new ideas which are ready to appeal to force always introduce an incongruous and explosive element into the peaceful process of social thought and persuasion. This is only a 'dusty answer'. But it is also the only answer which the mind can ever get, however hot for certainties it may be.

E. Bakers

4

Law

INTRODUCTION

Will of State in Terms of Law. The state acts through its instrument the government, which interprets its will in terms of law. All individuals and associations shall obey law or suffer punishment as prescribed by law.

Law as Vehicle of Sovereignty. Law can be regarded as the vehicle of sovereignty. The ordinary individual finds sovereignty as something which is abstract. But when he obeys law, he respects the sovereignty of the state without actually knowing about it. Eddy Asirvatham says on page 324 in *Political Theory* (1957): 'Any discussion of sovereignty involves the question of law. Sovereignty is a mere theoretical principle and does not have much meaning unless it expresses itself in and through law."

Law as Instrument of Changes, Development and Social Justice. It is not enough, if the state uses its sovereignty through law for the maintenance of peace and order. It has to do much for realizing the purposes for which the state came into being. The state has to promote the welfare and happiness of its citizens, introduce reforms, bring about development and uphold social justice. All this can be achieved by using the tool or instrument of law. Great changes can be brought about in a state in a peaceful manner with the help of law.

DEFINITION, MEANING AND FEATURES OF LAW

Rule of State for Regulation of Social Life. Law is a written rules made by state for regulating the conduct and behaviour of its members. Punishment is prescribed for violating the rule. T. E. Holland, says on page 40 in *Elements of Jurisprudence* (1906) that law is "a general rule of external human action enforced by a sovereign political authority." Social life cannot be peaceful and orderly unless rules are made to bring about a minimum uniformity. A definite pattern of social behaviour is prescribed by a set of rules made by the state. These are known as laws. They create orderly conditions for civilised social activity. Without laws, there would be anarchy. R. H. Soltau says on page 76 in *Introduction to Politics* (1961): "A law is a rule of behaviour for the members of a state, the disregard of which meets with a penalty, which will be enforced by the state's machinery of power." R.N. Gilchrist points out on page 160 in *Principles of Social Science* (1961) that the term law is derived "from an old Teutonic root *lag,* which means something which lies fixed or evenly."

All Rules Not Laws. All rules and principles in society are not laws, though they may have the backing of the family or religion or public opinion. The state, which alone can make laws lays down clearly in the written form that certain rules are laws. R.N. Gilchrist says: "In other words, a law is a law because it is declared to be so by the state through the proper law-making organs, whether will of autocrat, act of Parliament, or decision of Supreme Court. It is not the issuing of the law that makes the state a state; it is the force of the state that makes law, *law* as Hocking puts it."

Difference between Law and Social Rule. The difference between law and social rule or custom may be noted. Sovereignty is behind law, whereas public opinion is behind sovereignty. Man is exposed to social censure, when he violates customs, and his prestige in society may get eroded. Society, however, has no power to punish him by way of imprisonment or fine, as it lacks sovereignty, that is, the power to coerce and punish. On the other hand, the state, which has sovereignty punishes him, when he violates law.

Basic Features of Law

We may briefly mention the following basic features of law:

1. *Equality Before Law.* Laws are universally applicable to all individuals and associations in a state without any exception. In a democratic state, there is perfect equality before the law. Law rewards or punishes all individuals in same manner in the state.

2. *Sovereignty Backs Law.* Law is backed by sovereignty or coercive authority of state. In a modern state, the legislature makes laws, the executive enforces them and the judiciary interprets them while settling disputes.

3. *Law as Expression of State Will.* The will of the State is expressed in terms of law, which may be regarded as the vehicle or carrier of sovereignty.

4. *Written Form.* Law is written and is supposed to be known to all. No person can escape punishment on the plea of ignorance of law. Ignorance is no excuse for violating aw.

5. *Concerned with External Acts.* Law is concerned only with the external acts of the individual. It does not take into consideration the inner decisions and motives of the individual. T.E. Holland say that "a law is a general rule of action taking cognizance only of external acts, enforced by a determinate authority, which authority is human and among human authorities is that which is paramount in a political society: or briefly a law is a general rule of external human action enforced by sovereign political authority.

6. *Law Not a Mere Command.* John Austin is wrong when he states that law is the command of the sovereign, "who is a determinate human superior." He completely ignores customs and traditions, whose importance is recognised even by courts of law. Sir Henry Maine, the historical jurist, who regards Austin's definition as very narrow, says that law is based on political authority, customs and usages, and popular consent. Woodrow Wilson, who brings about a compromise between the analytical view of Austin and the historical view of Henry Maine says that "law is that portion of established thought and habit, which has gained distinct and formal

recognition in the shape of uniform rules backed by the authority and power of government."

Different Meanings of Law and its Importance

Law Understood in Different Senses. The term Law is used in various subjects in different senses. Amar Nandi says on page 116 in *An Introduction to Political Science:* "It means one thing in political science and quite another in physical science. Thus we speak of the Law of England, law of crimes, as well as of the Law of Gravitation and the laws of motion. The word Law in the first two expressions means certain uniform rules of conduct enforced by a political authority, while in the last two it means certain uniformities in the process of nature. We also hear of Laws of Honour, Law of God, Law of Nature, Laws of Chess and so on. " Law also means a moral principle.

Importance of Law in Regulating Human conduct and Maintaining Peace and Order. The importance of Law is indeed great in regulating human conduct and in maintaining peace and order in the state. R.M. MacIver says on page 61 in *The Web of Government* (1959): "Without law there is no order, and without order men are lost, not knowing where they go, not knowing what they do. A system of ordered relationship is a primary condition of human life at every level. More than anything else it is what society means. Even an outlaw group, a pirate ship, a robber gang, a band of brigands had its own code of law, without which it could not exist."

DIFFERENT SCHOOLS OF JURISPRUDENCE

Different schools of jurisprudence view law from different angle. These schools are: (1) Historical, (2) Analytical, (3) Philosophical, (4) comparative, and (5) Sociological.

1. Historical School

Law Not Made by State But by Customs and Usages. Frederick von Savigny (1799-1861), Sir Henry Maine, Sir Frederick Pollock, Gustav Von Hugo (1764-1844), G.F. Puchta (1798-1846), F.W. Maitland and other scholars belong to this school. They say that the state cannot be regarded as the maker of law. It is the people who are law-makers. Law is the product of historical forces and influences silently working in society. Since primitive times people evolved habits, customs and usages, which provided a basis for the laws of the State. The State only enforced what the people themselves had evolved and accepted for obedience. Even today, no law can stand the test of time, unless it serves the purpose of the people and unless it is the product of their genius, customs and needs. A law totally divorced from customs and usages may not be obeyed by the people, but may remain only a dead letter. Frederick von Savigny say: "Law is the organ of folk-right. It moves and grows like every other expression of the life of the people; it is formed by custom and popular feeling, through the operation of silent forces, and not by the arbitrary will of a legislator."

Criticism of Austin. The jurists of the historical school criticize Austin, who regards law as sovereign's command and who overlooks historical forces without giving due importance to customs and usages.

Evaluation. We may make a brief reference to the merit and drawbacks of the historical school.

Merit. The great merit in the view of the historical jurists is that they explain the tremendous importance of customs, traditions and usages in the evolution of law.

Defects. The view of the historical school has drawbacks: (1) It does not speak the whole truth. It ignores factors other than customs in the making of law. (2) Its view is very conservative. It does not give due credit to good laws enacted by legislatures for the reform and betterment of society. (3) It forgets that every law is backed by sovereignty. There can no law without sovereignty, and every law is command of state, whatever may be its source.

2. Analytical School

Law as order of Sovereign. Jeremy Bentham, John Austin and other scholars belonging to the analytical school says that law is an order issued by the sovereign of the state (who is a determinate human superior and whose power is absolute) to the people, who are all inferior to him. This school is strongly influenced by the ideas of Hobbes.

Drawbacks. The view of the analytical school has been vehemently criticised on various grounds. We may briefly summarise the points of criticism.

1. *Law Not a Mere Command of a Superior.* It is incorrect to say that law is nothing more than a mere command given by a superior to his inferiors. Law, which has its roots in the past, is the product of various factors and influences of history.

2. *Great Difference between Law and Command.* Law and command are not synonymous. There is much difference between them. MacIver says that law is the anti-thesis of command, because command seeks to separate the giver from the receiver, while law unites the legislator and the ordinary citizen through its general applicability to all.

3. *Sovereign Not above Law.* Austin's sovereign is above law and is absolute. But this is not the case in a democratic state, as law-makers also are subject to law. Members of legislatures, ministers and judges have to obey laws, and are not above it. In the modern state, law which is universally applicable unites the law-marker and the rest of the people.

4. *Temporary Tenure of Commands.* It seems that commands or orders in the Austinian sense have only a temporary tenure; but law lasts for a long time and we give it the attributes of relative stability and permanence. It is only in the day-to-day administration that officials issue temporary orders for the smooth and efficient functioning of the government machinery.

5. *Artificial.* Law as conceived by the analytical school looks artificial. Its source is the supreme power of a determinate superior. It is not natural, as it does not give due importance to customs, traditions and usages.

6. *Conservative.* The ideas of the analytical school are conservative and static. They are not in tune with a fast moving and dynamic society. The analytical jurists overlook the contribution made by the historical or evolutionary process to the growth of law.

7. *All Laws Not Created by State.* It is wrong to say that the state made all the laws through a determinate superior, because even before the state was born there were laws. James Bryce says on page 249 in *Studies in History and Jurisprudence,* Vol. II: "Law cannot be always and everywhere the creation of the state, because instances can be adduced where law existed in a community before there was any state."

3. Philosophical School

Ideal Legal Systems Breathing Spirit of Justice. The German scholar Joseph Kohlar (1849-1919) and others belong to the philosophical school, which is of the view that philosophical standards should be applied to the juristic systems. It believes in the law of nature of the eighteenth century and is in favour of ideal legal systems breathing the spirit of justice. Kohler says that "the juristic philosopher is as much concerned with the ideal as with the actual content of the law. Law is both the product of culture and a means for furthering it."

Criticism. The view of the philosophical school can be easily criticised. It deals with abstractions far removed from the real state of affairs. It is difficult to apply its principles in practical world.

4. Comparative School

Macking Comparative Study of Legal Systems. Scholars of the Comparative School whose main exponent is Paul Vinogrodoff of Britain have made use of the material in biology, comparative philology, anthropology and other subject for comparing the different legal systems of the past and the present. The inferences drawn by the school have been of immense practical value to the political scientist.

5. Sociological School

Law Pre-Political and Connected with Social Ends. Leon Duguit in France, Krabbe in Holland, Gumplowicz in Austria, Holmes in the USA and others belong to this school. Their approach is sociological and pragmatic. Quite unlike Austin and other analytical jurists, they say that law, which is not the command of the sovereign existed even before the emergence of the state. They firmly believe that law should serve social ends. Law grew spontaneously as a result of social forces with the purpose of serving the needs of the people. R.G. Gettell says: "In contrast to the analytical jurist who fund the sanction of law in the command of the state, to the philosophical jurist who found its sanction in inherent justice and to the historical jurist who found its sanction in established habit and custom, the sociological jurist finds the sanction of the law in the social needs and interests it serves."

State Not Creator of Law. The state cannot be regarded as the creator of law. Duguit points out that human beings as members of society observe certain rules and regulations, which gradually assume the form of laws. Krabbe says that law is superior to state and is also independent of it. The human mind is the source of law.

Reason for Obeying Law. People obey law not owing to the fear of suffering punishment but because they are naturally conscious of its need. Psychologically or by nature people are inclined to be law-abiding, and that is why they evolve customs and rules, which become the basis for law.

Law Connected with Man's Inner Nature and Justice. Krabbe says that law is concerned with man's inner nature. Man obeys law because he feels it is just and good. Laski, who also thinks along similar lines, *says on page 276 in A Grammar of Politics:* "For the end of law is the satisfaction of human wants. That means not the wants deemed right by those applying the law, but the totality of wants encountered by law. Law, therefore, to be justice, must be the expression of relations found adequate in the experience of men." The human mind gives its willing consent to obey law, for it does good to human beings, fulfils their desires and meets their requirements.

Evaluation. We may briefly refer to the merit and defects of the views of the sociological school.

Merit. The sociological school is right, when it says that law is not a mere command of a sovereign and that it arose to serve social purposes.

Defects. The following serious defects in the view of the sociological school can be mentioned:

1. Customs and usages may be pre-political, but law is not. It has to be emphasised that a state is organised for law.
2. Law has sovereignty or coercive power behind it, and therefore it is incorrect to say that law is not the command of the sovereign.
3. All laws do not meet the needs of society and may not serve a good purpose. Some laws may be unjust and oppressive.
4. Law, which is the vehicle of sovereignty, cannot be independent of state.

6. Conclusion Regarding Views of Various Schools

The following conclusions can be drawn regarding the views expressed by the different schools of law:

1. The views of each school contain grains of truth, and an adequate explanation about the nature of law can be had by collecting these grains of truth
2. Each school of law has made its own distinct contribution to the study of law.
3. None of the schools speaks the whole truth, as each studies only one aspect of law.
4. The views of each school have drawbacks. All laws are not commands of the sovereign; all laws are not customary; and all laws are not the means of promoting human welfare.

Sources of Law

Legal Sense. In the strict legal sense, the state is the sources of all laws. But this explanation is extremely simple and inadequate.

Plurality of Sources. Law has emerged from a plurality of sources. In the remote past, law was customary and very simple, as the needs of society were few. But in the course of centuries great changes took place in society. Then social needs multiplied and problems became complex. Then law itself had become more and more complex to meet the challenges of a dynamic society.

Various Sources of Law. Law has come from various sources. Prof. T.E. Holland mentions six sources of law: (1) Religion, (2) Custom, (3) adjudication, (4) Scientific Commentaries, (5) Equity, and (6) Legislation.

1. Source of Religion

Role of Religion. As religion played a vital role in the evolution of state and law, we regard religion as an important source of law. In primitive society, law was customary with religion as the driving force behind it. Religion was a matter of life and death for human beings, and no custom could have any validity without its sanction. It was very difficult to distinguish between religious law and customary law.

Power of Priest Kings. The earliest kings were either priests themselves or were strongly influenced by priests, sorcerers and magicians. Priest kings, who became law-givers, could easily win the loyalty and obedience of the people, as primitive men believed that law had a divine origin.

Sanction of Religion behind Law. Religion was the powerful sanction behind law in the ancient states of Egypt, Mesopotamia, India, Greece and Rome. The great king Hammurabi (c. 2200 B.C.) of Babylonia, who wished to have divine sanction for his Code made his subjects believe that it (the Code) was a divine gift to him. The Codes of the *Pentateuch* or the first five books of the *Old Testament* also referred to God's authority. Even in modern times the influence of religion on law is great. In India Hindu law is based of the *Code of Manu* and Mohammad an Law on the *Koran*.

2. Source of Custom

Meaning of Custom: Webster's Unified Dictionary and Encyclopedia says that custom means common usages or practice.

"Custom carries the authority of long-standing and public acceptance." "Practice is the repeated doing of something or the way of doing something." When an act is frequently repeated it becomes a custom. Amar Nandi says on page 120 in *An Introduction to Political Science* (1955): " When a person invents a particular method of doing thing and is limited by others, a custom gradually comes into existence. A custom, as Prof. T.E. Holland points out, is formed in much the same way a path formed across a field.

Conduct Governed by Custom. The behaviour of conduct of individuals in families, clans and tribes is regulated by unwritten customary rules. Our behaviour in the family and in society in general conforms to well established customs and usages even now.

Early Law Customary. Early law was customary. In primitive society those in authority settled disputes under the privailing social customs. Even when law-givers tried to put law in the written form, they gave much importance to customs and traditions. The attitude of law-givers made customs to have almost the same status as law, and therefore laws breathe the spirit of long-standing customs and usages, whose importance has been recognised directly or indirectly by the different schools of jurists. What is done repeatedly by people generation after generation for the sake of meeting their needs conveniently and easily becomes a custom; and people instinctively obey the dictates of custom with which they are familiar. Customs are evolved because they serve a social purpose making the day-to-day life smooth and easy. Before man knew the art of writing, laws were customary. Even after the art of writing was learnt, customs played a very important part in a state; for when the king issued orders to put law in a different form, the age-old customs and usages had to be taken into consideration. Hammurabi's Code in Babylonia, the Codes of Lycurgus, Draco and Solon in ancient Greece and the *Laws of the Twelve Tables* in ancient Rome give great importance to customs. In India Manu, Yajnavalkya and other law-gives gave due prominence to the role of customs and usages, while preparing their respective codes. Even now, in all states of the world, customs and usages, which really form a code of unwritten law, are given their due weight by law courts in the administration of justice. An excellent example of the unwritten code is the Common Law of England. Customs acquire the stats of law when they are recognised by government, and judges follow them in giving justice.

Need of Eradicating Obnoxious Customs. It has to be noted very clearly that all laws are not based on customs. All customs are not wholesome and beneficial. Some of them are a curse. All customs having their roots in the remote past are not recognised and law is not written on the basis of all of them. On the contrary, laws have to be enacted to eradicate cruel, unjust and evil customs, which are baneful to the community. In India, Lord William Bentinck's government had to pass laws abolishing *sati,* female infanticide and child marriage. Similarly, under the Constitution of India (1950) and the laws based on it, the practice of untouchability is a cognizable offence though the evil of this pernicious custom has the sanction of many centuries. In England, only customs which are reasonable and not against law and morality and those which refer to legal relations are given importance and recognition by law.

3. Source of Adjudication or Judicial Decision

Creation of Law by Judges. The main function of a judge is to declare the law and interpret it while settling disputes. The main function of the legislature is to make law. But it should be noted here that judges consciously or unconsciously make new law in the course of judicial proceedings. Therefore their adjudication or verdicts are considered as a source of law.

Judicial decisions or verdicts given by the tribal leader in settling disputes between individuals or groups in primitive society became a source of law, as these became precedents for the future. At times, when the tribal leader acting as judge found no precedent to guide him, he used his own common sense or individual discretion to settle the cases fairly and impartially.

When the art of writing was discovered, records of the verdicts given by judges could be kept for the guidance of future generations. Law-makers made use of these records in the preparation of law codes.

3. Source of Scientific Commentaries

Scientific commentaries by learned and experienced judges, lawyers and jurists on customs, conventions, traditions, laws and verdicts of law courts form another important source of law. R.G. Gettell says: "By collecting, comparing and arranging in logical form past customs, decisions and laws, writers on law are able to arrive at general principles which may serve as the basis for further enactment, to indicate the gaps that need filling, to point out discrepancies, and in so far as their ideas are enforced by the courts to create law." In the course of their commentaries, jurists point out the drawbacks in law and what should be done to rectify them. Commentaries are to be differentiated from judicial verdicts. The former do not bind anyone, and they do not have government authority behind them. They are written for enlightening the readers on points of law. But the latter given by courts are binding on the parties to disputes. Great value is attached to the scientific commentaries given be eminent jurists, as they carry much weight of their vast learning, long experience and great reputation. The commentaries of jurists acquire importance only when they are accepted as laws by judges. Their usefulness is practically proved when they are referred to by judges and lawyers in open courts. They are recognised by government as works of high standard and are given the respect or attention due to judicial decisions. A. Appadorai says on page 68 in *The Substance of Politics* (1957): "The opinion of learned writers on law have often been accepted as correct law; in England, for instance, the opinions of Coke and Blackstone, in America of story and Kent; and in India of Vijnaneswara and Apararka." In settling cases pertaining to Hindu personal law, the *Mitakshara* and the *Dayabhaga* are useful.

4. Source of Equity

Another source of law is equity, which in common usage means justice or fairplay or "moral justice of which laws are the imperfect expression." It implies impartiality, equality and moral uprightness. Judges give verdicts on the basis of law and judicial precedents. But at times they are at their wits' end when an unusual or unique case without any precedent is to be heard by them or when they are to give their opinion on a law point in the course of the unprecedented proceedings. To tide over the difficulty created by the extraordinary case of law point, the judge may apply his own sense of justice and fair play in giving his verdict. Here the judgemakes a new law to mete out impartial justice. The importance of equity as a source of law is realised when the existing positive law is proved to be inadequate in a changing and developing society. Positive law meets the requirements of a simple society; but it cannot cope with the needs of a society which becomes complex. The gaps and inadequacy in the positive law have to be filled by equity. The principle of equity is tantamount to an informal method of creating new law or amending an old one. The collection or body of newly created laws is known as equity. Equity not only adds to the existing laws but makes them flexible. It is the result of the attempt to reduce the severity of rigid application of common law, rules, principles and verdicts. Amar Nandi says on page 123 in *An Introduction to Political Science* (1955): 'Equity comes into existence when civil law becomes rigid and inelastic and it found difficult of adaptation to new conditions."

According to Sir Henry Maine, equity is any body of rules existing by the side of the original civil law, founded in distinct principles and claiming incidentally to supersede the civil law in virtue of a superior sanctity inherent in those principles." Regarding the importance of equity, R.N. Gilchrist says on page 167 in *Principles of Political Science* (1961): "Equity is exclusive where it recognises rights not recognised by common law; it is concurrent, where the law recognizes, the right but does not give adequate relief; and auxiliary, where the necessary evidence cannot be procured.

Equity in Rome and England. In ancient Rome, when cases (to settle which the existing law was found inadequate) came before law courts, judgements based on common sense and fairness were given. Thus new principles of law known as equity were laid down. The Praetor in ancient Rome and the Lord Chancellor in England created principles of equity. It must be noted that equity applies to civil cases only and not to criminal cases. *Webster's Unified*

Dictionary and Encylopedia says: "Equity is a branch of law which slowly developed as a supplement to common law; an effort through courts of equity to furnish a remedy whenever, within the bounds of precedent and legal principle it could meet obvious demands of natural justice....Thus equity does not control, alter, or replace common law, but merely supplements it with special attention to the circumstances of each individual case. Judges are allowed a good deal of latitude in expounding the law of equity, especially in expounding it to meet unprecedented conditions." R.N. Gilchrist says on page 167 in *Principles of Political Science* (1961): 'In England the beginning of equity legislation is to be traced to the custom of giving to the Lord High Chancellor, complaints addressed to the king which were not met by the existing common law. These appeals were made to king's justice or conscience, and were referred to the *keeper of the king's conscience,* or the Lord High Chancellor (Modern Lord Chancellor, who received powers to remedy injustice according to equity or fair dealing or the moral law."

6. Source of Legislation

Legislation became the most important and prolific source of law overshadowing the other sources. Most of the laws are passed by the legislative branch of government in the modern state. The other sources have lost their original importance and have only minor roles. The legislature in which the representatives of people sit understands the needs of a dynamic society. It is called upon to legislate widely on a large variety of subjects. As the role of the legislature assumes greater and greater importance in law-making, the importance of the other sources of law decreases. In the past, laws were few, and the individual enjoyed much freedom. But in the modern state, which has to shoulder the responsibility of promoting people's welfare, the individual finds that his freedom is being more and more restricted by many laws made by the legislature to regulate his activities. Legislators have to bear in mind the big historical background of custom, religion, equity, precedents and other factors while making law. If there is urgent need of legislation, when the legislature is not in session, executive in the modern state issues decrees or ordinances, which have the force of law.

Development of Modern Law

The development of modern law took a long time. We may briefly examine here how it took place.

1. European Law

Modern European law was derived from roman and Teutonic sources of law.

Roman Law. Rome gave a uniform system of law all over her mighty empire. Law was enforced through the agency of a hierarchy of government officials.

Blending of Roman and Teutonic Laws. The Roman Empire was destroyed by the Franks, Goths and several other barbarian groups towards the end of the 5th century A.D. and for about five centuries (from the 6th century of the 10th century) Europe had the Dark Age during which Roman law yielded place to the tribal law of conquerors. This was known as Teutonic law. Teutonic law could not displace Roman lav altogether because during the long rule of Rome, Roman law had struck deep roots. Teutonic judges were compelled to recognize the importance of Roman law while settling disputes. Thus in course of time Teutonic law and Roman law were blended to make the administration of justice smooth and efficient. While the amalgamation of the two types of laws took place in Europe, this did not happen in England owing to its insular position.

Causes of Survival of Roman Law. Between Roman Law and Teutonic Law, the former became more important in Europe after surviving the barbarian onslaughts. The barbarians were unable to wipe out the influence of Roman Law owing to certain causes. (1) Roman Law was in Latin, the language of classical scholars and jurists. (2) The Code of Justinian was the standard code for easy and ready reference by law courts. (3) The Church played a great part in preserving Roman influence. It followed the organisational methods of the Roman Empire and became powerful unifying force in Europe. (4) Lawyers all over Europe studied Roman Law and did much to continue the Roman form and spirit.

Influence of Roman Law on Europe. Roman Law profoundly influenced the law codes of modern Europe. The Codes Napoleon of France and the legal systems of Spain, Holland, Germany, Italy and other European countries bear the imprints of Roman law. If Teutonic principles influenced public law, Roman principles influenced private law in Europe.

2. Law in England

Development of an Independent System. England developed her own systems of law under the influence of Teutonic customs. Two systems of law grew side by side: (1) Common Law, (2) Civil Law.

Attitude of King and Clergy. The king and clergy favoured the Roman system, as it could give them more power and prestige. Ecclesiastical courts preferred Roman law. But the will of the king and the clergy could not prevail against the independent legal system evolved by the English courts.

Common Law. In the course of a long time England evolved a system of unwritten law known as Common Law. It was based on long-standing customs and usages. *Webster's Unified Dictionary and Encyclopedia* says that the Common Law is the "legal system produced by English court decisions of Court of Common Pleas, Exchequer and King's Bench. More precisely, it is the part of that system which is not included in statutes or codes by depends on precedents (past decisions of the courts). It received its name in the 13the century as it was law common to all parts of England... Much of the common law has been superseded by statutes especially in criminal and commercial law." The system of common law was different from the civil or Roman Law and the canon or ecclesiastical law. J.A. Corry says on page 431 in *Democratic Government and Politics* (1951): "The common law is unwritten in the sense that there is nowhere to be found a compendious set of written rules that authoritatively state that law. Plenty of books have been written on all branches of the common law and they are of great assistance in finding the law. Yet none of them is in any sense binding on the courts, which must always base their decisions on some earlier decision of a court, called precedent."

Civil Law. In Britain, civil law is written law, and it takes the form of an authoritative code of general rules. J.S. Roucek and others say on page 154 in *Introduction to Political Science* (1958): "The term 'civil law' is a confusing one. Uncapitalised, the term refers generally to that part of the law which governs claims made by one person against another, usually for compensation, where damage has been inflicted or contracts have been violated. When capitalised, Civil Law refers to the law of the European continent and non-English-speaking America."

4. Law in India

When the British became rulers in India, they saw two types of legal systems *viz.*, Hindu and Mohammadan.

Hindu Law. The Hindu Law was based on Codes of great ancient law-givers like Manu.

Mohammadan Law. The Mohammadan Law was based on the *Koran* and its commentaries.

Legislation by British Rulers. The British rulers respected the ancient customs and traditions in India, but got rid of evil customs like *sati,* The Declaratory Act of 1780 passed during the rule of the British East India Company recognised in India laws pertaining to succession and inheritance. Laws were codified along British lines, and various Acts like the Evidence Act and the Penal Code were passed.

Kinds of Laws

MacIver's Classification of Laws. MacIver says that Political Law is of two types: (1) National, and (2) International.

National Law is of two categories; (1) Constitutional and (2) Ordinary.

Ordinary Law is of two kinds: (1) Public, and (2) Private.

Public Law is classified into two types: (1) Administrative, and (2) General.

We shall briefly examine the meaning of various kings of law: (1) National Law and International Law; (2) Constitutional

Law and Ordinary Law; (3) Municipal Law; (4) Common Law and Civil Law in England.

1. National Law and International Law

National Law. The law of the state, whose jurisdiction is over all the people within the state, is called national law. All shall obey national law, and its violation is punishable. In ancient times, national law was called municipal law. National law is made and enforced by the (sovereign) state.

International Law. International law, which is meant for regulating thc conduct of and relations between the various states in the world, has no sovereignty behind it. All states are sovereign, and are on an equal footing, and theoretically none can be coerced into submission by any power on earth. International law has force only to the extent to which it is recognised and voluntarily accepted by the different states of the world. No state can be coerced into submission or obedience by any international court. Only when a world federation is formed in the future and all states surrender their sovereignty to it, world courts might be able to enforce the laws of the world state.

2. Constitutional Law and Ordinary Law

R.M. MacIver says that "the state is both the child and the parent of law. There is the law which governs the state and the law by means of which the state governs." Here MacIver makes a reference to constitutional law and ordinary law.

Constitutional Law. Constitutional law is the basic law of the state. A collection of basic principles according to which government is conducted in a state is known as constitution. The structure of government, the distribution of power, the scope of authority and other basic matters are given in the constitution or constitutional law. A constitution is either the product of history or the work of an individual or a committee or a constituent assembly. Government can exercise power only according to the written or unwritten principles of the constitution.

Ordinary Law. The law according to which the people in a state are governed is called ordinary law. Ordinary law lays down the relations between the government and the citizen as also between one citizen and another. It has its roots in the past and it influenced by the forces of religion, customs and usages. In modern times, legislature enacts ordinary law according to the procedure laid down by the constitution.

Ordinary law is of two categories: (A) Public Law, and (B) Private Law.

(A) Public Law deals with the relations between the individual and the state. The individual is obliged to obey this law under threat of punishment.

In some states Public Law is of two kinds: (1) Administrative Law, and (2) General Law.

Administrative Law regulates the relations between the state and its officials and General Law regulates the relations between the state and its private citizens.

(B) Private Law deals with the relations between one individual and another. Just as between individual and state relations are regulated, relations among individuals themselves are regulated. Every individual is given rights by law. Rights are not absolute, but subject to reasonable restrictions.

3. Municipal Law

Combination of Public Law and Private Law. The term Municipal Law was used in ancient times. It is the law of a state dealing with individuals and associations. Hence, it is a combination of public law and private law. Now this law is generally called national law.

4. Common Law and Civil Law in England

Common Law. Common law is unwritten law in England, and, as stated earlier, no book of law can authoritatively explain the contents of Common Law.

Civil Law. Unlike Common Law, Civil Law is in written form; and judges have at their disposal an authoritative code of civil law.

Law, Morality and Justice

It is necessary to know the difference between law and morality, and law and justice.

1. Law and Morality

Comparison. Law and morality are closely related, and some writers do not find a clear margin between what is illegal and immoral. R.G. Gettell says that "in origin they were both identical, both arising as a result of habit and experience in that primitive social life when moral and political ideas were not separated."

Ernest Barker holds the view that the house of ethics has around it the fence of law for protection.

Difference. The following points of difference between law and morality may be noted:

1. Law is concerned only with the external acts of man and not with his inner decisions and motives; but morality which is concerned with the whole life of man covers inner motives as well as external acts.

Though the state does not directly deal with principles of morality, and is not concerned with making people morally good, it can go a long way in creating conditions conducive to the growth of moral principles. Political science dealing with state and government, and ethics dealing with morality are both social sciences, and both with man and his general welfare, though they lay emphasis on different aspects of man's social life.

2. Law is the concern of the state; but morality is the concern of individual conscience. Sovereignty is behind law, and public opinion and individual conscience are behind morality.

3. Law deals only with a part of man's life; but morality deals with the whole of man's life.

4. Violation of law is punished by the state; but violation of moral principles does not meet with punishment. Law can be enforced, but not morality. The sanction behind morality is the authority of public opinion, which may not be always

effective. Criminals are punished according to the law; but violation of moral principles, so far as it does not disturb peace and order is not punished by law. Greed, ingratitude, meanness and cunningness are not punished. Telling a lie or breaking a promise is immoral, but not illegal. It becomes illegal only when it results in loss or injury to anyone as proved in a court of law. Society cannot punish but develops a bad opinion of individuals, who violate moral principles. At the most a man who violates moral principles may be boycotted by society.

5. Law is backed by the coercive power or sovereignty of the state: but morality is not supported by any coercive power. Only moral force, fear of God, conscience, public opinion and social censure stand behind moral principles.

6. Law is definite and precise. But we cannot say precisely what is moral or immoral at times. Many matters in the moral field are vague. MacIver say on page 257 in *The Modern State* that law is made "objective and ethically neutral" for avoiding the possibility of making subjective interpretations. Ethical principles are subjective. The meaning of law is the same for all and it cannot change from person to person. But in the case of moral principles, there can be a difference. What is immoral for one individual, may be perfectly moral for another individual. R.M. MacIver says: "There must be one legal code for all, but moral codes vary as much as the individual characters of which they are the expression.

7. The law of a state is applicable only within the frontiers of a state. But moral principles cross state boundaries and are universally applicable.

8. Law which is enacted for convenience and expediency does not demand absolute standards as morality does. Law is enacted for specific purposes; but here is nothing like enacting moral principles, which are already prevalent in society. Law, which is backed by the mighty power of the state, may not always be just and fair. At times it may be manifestly oppressive and

unjust. All the same it has to be obeyed by all. Government, which is unable to trace criminals in a village after repeated efforts, may impose very heavy collective fine on the entire village through a law or decree or ordinance. Here poor and innocent villagers may suffer. This law is immoral, but it is made for the sake of expediency. Owing to peculiar problems a government is compelled to face, its laws may have to compromise with convenience and expediency. Moral principles which cannot tolerate what is wrong and unjust cannot make such a compromise.

9. What is legally wrong need not necessarily be morally wrong, and what is legally right may at times be morally wrong. What is morally wrong may or may not be legally wrong. Parking a car at a wrong place or smoking in a cinema theatre is legally wrong; but morally it is not so. Prostitution is legally right, if the state enacts legislation to legalize it. But morally it is condemned. Adultery is not illegal in England, though it is immoral. The immoral and degrading institution of slavery was perfectly legal in the USA before the Civil War (1861-65).

10. In a state there is a group of persons for making law, another group for enforcing it and a third group for interpreting it and administering justice. On the other hand, there are no such bodies for making, enforcing or interpreting moral law.

Bringing Law and Morality Nearer. Though the state should not pass legislation to reform the morals of the people, it owes a duty to them to create conditions for improving their moral tone. Therefore the state should see that law is not divorced from morality. Law and morality should be brought nearer to each other, and efforts should be made towards that end. A law cannot command loyalty, if it is immoral according to the generally accepted standards of society. Immoral laws or laws which are not conducive to the growth of morality are harmful to society. Human beings are moral agents and, therefore, if they are bad or immoral, the state can never be good. The state functions for the welfare of the individual on whom depends its nature. There cannot be a great state, unless individuals have great minds and are concerned with principles of morality. In ancient times, a great Greek philosopher aptly said: "The best state is that which is nearest in virtue to the individual. If any part of the body politic suffers, the whole body suffers."

Need of Repealing Bad Laws and Eradicating Evil Customs. The state should repeal bad laws and enact legislation for eradicating evil customs, which are harmful to the people. Enlightened British Governors-General in India took steps to improve the condition of the people by passing laws aiming at wiping out obnoxious social traditions and usages. Here is special reference has to be made to Lord William Bentinck (1828-35) who boldly passed legislation to eradicate the revoltingly cruel custom to *sati*.

Good Laws for Welfare State. Under British rule in India, government enacted legislation favourable to British industry and trade. This resulted in ruthless exploitation of the poor. Though British laws were valid in the legal sense, morally they were condemned. Since independence and after the commencement of the Constitution of India (1950), the Union and State Governments have to follow the concept of the welfare state. Now states all over the world with a new awakening try to make laws, which are just not only in the legal sense but also in the moral sense.

2. Law and Justice

Law Not Justice Itself. The term 'justice' which is used in connection with law and social morality stands for the entire field of principles and procedures that should be followed. In legal terms, the system of law as a whole is often called the system of justice. Law seeks to give justice, but it is not justice itself. Courts of law are often incorrectly referred to as temples of justice. A judge with all his keenness and detachment to be just, fair impartial may not be able to do full or even partial justice, though he is just in the legal sense and his verdict may be legally sound. A judge is not a law-maker. He has to settle disputes and give verdicts according to the prevailing law of the land, which may be tilted in favour of the rich and may do injustice to the poor. Therefore it is said that people get law and not justice in courts. A court of law gives justice in the legal sense and not in the moral sense. Law makers in a state should try to narrow down the gap between justice in the legal sense and justice in the moral sense.

Resistance to Law

Sovereignty for Making any Law. The state has sovereignty or supreme power to make any law, good or bad. Sovereignty in a state may be misused by those who are in power. Power-hungry, corrupt and morally low persons in authority may enact thoughtless legislation subjecting people to tyranny and hardship.

Disobeying Law a Crime. Every citizen is expected to obey the laws of the state. Disobeying law or offering resistance to law, even if it is a bad one, is legally speaking a crime, and the guilty person shall be punished according to the provisions of law. Most of the people in a state obey law. They are aware that they cannot violate it unless they are ready to get punished. Law is only a means to an end, and not an end in itself. At times a law may be passed for a bad purpose, and it may cause great hardship and suffering to the people. The question arises whether an individual is justified in resisting or violating such a law. From the point of view of the state, that is, in the eyes of law, resistance is a crime. But from the point of view of the people and on the basis of moral principles resistance to a bad law become a moral duty, particularly after all efforts to convince the rulers that the obnoxious law should be repealed have failed.

Justification for Offering Resistance to Law. It is difficult to judge when exactly a citizen becomes competent to resist law as a matter of moral obligation, as there is no criterion to know what is just or unjust. Justice, many a time, may be something that is subjective. What is regarded as just by a citizen, who wishes to offer resistance to the state may be considered unjust by others. An individual may be overwhelmed by emotion or may be politically motivated to offer resistance. Instead of being thoroughly objective and detached, he may be selfishly subjective. Those who resist law say that they obey the dictates of conscience; but those in power in a state claim that they are competent to put down firmly any opposition to the duly constituted state and violation of its laws. Matters of conscience are many a time highly controversial. Conscience or inner voice differs from individual to individual. What an individual does according to his conscience maybe harmful to the community at large.

Disobedience as the Last Resort. Disobedience should not be made a routine affair or taken lightly by those who are dissatisfied with a particular law. Only under extraordinary conditions and as a last resort resistance to law maybe offered. A person offering resistance should satisfy himself fully that his action in the larger interests of society and that he has no other alternative.

The following principles may be laid down for the guidance of those who desire to resist law:

1. A law should not be disobeyed merely because one dislikes it for personal reasons.
2. The precise objective of resisting law should be clear. The aim should be absolutely selfless and the motive should be to serve society.
3. Resistance should be open and never covert. As the purpose of defying law is to focus public attention and create an awakening about the real injustice in law, secret, resistance is absurd and meaningless.

Views of Eminent Men of Resistance

We may make a brief reference to the views on resistance of eminent men like T.H. Green, H.J. Laski and Mahatma Gandhi.

1. View of T.H. Green

Resistance only under Certain Conditions. T. H. Green in his *Principles of Political Obligation* concedes the individual the right to resist law, but only under certain conditions. He should not offer resistance, if the law, which he does not like, may be linked by the bulk of the people, as it is in their larger interests. Resistance may be offered, if he finds that the law is contrary to the interests of all or of an overwhelming majority of people. But before offering resistance, he should make use of all the legal and constitutional methods of getting it repealed. These methods may taken much time, but he should patiently wait, because offering resistance in unseemly haste, may do more harm than good. Till the bad law is repealed, as a good citizen, the individual should continue to obey it.

Resistance not a Right, but a Painful Obligation. A democratic government may turn tyrannical, inefficient and corrupt. It may be unsympathetic towards the people and may make laws for favouring a few at the cost of the many. An individual may offer resistance as a last resort to get an unpopular and oppressive law repealed. But this has to be regarded not as a right, but as a painful obligation.

Requirement of Moral Competence. Green says that the individual who wants to resist a particular law or laws should do self-introspection to see whether he is morally competent and justified in offering resistance. He should ask himself the following questions to find out for himself whether the contemplated stop of offering resistance should be taken or not.

1. Have I used all the legal and constitutional methods of getting the bad law repealed?
2. Is my contemplated step the result of cool judgement?
3. Are the people for whose sake I think of offering resistance fully satisfied that resistance is the right step?
4. Do I have the necessary moral caliber to launch resistance against the law?
5. Is the law against which resistance is planned really so bad as to require resistance?
6. Are my aims enlightened and selfless, or selfish and egoistic?
7. What will be the results of resistance, and will the situation improve and benefit society by my action?

Resistance after Deep Thought under Exceptional Circumstances. From all this, one can realize that Green permits resistance only under exceptional circumstances, and by individuals who are morally competent and motivated by a spirit to serve really noble ends. Those who fully qualify themselves to undertake the job of resistance must be very few and far between. Sometimes, an individual may have to resist, even if the prospects of success are dim. A person belonging to a small minority may think of offering resistance after feeling that he is morally justified in offering resistance and that he will be failing in his moral duty as a citizen, if he continues to obey the bad law.

2. View of H.J. Laski

Satisfaction of Conscience. Harold Laski is in favour of the individual offering resistance, if his conscience is fully satisfied. Before resisting, the individual will have to try all constitutional methods to get bad laws repealed. If all these methods fail, he is justified in offering resistance, because obedience to tyrannical and evil laws is a greater evil than disobedience.

3. View of Mahatma Gandhi

Great and Noble Citizen. Mahatma Gandhi was a great and noble citizen, who felt that he would be failing in his duty, if he did not offer resistance to bad and unjust laws.

Resistance in South Africa. In South Africa he offered resistance to uphold the cause of justice and equality on behalf of Indians, against whom the most degrading and the meanest type of discrimination was practised.

Resistance Movement Part of Swaraj Movement. In India Gandhiji repeatedly appealed the British Government (which was ruthlessly exploiting India) to be fair and just, but it turned a deaf ear to him. Therefore he thought that the only course open to him was to offer resistance to the unjust, tyrannical and oppressive laws. The resistance movement of Gandhiji became a part of the larger movement for *Swaraj*. He was fully successful and ultimately India won *swaraj* on 15the August, 1947.

Strict Standards. Mahatma Gandhi followed very strict standards of conduct, and all were convinced that he was acting as a true *mahatma,* a great soul. His resistance was completely non-violent and was based on uncompromising truth and sincerity.

BOOKS FOR FURTHER READING

1. Appadorai, A., *The Substance of Political*—1957.

2. Asirvatham, Eddy, *Political Theory*—1957.

3. Barker, Ernest, *Principles of Social and Political Theory.*

4. Brown, W. J., *The Austinian Theory of Law*—1931.

5. Bryce, James, *Studies in History and Jurisprudence,* Vol. II—1901, Oxford.

6. Coker, F. W., *Recent Political Thought*—1966, The World Press, Calcutta.

7. Corry, J. A., *Democratic Government and Politics*—1958.

8. Dicey, A. V., *Law and Public Opinion*—1919.

9. Duguit, Leon, *Law in the Modern State.*

10. Friedmann, W., *Legal Theory*—1953, Stevens & Sons.

11. Gettell, R. G., *Introduction to Political Science.*

12. Gilchrist, R. N., *Principles of Political Science*—1961, Orient Longman.

13. Holland, T. E., *Elements of Jurisprudence*—1906, Oxford.

14. Kantorowicz, H., *The Definition of Law*—1958, Cambridge University Press.

15. Kelsen, Hans., *General Theory of Law and State*—1949, Harvard University Press.

16. Laski, H. J., *A Grammar of Politics*—1957.

17. Laski, H. J., *Studies in Law and Politics*—1932, Yale University Press.

18. MacIver, R. M., *The Modern State*—1950.

19. Nandi, Amar, *Introduction to Political Science*—1959.

20. Ross, Alf, *On Law and Justice*—1959, Stevens & Sons.

21. Roucek & Others, *Introduction to Political Science*—1954.

22. Sidgwick, H., *The Elements of Politics*—1908.

23. Soltau, R. H., *Introduction to Politics*--1959.

5

Liberty

Meaning, Features and Importance of Liberty

The word 'liberty' is derived from the Latin term *liber,* which means free.

Apparently Easy Word Used by All. 'Liberty' is an apparently easy word with which all are familiar. It seems everybody knows the correct meaning of the word. The man in the street, the housewife, the office-goer, the factory-worker, the grocer, the farmer, the poet, the artist, the political researcher, the scholar, the politician, the philosopher and everybody else freely use the term. R.N. Gilchrist says on page 119 in *Principles of Political Science* (1961): 'Every one has a vague notion of liberty of some kind and a desire for it, but among ten people using the word, perhaps no two will be able to say exactly what they mean, or, if they do say it, will agree with each other in their definitions."

Giving Precise Meaning Difficult. 'Liberty' has different connotations to different people, and it is used very often loosely and carelessly. In political science, which is an inexact social science, great difficulty is experienced in furnishing exact definitions and meanings of concepts like liberty, equality, sovereignty, and nationalism. Stephen Leacock says on page 67 in his *Elements of Political Science* (1932): "Let us begin by observing that such terms as *liberty, freedom* and *free* are used in a variety of senses and great latitude of connotation........the term *liberty* is used also as a vague generality to stand for something evidently desirable, and yet so simple in its nature as to need no further definition. It is freely assumed that everyone ought to have complete liberty and that every violation of liberty is an injustice without the need being felt for any special inquiry into the meaning of liberty itself."

Difficult to distinguish between Liberty and Freedom. It is difficult to distinguish between the two terms *liberty* and *freedom.* They are generally used as synonymous terms, though there are writer who make a distinction; but even such writers are unable to explain any clear and significant difference. Their hair-splitting arguments add to the vagueness instead of making any lucid and meaningful difference. R.H. Soltau says on page 127 in *An Introduction to Politics* (1959): "We are unable to make a satisfactory distinction between the term *freedom* and *liberty;* the only difference is that one is English, the other Latin; and we cannot follow Mr. Carrittt when in his *Morals and Politics* he defines freedom as 'unconstraint from human action; especially from socially organised and legal constraint, and liberty as a voice in deciding among claims to unconstraint and between ourselves and others'."

Freedom from Restrictions. Basically liberty means absence of restraints. *Chamber's Twentieth Century Dictionary* says that liberty is "freedom from constraint, captivity, or tyranny; freedom to do as one pleases; the unrestrained enjoyment of natural rights; power of free choice; privilege; permission; free range; leisure; disposal; the bounds within which certain privileges are enjoyed: (often in pl.) a limited area outside a prison in which prisoners are allowed to live; presumptions or undue freedom; speech or action, violating ordinary civility." This dictionary meaning shows the varied uses to which the term is put. The quintessence of liberty is freedom from restrictions or restraints. This does not mean that liberty enables an individual to do whatever he likes regardless of others. A person cannot rob others or be a nuisance to others. He has to subject himself to restraints prescribed by law and custom. Therefore liberty means absence of arbitrary, illegal and unreasonable restraints. It seems liberty is a word of negative sense, but a close examination of its scope shows that it is also a term of positive meaning. Liberty positively stands for the presence of favourable conditions for the development of human personality.

Liberty as Key Concept of Constitutionalism. The liberal theory of freedom is a key concept of what we call constitutionalism which emerged in modern times. An individual enjoys liberty or freedom, when his thoughts, speech, writing, movements, pursuits, occupation mode of worship and way of living in general are not subject to unjust arbitrary restraints of government. Power is distributed among organs of government according to written or unwritten constitutional principles. Government exercises its coercive power constitutionally and not arbitrarily. The individual is ensured the enjoyment of certain minimum civil, political and economic rights, on which his liberty is based.

Liberty a Priceless Possession. Liberty is a condition which powerful attracts the individual and masses of people. It is a priceless possession to secure which mankind has sacrificed much. Nations have sung its praise and have placed it among their most valuable assets. Liberty gives the highest form of emotional satisfaction. A person has liberty, when he finds himself in a state in which he can give full expression to what all he wills. History has recorded many battles and shedding of much blood all over the world for winning the highly coveted treasure of liberty. Rousseau goes to the extent of saying that "to renounce liberty is to renounce being a man, to surrender the rights of humanity and even its duties."

Important Definitions of Liberty

We may make a reference to certain important definition of liberty.

Free Choice. Massimo Salvadori says on page 21 in *Liberal Democracy* (1957): "Liberty is free choice, each individual's own decision concerning his own course of action: it belongs to himself, not to the external world that surrounds him."

Power to Think their Own Thoughts and Act Upon Them. Ramsay Muir Says: "By Liberty I mean the secure enjoyment by individuals, and by natural and spontaneous groups of individuals, such as a nation, church, trade union, of the power to think their own thoughts and to express and act upon them, using their own gifts in their own way under the shelter of the law, provided they do not impair the corresponding rights of others."

Liberty a Product of Rights. Harold Laski says: "By liberty I mean the eager maintenance of that atmosphere in which men have the opportunity to be their best selves Liberty therefore is a product of rights."

Liberty not Absolute but Conditioned in Social Context. Liberty cannot be absolute and unrestricted, as it has to be understood in a special context, in which the needs of the individual should be in harmony with those of society. Man can have rights only when he has social relations. Stephen Leacock says on page 69 in *Elements of Social Science* (1932): "The utmost freedom of action that each and every individual can enjoy upon like terms at the same time is to be completely unrestrained in his action in so far as they do not interfere with the like freedom of his fellows." It is impossible for all persons in society and state to enjoy liberty in the absolute sense; in case one person is allowed to have absolute and unrestrained liberty, others will have no liberty worth the name. Ernest Barker says on page 145 in *Principles of Social and Political Theory* that liberty is "not the indefinite liberty of an undefined individual but is the definite liberty of a defined personality, seeking to realize specific capacities." Liberty prevails when people have respect and goodwill for each other, and when they behave with others in the same way in which they want others to behave with them. They want liberty for themselves by enjoying rights, but at the same time they would allow others too to enjoy their rights, which create liberty for others. Unrestrained and unregulated liberty would mean the law of the jungle and the unbridled licence to do anything dictated by men's passions. If the physically strong man sees no restraints in society and state, he is likely to condemn other people to slavery without any compunction. Human beings enjoy liberty in society under well defined laws, customs and usages.

Features of Liberty

We may briefly discuss the important features of liberty.

1. *Not Static.* The content of liberty is not static: it changes with the moving times, though "its large outlines may have a permanent character." R.K. Carr and others say in *American Democracy in Theory and Practice* (1961): "What one generation regards as an indispensable liberty, another may feel it should be sacrificed to the needs of the changing times and conditions." Cotton-planters in the USA had the freedom to buy, keep and sell slaves. But this liberty was regarded as a crime, when slavery was banned by legislation. Factory-owners at one time had the liberty to engage children and women for long hours at night. But when laws were passed against such employment, they lost the liberty. Concepts of social decency and justice change from generation to generation. So also the content of liberty.

2. *Against Political Subjection.* The *Encyclopedia Britannica,* Vol. III (1947) page 1005 gives the meaning of liberty "as a state of freedom especially opposed to political subjection, imprisonment or slavery. Its two most generally recognised divisions are civil and political liberty." At the altar of liberty individuals and countries have prayed and agreed to fight relentlessly to secure it. It was the love of liberty that provoked the people in England to revolt against the tyrannical Stuarts, American colonies against George III's oppressive government in England, the French against the ruthless and bankrupt Government of Louis XVI and the people in Latin American countries against the exploiting imperialist masters of Europe. Patrick Henry, the revolutionary leader, raising his voice in the American colonies against Britain said: "Give me liberty or give me death." The French revolutionaries profusely shed blood for the sake of the magic words Liberty, Equality and Fraternity. Obviously the various movements, revolts and revolutions in Europe were inspired by the strong urge to break the chains of restraints arbitrarily and unjustly bound around the hands and feet of the people by their relentless rulers.

3. *Greek Concept of Group Protection and Full Realisation of Ideals.* The ancient Greeks in city-states like Athens claimed that they were lovers of liberty of thought and action. "The basic idea of liberty as a part of the armoury of human ideals goes back to the Greeks and is born, as the funeral oration of Pericles makes abundantly clear, of two notions; the first is the protection of the group from attack, the second is the ambition of the group to realize itself as fully as passible." (See *Encyclopedia of Social Sciences,* Vol. I—1954, p. 442) The Greeks did not know the concept of liberty *as we understand it now;* they did not differentiate between state and society, state and government, and thought in terms of life-partnership with the state. They did not have any rights as such against the state; and individual liberty, the product of rights as we know it and enjoy it in the modern state now, did not exist. In another sense in Greece, liberty as a positive concept meant the right and obligation to participate in the making of political decisions, the right to vote, the right to hold office and so on.

4. *Absence of Restraints and Favourable Positive Conditions.* Liberty does not merely mean an absence of restraint from anyone; it also implies the prevalence of positive conditions for the growth of the personality of one and all. "The positive concept of liberty.......admits that there must be compulsion if liberty is to have a practical meaning......whereas the positive view of liberty expresses the freedom to do something, the negative aspect connotes the freedom from having to do something." A person may sit in the park, enjoying the cool breeze in the evening. The policeman has no power to ask him to work on the ground that he is idling his time. The person here has the liberty of not doing any work at that time against his will.

5. *Liberty Inseparable from Rights.* Liberty is present, when people have rights, and therefore liberty is regarded as the product of right. (The rights of the individual are discussed in Chapter 19.) H. J. Laski says on page 144 in *A Grammar of Politics* (1957): "Freedoms are therefore opportunities

which history has shown to be essential to the development of personality. And freedoms are inseparable from rights because otherwise their realisation is hedged about with an uncertainly which destroys their quality."

6. *Liberty Essential Condition for Personality Development.* Liberty ensures conditions, which are most congenial to the free expression of thought and freedom of action and to the full development of the individual's personality. J.A. Corry observes on page 29 in *Democratic Government and Politics* (1958); "Individual freedom or liberty is the necessary condition for the realisation of the potentialities of personality. The sheltered protected person, like the slave, whose choices are made for him by others, is likely to be a colourless, starved, and even weak personality. It is the making of moral choices in which we assess the alternatives and then have to abide by the consequences of the decision that develop character and make life rich and meaningful. The long struggle for individual freedom arose from the claims of even larger number of men seeking to secure for themselves this means to the enrichment of their lives."

7. *Liberty Found Only in Democracy.* Liberty finds an important place in the study of democracy as a form of government and a way of life. It is only under a democratic government that the individual enjoys full liberty. There is no liberty under a totalitarian government or absolute monarchy or dictatorship. Liberty cannot be taken for granted in countries in which there are no representative institutions. A person living in a democratic state has an experience quite different from the one a man has under a tyrannical government. In the former the individual has various kinds of rights, whose product is liberty, and in the latter the individual is denied rights and feels the conspicuous absence of liberty. Ernest Barker says on page 140 in *Principles of Social and Political Theory* (1952): "The procedural rule or principle of liberty means that the state treats each and every moral person as a free agent, capable of developing his own capacities in his own way, and therefore capable of enjoying and exercising the rights which are the conditions of such development."

8. *Liberty Accompanied by Responsibility.* Liberty is always accompanied by responsibility. It is contrary to unbridled activity, which is harmful to the general interests of society. Liberty carries with it a great sense of responsibility of choosing the right types of restraints. Rodee, Anderson and Christol say one page 91 in *Introduction to Political Science* (1957): "Liberty implies restraint which, in a democracy, means social self-restraint to be exercised where necessary for the security and welfare of the community and in accordance with the will of majority as expressed through democratic processes. In other words, liberty implies personal and group responsibility." The liberty of one man has to be consistent with an agreeable to the liberty which other men enjoy. Liberty unaccompanied by reasonable restraints ceases to be liberty and comes in the way of the liberty of others. Herbert Spencer aptly observes: "Every man is free to do that which he wills provided he infringes not the equal freedom of any other man."

Importance of Liberty

The meaning and features of liberty speak volumes of its tremendous importance to the individual, society, and nation. The individual needs it for the development of his personality, society needs it for its growth and progress, and the nation needs it for independence. It is a highly valued and treasured possession to secure which much sacrifice has been made all over the world. Human life is worthless without liberty.

CATEGORIES OF LIBERTY

Liberty Conveying Wide Range of Ideas. Liberty is a term conveying a wide range of ideas, and one can speak of different types of liberty. R.M. MacIver says in *The Modern State* (1950): 'Liberty itself is not one but manifold. There are many forms of liberty: liberty of thought and of its expression, liberty of action in hundred external spheres, civil liberty, economic liberty and so forth, each of these again having many divisions, such as in the economic field, the liberties of contract and of competition."

Broadly understood liberty can be brought under 5 categories: (1) Natural Liberty; (2) Civil or Personal Liberty; (3) Political Liberty; (4) Economic Liberty; and (5) National Liberty.

1. Natural Liberty

Synonymous with Anarchy. As generally understood, natural liberty means the unrestrained freedom to do what one pleases. Such a type of freedom does not and cannot exist in a state, as no individual can be allowed complete freedom to do anything he likes without harming the interests of others. Unrestrained liberty is the very negation of true liberty. Natural liberty is pre-social, that is, it must have existed at a time, when there was no society. There can be no natural liberty in a civil society. Contractualists like Hobbes, Locke and Rousseau speak in terms of a state of nature, in which there were no restraints. The primitive man did whatever he liked and only the superior brute force of this opponents could curb his natural liberty. With the emergence of society and state, and with the rise of several restraints, natural liberty had to end. While in a state the weak are protected, in a condition of natural liberty, the weak were thrown at the mercy of the strong. Natural liberty is synonymous with injustice and complete anarchy. It is illusory as there can be no true liberty when there is natural liberty.

As Understood in Proper Spirit. If understood rationally and in a proper spirit, natural liberty may be taken to mean the freedom given by nature to all, the need to treat all as equal in society, and the prevention of any one from taking undue advantage of his position and from claiming rights which others do not have. It requires a great mind to understand and appreciate the philosophical meaning of natural liberty. Ordinary men and women, who cannot understand it, cannot subject themselves voluntarily to self-restraint. If all people happen to be good and noble, coercive power is not necessary. No police force is required, and courts and jails would be superfluous; the trouble is that the ordinary man by his very nature needs someone to order him to behave in a manner which does not inconvenience and annoy others.

Natural Liberty Connected with Natural Law. Natural liberty is intimately connected with natural law. The stoic philosophers in Greece and the Roman thinkers, who were profoundly influenced by them, spoke of the law of nature, which they believed was based on justice and reason. Cicero says that "there is a single law or system of law governing the whole universe; it applies to everything that exists in divine creation, animate as well as inanimate, rational as well as non-rational. It is as old as time and is the source of the state itself; the state is partnerships of law." While governing a mighty empire, the Roman Statesmen thought in terms of natural liberty as connected with natural law. In governing diverse people of different races and cultures, the wise and practical-minded Roman statesmen were influenced by natural law. In the evolution of Roman law, *Ius Naturale* or Natural Law was blended with *Ius Civile* or Civil Law and *Ius Gentium* or Law of Peoples.

Natural Law in Medieval and Modern Times. The concept of natural law travelled beyond the barrier of the ancient times, and found a place in the writings of medieval church thinkers, who found natural law in the law of God and the law of the Church. In modern times, through the writings of Locke and Rousseau, natural law exerted its influence. The American and French revolutionaries were inspired by the ideas of liberty equality and fraternity as could be discovered in the law of nature.

2. Personal or Civil Liberty

Product of Several Civil Rights. Personal or civil liberty is the product of several rights including right to think freely, right to speech, right to free movement, right to property right to live freely, and right to have one's own culture.

To live Freely without Arbitrary Restraints. Civil liberty, which is enjoyed by a person in his capacity as an individual in the private relations of social life means the absence of unreasonable and illegitimate restraints. Civil liberty prevails in a state when authority is legitimate and restraints are imposed on the people in accordance with the law and the constitution. Civil liberty, includes among freedoms the basic freedoms of physical freedom, intellectual freedom and practical freedom.

Freedom from Arbitrary Imprisonment. A. V. Dicey says on page 207 in *Introduction to the Study of the Law of the Constitution* (1956): "The right to personal liberty as understood in England means in substance a person's right not to be subjected to imprisonment, arrest or other physical coercion in any manner that does not admit of legal justification."

Physical, Intellectual and Practical Freedom. Ernest Barker says that "civil liberty consists in three differently expressed articles: Physical freedom from injury or threat to the life, health and movement of the body; intellectual freedom for the expression of thought and belief; and practical freedom from the play of will and the exercise of choice in the general field or contractual action and relations with other persons." These three freedoms give a wide scope to civil liberty.

Importance of Personal Freedom. As stated above, civil liberty includes personal freedom, which is of tremendous importance of the individual. A state, which values and upholds freedom, will treat with respect the personality of the individual. Every human being, whether male or female, rich or poor, strong or weak, has an importance as an individual and this has to be fully recognised. Every individual should have the maximum freedom, which however should not be a hurdle to the freedom of others. There should be a balance between the freedom of one individual and the freedom of others. This is possible only when all individuals are law-abiding and respect the rights of others. F. A. Hayek says on page 11 in *The Constitution of Liberty* (1959) that freedom or liberty is a "condition of men in which coercions of some by others is reduced as much as possible in society.....The state in which a man is not subject to coercion by the arbitrary will of another or others is often also distinguished as individual or personal freedom."

Importance of Civil Liberty in Britain and the USA. In states like England and the USA, people attach great importance to civil liberty including personal freedom and resent the least encroachment on it. Englishmen and Americans do not like to be dictated by the state as to how they should live, what religion they should follow, what avocation they should pursue, what opinion they should have, how they should dress, and how they should plan their life in general. They want to be left completely free to live in their own way, and develop themselves according to their own ideas, tastes and values. The Englishman is ever jealous of his rights as a person and wants his home, which he proudly regards as his castle, to be free from any outside interference. J.S. Mill was a staunch advocate of freedom and great champion of individual liberty and his essay *On Liberty* has been regarded as a masterpiece. Mill pleads for tolerance for various points of view and ways of living. Mill's opinion has to be understood in the light of the fact that in a modern democracy, power falls into the hands of the majority party. Every individual, whether he belongs to the majority or to the minority, should be given complete personal liberty and tolerance. Mill says: "If all mankind minus one were of one opinion and only one person were of the contrary opinion, mankind would be no more justified in silencing that one person, than he, if he had the power, would be justified in silencing mankind." In the 20th century, the eminent British philosopher Bertrand Russell underlined the tremendous significance of personal freedom, which is preferred even to political freedom.

Roosevelt's Stress on Four Freedoms. The rise of Fascism in Italy under Mussolini and Nazi totalitarianism under Hitler in Germany proved to be a great threat to democracy and freedom, and therefore in declaring the war aims in 1941 (during the Second World War 1939-45) President Franklin D. Roosevelt of the USA eloquently spoke for the cause of liberty by upholding his celebrated Four freedoms: (1) Freedom of Speech and Expression; (2) Freedom of Religion; (3) Freedom from Want; and (4) Freedom from Fear. (In this connection, it may be stated that religious freedom took longer to be recognised than other types of freedom. For ages religion was controlled by the State.

Protection of Civil Liberty. Civil liberty in democratic countries is protected by: (1) the recognition of the distinction between state and government; (2) a democratic constitution written or unwritten; (3) the actual definition of the rights of private action; and (4) the recognition of fundamental rights. Full protection of civil liberty is an important obligation of government. Law protects the individual's liberty from encroachment from others. The individual has to be protected also from any government action which is dangerous to his civil liberty. A Bill of Rights as in the USA or a list of Fundamental Rights guaranteed by the Constitution as in India protects the individuals from any encroachment by the state. In the USA and India, which have written constitutions, the judiciary can declare laws of government as *ultra vires,* if they violate the provisions of the constitution. Britain has not drawn up a list of fundamental rights; but even then the British courts are equal to the task of affording complete protection to the civil rights of the people. In England there is no difference between constitutional law. Parliament is supreme in England, where the judiciary is not competent to question the validity of laws passed by it. The eternal vigilance of the British people is the surest guarantee of civil rights.

Negation of Liberty in Totalitarian States. In totalitarian states like Fascist Italy, Nazi Germany, Communist Russia and Communist China, liberty is denied to the people. In these states the liberties of the people are ruthlessly suppressed and the individual is regarded as the tool of the state. Individuals resorting to resistance even in a peaceful manner are arrested and imprisoned after a "trial" or punished in other ways.

3. Political Liberty

Product of Political Rights. Political liberty is the product of political rights like: (1) right to vote; (2) right to contest elections; (3) right to hold public office; (4) right to criticize government. Political liberty is enjoyed by the citizens of a state and not by foreigners.

Political Liberty Synonymous with Democracy. Political liberty, or constitutional liberty as some would like to call it, is considered synonymous with democracy. A citizen having political liberty secures opportunities to take part in the political affairs of the state and share power. Ernest Barker says on page 11 in *Reflections of Government* (1958): "If a man is free to advocate his thoughts, and to associate himself with others for their common advocacy, he must be free to advocate personally thoughts of his own about the affairs of Commonwealth and not only so, but also to form or join political parties by which such or similar thoughts are generally advocated." Political liberty without which civil liberty has no basis and meaning makes democracy real and enables the individual to have a share in shaping government polities directly or indirectly. In a democratic state, sovereignty is vested in the people. They can effectively use sovereignty only when they are fully guaranteed political rights, with the help of which they can contest elections, enter the legislature, climb to seats of power and take important decisions.

Recognition of Political Liberty. Political liberty should be constitutionally and legally recognised, and proper conditions should be created to give it the maximum scope. The spread of education, the formation of political parties and the freedom of the press go far in increasing the scope of political liberty. The people in a state can make provision in their constitution for the enjoyment of guaranteed political rights, which automatically create political liberty. In states like the USA, Britain and India, the individual enjoys full political liberty.

4. Economic Liberty

Product of Economic Rights. Economic liberty is the product of economic rights, which include: (1) right to work, (2) right to living wages, (3) right to adequate leisure, (4) right to benefits against accidents, sickness and unemployment, and (5) right against exploitation. These right satisfy the basic economic wants of the individual and provide him with a sense of reasonable economic security, without which the individual's mind will be haunted by constant anxiety, insecurity, and tension.

Meaning and Importance of Economic Liberty. H.J. Laski gives the meaning of economic liberty on page 148 in *A Grammar of Politics:* "By economic liberty, I mean security and the opportunity to find reasonable significance in the earning of one's daily bread. I must, that is, be free from the constant fear of unemployment and insufficiency which, perhaps more than other inadequacies sap the whole strength of personality. I must be safeguarded against the wants of tomorrow." A person, who does not have adequate food, clothes and housing, cannot enjoy full civil or political liberty.

More Important than Civil and Political Liberty. Any type of liberty is barren, unless there is economic liberty. Therefore economic liberty is more important than civil and political liberty, which mean little to hungry stomachs facing economic degradation. Political liberty and civil liberty do not prevent the ruthless exploitations of the poor by the rich. In several states, persons in seats of political power misuse it and exploit the people (who enjoy civil liberty and political liberty) without any hindrance. While in democracies people have the right to vote and the right to free movement, not to speak of other rights, they may not have economic liberty which alone can make them free from hunger and economic exploitation. People do not care much for the right to vote or the right to form associations or freedom of expression, if they do not have freedom from want or economic liberty. Civil and political rights are of little avail for people suffering from long spells of unemployment.

Democracy Made Meaningful by Economic Liberty. Democracy is meaningless and has no significant content without economic liberty. Without adequate economic security, the individual cannot develop himself and can have no interest in life even in a democratic state. It has been rightly said that democracy should enter the economic field and guarantee employment and minimum wages to workers. Laski says on page 148 in *A Grammar of Politics:* "Economic liberty, therefore, implies democracy in industry. That means two things. It means that industrial government is subject to the system of rights which obtain for men as citizens, and it means that industrial direction must be of a character that makes it the rule of laws made by co-operation and not by compulsion."

Safeguarding Economic Liberty. Broadly speaking, economic liberty can be safeguarded in certain ways: (1) by defining the economic rights of the people; (2) by recognizing the status of the worker and providing scope for the development of his personality;

(3) by guaranteeing the individual's right to work; (4) by making provision for minimum wages; (5) by providing adequate leisure; and (6) by shieiding workers from the anxieties of unemployment, accident, sickness and old age.

Representation of Labour on Management. Over and above all these, workers may be given representation on the management of industrial and other concerns so that their interests may be protected. This will also bring legitimate pride among workers with the feeling that they are not a negligible quantity, and there will be sufficient reason for workers to show their initiative and drive in any work they undertake.

5. National Liberty

Complete Independence. National liberty is equivalent to national freedom or independence. When a state is not subject to a foreign power, it enjoys what we call national independence. Like individuals, groups of people can also think in terms of liberty. The people in a state can think of liberty in a corporate capacity. When all people have liberty as individuals belonging to a nation, liberty becomes national.

Importance of National Liberty. National liberty is of great importance, as it provides a basis for civil, political and economic liberty. There is national liberty in a state, when people are completely free from any foreign control, and have a government of their own. In other words, when a state attains a full sovereign status, national liberty is possible. Indians did not have national liberty before India became completely independent (August 15, 1947).

Safeguarding Liberty

Need of Safeguarding Liberty. Owing to various causes, people all over the world became conscious of their rights and fought for liberty in modern times. In ancient and medieval states, people did not have liberty, as they have now. In highly advanced countries, where people paid a heavy price to earn liberty, it was felt that special measures should be adopted to safeguard liberty. Liberty may be lost in the absence of adequate safeguards.

Laski's Emphasis on Special Guarantees. Laski has rightly emphasised the need of having adequate guarantees of liberty. He makes certain significant observations and makes out the following points on pages 141 to 151 in *A Grammar of Politics* (1957):

1. "Freedom will not be achieved for the mass of men save under special guarantees" and it cannot "exist in the presence of privilege.
2. Special privileges and freedom cannot coexist. "Special privilege is incompatible with freedom because the latter quality belongs to all alike in their character as human beings."
3. All should be guaranteed rights and nobody should be made to depend on others for their rights. Liberty cannot be reaslised in a state in which "the rights of some depend upon the pleasure of others."
4. State action is necessary for safeguarding liberty. Certain persons in society are likely to destroy the livelihood of others and may through maldistribution of wealth impair the interests of others. "At every point, therefore, where the action of a group of men may impinge upon the exercise of rights a control is wanted which will frustrate their power to so impinge." The state should make laws for diffusing economic power and providing social justice.

Essential Conditions for Liberty

People can enjoy full liberty only under certain essential conditions, which may be enumerated as follows:

1. *Strong Urge for Liberty and Eternal Vigilance.* First of all people in a state should themselves have the urge for liberty, and be ever vigilant to guard it, when it is secured. Love of liberty cannot be artificially thrust into the hearts of people from outside; it should spontaneously rise from within. If the people themselves do not show their keenness to have, preserve and safeguard it, they are sure to lose it sooner or later. The people must feel in their heart that nothing is so

precious to them as liberty. If the individual is not vigilant, he will surely forfeit his liberty, and if a nation goes to slumber, it will also lose its liberty before long. No nation can retain its liberty, if the people recklessly throw it away to foreigners. Foreign states may commit aggression, if people lack vigilance. As Byron has aptly put it, "Eternal vigilance is the price of liberty." People should always be watchful and vigilant, lest national liberty is snatched away be a foreign power or lest the government itself deprives the people of liberty. People have to watchfully guard themselves against their own government and foreign governments.

2. *Democratic Government with Fundamental Rights.* Government should be truly democratic, and power should be vested in persons, who are accountable to the people. The constitution should have a list of justiciable or guaranteed fundamental rights, which should be beyond the reach of those who are in power. Provision should be made for easily getting these basic rights enforced, and there should be no possibility for the executive or the legislature to encroach on these rights.

3. *Principle of Separation of Powers.* The introduction of the principle of separation of powers will also ensure liberty. One organ of government should not be under the complete control of other organs. The judiciary should not be put under the control of the executive or the legislature. Powers should be so distributed among the three organs of government (executive, legislature and judiciary) that the basic rights of the individual are safely preserved.

4. *Restricting Powers of Executive and Legislature.* The powers of the executive need restriction. The sphere of the executive should be clearly marked out, and it should be prevented from usurping the powers of other branches of government. Ivor Jennings believes that besides limiting the powers of the executive, it is necessary to check the powers of the legislature, which claims to represent the opinion of the majority of the people. Not always does a legislature reflect

public opinion, and the majority party dominating the legislature in a parliamentary democracy may totally ignore the interests of or work against the wishes of the minorities. Legislature may be the handmaid of the party in power, and it may trample with impunity on the rights of the minorities. Ivor Jennings says on page 214 in *The Law and the Constitution* (1955): "It is therefore usually regarded as desirable not only that the ordinary law shall protect the right of free speech, the right of public meeting, but also that the powers of changing the law whether by legislation or administrative regulation shall be so restricted that these rights may not be interfered with." "Constitutions should clearly define the powers of the legislature bearing in mind the rights of all including those of minorities.

5. *Rule of Law.* The rule of law, which provides equality before the law to all, is supposed to be a sure guarantee of liberty. The USA has a written constitution, and there is a list of the most important rights called the Bill of Rights. Britain does not have a written constitution or separation of powers, and no court of law can sit in judgement on a law passed by Parliament; yet Britain does not have less liberty than the American. This is because England has the rule of law, which is regarded as the key to British liberty. In Britain, power is exercised, not arbitrarily, but according to law and principles of the constitution. A. V. Dicey observes: "There is in the English Constitution an absence of those declarations or definitions of rights so dear to foreign constitutions... In England the right to individual liberty is a part of the constitution because it is secured by the courts, extended or confined as they are Habeas Corpus Act."

6. *Strong Public Opinion and Free Press.* Vigilant people and vigilant press can go far in creating the right conditions for the enjoyment of liberty. When government rules arbitrarily and wantonly and stubbornly erodes the rights of the people, they should assert themselves against the government and make use of all agencies of public opinion to bring strong

pressure on the government in favour or rights. A vigilant electorate and a free, fearless and unfettered press can safeguard liberty. In the Western countries, the power of the press is truly great. Rulers watch and hear what the press says. Rodee, Anderson and Christol say on page 191 in *Introduction to Political Science* (1957): "In the final analysis public opinion is the ultimate sanction, behind all bills and declarations of individual liberties. Courts, as well as legislative assemblies, reflect (whether promptly or belatedly) the temper of the popular mind." In the USA, Resident Richard Nixon had to step down owing to the strong pressure of public opinion built up by the press. Americans resented actions of Nixon which resulted in retrenchment of their rights.

7. *Strong Political Parties.* Political parties, which are extra-constitutional in growth, have become indispensable in modern democracies. A strong political party with the backing of large sections of the people can overthrow a government which encroaches on the liberty of the individual.

SOVEREIGNTY, LAW AND LIBERTY

Anarchists, Syndicalists and Guild Socialists Against Sovereignty. Anarchists, who want the state to be abolished altogether, say that sovereignty and law, its vehicle, go against liberty. Syndicalists also think that liberty and law are antagonistic to each other. Guild socialists are against the monistic theory of sovereignty, and they want guilds to be permitted to regulate their own affairs. They opine that laws made by the state are against the freedom of the individual.

Sovereignty not Antagonistic but Friendly toe Liberty. Critics of the monistic theory of sovereignty point out that the sovereignty of the state is inconsistent with the liberty of the individual. It is made out that liberty and sovereignty cannot co-exist. For instance, pluralists like Laski and MacIver, who underline the importance of the role of various associations in political and social life and claim co-sovereign status for them are against giving indivisible sovereignty to the state. But here pluralists are wrong, as they overlook the fact that it is sovereignty that provides content to liberty, and without sovereignty liberty will be empty. Though apparently liberty and sovereignty cannot be friendly, a close examination of the needs of society makes it clear that liberty is not possible without the sovereignty of the state. Liberty, which does not mean the right to do anything in the community, needs sovereignty. The state alone can protect the liberty of the individual from those who encroach on it by making use of sovereignty or supreme coercive power. Liberty is undoubtedly at stake only when the sovereignty of the state is expressed through an irresponsible despot or dictator. Sovereignty is essential for liberty; for without it the sate would have no power to punish law-breakers, and there would be complete anarchy and negation of freedom. Liberty can never go without reasonable restraints. Dewey says: "Freedom unrestrained by responsibility becomes mere licence. Responsibility unchecked by freedom becomes mere arbitrary power. The question then is not whether freedom and responsibility shall be united, but how they can be united and reconciled to the best advantage. This is indeed the central problem of all political philosophy and practice."

Good Laws Favourable to Liberty: Law creates the necessary conditions for the enjoyment of liberty. A significant question that can be asked is whether law and liberty are antithetical or friendly to each other. A direct answer to this question cannot be given. It depends upon the form of government people have, the spirit of the people and other factors. In a normal form of government, free from perversions, law aids liberty and actually becomes a favourable condition of liberty. Without law, which carries sovereignty, there can be no liberty. People have liberty, as the state is sovereign and is competent to impose legal limitations on the behaviour of individuals and associations. Though there are restraints on liberty, they are essential and reasonable, and they act as a bulwark of liberty. If good laws are favourable conditions of liberty, bad oppressive laws are dangerous obstacles to liberty. When bad and oppressive laws are made, the opportunities for the development of the individual's personality are narrowed down. This will explain why laws in the various states of the world do not provide the same content of liberty. In some states, laws are good media or conditions of liberty; in others they provide a limited range of liberty, and in another category of states, laws are antagonistic to liberty. So all laws cannot be reconciled with the liberty of the individual.

Avoiding Dangers of Despotism and Mob Rule: In a country like England, there is great harmony between law and liberty, and government and the people are able to strike a proper balance between sovereignty and liberty. But in backward or developing countries, it is difficult to maintain such a balance. In backward countries, people are not politically sensitive, conscious and vigilant, and an excess of law may result in the destruction of liberty and an excess of liberty may mean mob rule. To be successful, democracy has to avoid the two dangerous rocks of despotism and mob rule. R.G. Gettell says on page 98 in *Introduction to Political Science* (1956): "The balance between sovereignty and liberty is too nicely adjusted to be easily maintained and tends always towards despotism on the one hand and anarchy on the other. Constant vigilance is necessary to preserve the balance under changing conditions, and modern states are not agreed as to what is proper adjustment or how it may best be secured." The healthy relationship between sovereignty and liberty prevailing in Britain cannot be found in countries like India. In Britain are found all conditions essential for the smooth working of democracy; but not all of them are present in India.

Conflict between Law and Liberty. In Britain, which has the two-party system, there is no conflict between law and liberty. If the party in power tries to destroy liberty, the opposition party will be able to overthrow it. The same cannot be said about India, where by and large since the commencement of the Constitution in 1950, the Congress has been able to rule as it likes without the least fear of being thrown out of power. The opposition is weak and pale, and cannot provide a safe alternative to Congress rule. In the elections of 1977, the Janata Party came to power at the Centre, but Janata rule lasted only for two and a half years (1977-80). Under Congress rule, the Constitution has been amended several times and the Fundamental Rights have been progressively eroded. The liberty of the individual has been cut down, and a conflict between law and liberty is clearly visible, as totalitarianism is slyly trying to enter through the back door. The erosion of rights and liberty that has taken place in India has not been witnessed in advanced democracies like Britain and the USA.

Essential conditions for Harmony between Law and Liberty. The relationship between law and liberty will be harmonious, if the following essential conditions prevail:

1. The government in a country is responsible and sympathetic to the people and understands their aspirations.
2. The opposition is effective, and it criticizes and warns the government from time to time.
3. The press is free and makes constructive criticism of governmental policies.
4. The courts of law function independently, fearlessly and impartially.
5. The people are always alert and vigilant.

Changing Relationship between Law and Liberty. The relationship between law and liberty cannot be static; it has to change with the changing times. Every state should realize that sovereignty is not to be bartered away, and at the same time the liberty of the individual is not to be thrown overboard. R.G. Gettell sayson page 149 in *Principles of Political Science* (1956): "Sovereignty carried to the extreme becomes tyranny and destroys liberty, and liberty carried to the extreme becomes anarchy and destroys sovereignty. The efforts made by states to reach a satisfactory compromise between these two equally undesirable extremes comprise a large part of the history of politics, and no permanent solution has yet been reached."

No Liberty under Absolute Monarchy, Dictatorship and Totalitarianism: Under absolute monarchy, dictatorship and totalitarianism there can be no liberty. In fact, liberty is conspicuous by its absence, as law never obliges liberty in states in which rulers are not accountable to the people. All activities of people are controlled by the arbitrary monarch, dictator or fascist boss. Any move of the people to secure liberty will be ruthlessly crushed, and people will be jailed or punished in other ways.

New Menace to Liberty

In the past, when there was no democracy, the scope for liberty was limited. With the emergence of democracy, liberty could have a wide scope; but in recent years even in democratic states a new menace to liberty is noted. This is from the side of government. Several factors are responsible for the rise of this new danger to liberty.

1. *Totalitarian, Trends for Social Welfare*: Though we are assured that democracy safeguards liberty, even in a democratic setup, in the name of the welfare state, governments all over the world are rapidly extending their power. It sounds paradoxical that in democratic states, totalitarian trends, if not naked totalitarianism, are clearly visible. Sardar K.M. Panikkar on page 15 in *The State and the Citizen* speaks of the tremendous growth of state power all supposed to be in the interests of the individual. The result of the state efforts is the loss of liberty of the individual. "it (State) speaks with a million voices on the radio. It overhears our conversations on the telephone. It pries into our secret thoughts be censoring our letters. It controls the water we drink, the food we eat, the lights we use, our modes of transport, and in fact practically everything in our lives. It gives with one hand and takes away with the other."

In modern times, the individual depends more and more on that state, and the functions and responsibility of the state are increasing. To discharge the numerous obligations, the state passes comprehensive legislation giving wider and wider powers to the government. All this has resulted in the progressive erosion of the liberty of the individual.

2. *Jungle of Laws.* The modern citizen lives in a jungle of laws. Legislatures are busy passing laws for various purposes. New laws and amendments to old laws are so many that it is difficult to keep track of them. Legislatures are overburdened with legislative work, and the load of bills is so heavy that they have found it necessary to delegate vast legislative power to the executive. The executive issues scores of orders and regulations to control the political, social and other activities of individuals. The passing of too many laws in rapid succession by the brute majority in the legislature is highly injurious to individual liberty. Besides restricting the scope of liberty, excessive legislation leads to greater red-tapism and its corollary, bribery and corruption.

3. *Thinking by Government.* In some states including those wedded to the democratic system, the government does all the thinking and tells the people what is good or bad for them. It does not respond to public opinion, and pay no heed to criticism. But it goes on asserting that its own views and policies are correct. Leaders in government profess democratic principles, but at the same time deny liberty to the people, whose cause they pretend to uphold. When government suppresses public opinion and arrogates to itself the function of thinking and speaking for the people, great damage is done to the cause of liberty.

4. *Tyranny of the Majority.* Individual liberty is restricted by the tyranny of the majority, which is possible when the opposition is weak. What people experience in several states is not democracy but the tyranny of the majority party, which controls the legislature treating the opposition with contempt. The thinker, who first formulated the idea of a *Tyranny of the majority* was Alexis de Tocqueville in his book *Democracy in America*. E. W. Martin says on page 9 in *The Tyranny of the Majority* (1961): "The tyranny which we fear and which Mr. De Tocqueville principally dreads is of another kind—a tyranny not over the body, but over the mind." Government based on a brute majority will trample

upon the liberty of the people unless the people themselves are able to exert their pressure on the government through the press, platform and other agencies of public opinion.

Books for Further Study

1. Barker, Ernest, *Political Thought in England.*
2. Barker, Ernest, *Principles of Social and Political Theory*—1953
3. Barker, Ernest, *Reflections on Government*—1953.
4. Carr, R. K. and Others, *American Democracy in Theory and Practice*—1961.
5. Cole, G.D.H. and Margaret, *A Guide to Modern Politics.*
6. Corry, J.A., *Democratic Government and Politics*—1958.
7. Denn and Peters, *Social Principles and the Democratic State.*
8. Dicey, A.V., *Introduction to the Law of the Constitution*—1962.
9. Gettell, R.G., *Introduction to Political Science*—1956.
10. Gilchrist, R.N., *Principles of Political Science*—1961, Orient Longmans.
11. Hayek, F.A., *The Constitution of Liberty*—1959.
12. Jennings, Ivor, *The Law and the Constitution*—1955.
13. Lacy, G., *Liberty and Law.*
14. Laski, H. J., *A Grammar of Politics*—1957.
15. Leacock, Stephen, *Elements of Political Science*—1933.
16. MacIver, *The Modern State*—1950.
17. Martin, E. W., *The Tyranny of the Majority*—1961.
18. Popper, *The Open Society and its Enemies*—Vol. I.
19. Raphael, D.D., *Problems of Political Philosophy*—1970, Macmillan.
20. Ritchie, D.G., *Natural Rights* (1903).
21. Rodee, Anderson and Christol, *An Introduction to Political Science*—1957.
22. Soltau, R.H., *Introduction to Politics*—1959.
23. Trueblood, Elton, *Declaration of Freedom* (1954).

6

Equality

Meaning and Features of Equality

1. Meaning of Equality

Disharmony and Imperfections in Society. The problem of social disharmony and social imperfections has always existed. To set right social drawbacks and solve social problems, thinkers contributed their own concepts or theories. One of these concerns the problem of inequality. Political thinkers analysed political social, economic and other problems and created the concept of equality. They thought that the concept of equality like the concept of liberty would go far in solving man's problems as a social and political animal. In modern times, human beings tried to come out of the conditions of privilege and inequality to the conditions giving the same rights or equality to all.

Difficult to Define Precisely. Equality cannot be defined easily and precisely, as the nature of its contents defy clear and exact definition.

Democratic Ideal of Equality Understood in Different Ways. Like liberty equality is a great democratic ideal, which has been understood in different way by different thinkers.

Many Facets. Equality has several facets. Giovanni Sartori says on page 326 in Democratic Theory (1965) that equality "has so many facets and so many implications, that after we have examined it from all angles we are left with a feeling of not having really mastered it." To some equality stands for political equality only, and to some it is nothing more than equality before the law. There are others, who understand it in the widest sense possible, and desire to bring political equality, social equality, civil equality and economic equality under the general heading of Equality.

Equality Does not Stand for Putting all Kinds of Persons on the Same Footing. The concept of equality does not mean that all persons irrespective of their capacities, talents, natural gifts and mental calibre should be put on the same level. A highly qualified surgeon is not to be put on a par with an unskilled cobbler on the roadside. Ernest Barker says on page 155 in *Principles of Social and Political Theory*: "Equality, after all, is a derivative value. It is derived from the supreme value of the development of personality—in each alike and equally, but each along its own different line and of its own separate motion." Up to a certain minimum level the state should enforce equality, but above that level difference in natural gifts, training, skill, ability and aptitudes has to be recognised. It is impossible to have equality at all levels among different types of human beings.

Basically a Levelling Process. The ideal of equality is basically all levelling process. Harold Laski says on page 153 in *A Grammar of Politics* (1957) "Undoubtedly it (equality) implies fundamentally a levelling process. It means that no man shall be so placed in society that he can overreach his neighbour to the extent which constitutes a denial of the latter's citizenship." Sartori refers pointedly on page 337 in *Democratic Theory* (1965) to the remark made by Brvce that in the USA equality first of all means "equality of estimation", that is in their "ultimate value" human beings are all equal. "For this reason American democracy, as a way of life, basically expressed in a general levelling status, in equal treatment and respect for the next man, whoever he may be."

Political Equality and Equality before Law. Some regard equality as nothing but political equality and quality before law. J.A. Corry says on page 33 in *Democratic Government and Politics* (1958): "The ideal of equality has insisted that men are politically equal, that all citizens are equally entitled to take part in political life, to exercise the franchise, to run for and hold office. It has insisted that individuals shall be equal before the law, that when the general law confers rights or imposes duties, these rights and duties shall extend to all; or conversely that the law shall not confer special privileges on particular individuals or groups."

Same Treatment and No Discrimination. Equality also means the same treatment for all from the state without any distinction between one individual and another up to a certain minimum level. The state shall show no discrimination among individuals while giving rewards and punishments. The principle of equality stands for a set of principles which do away with any type of discrimination between one citizen and another. One of the justiciable Fundamental Rights in the Constitution of India is the Right to Equality which includes: (1) equality before the law; (2) social equality; (30 equality of opportunity; (4) abolition of untouchability; and (5) no titles. Legally and constitutionally speaking, in India no discrimination can be shown against any individual, on the basis of religion, caste, creed or language.

Giovanni Sartori writes on page 338 in *Democratic Theory* (1965) on three principles: (1) juridico-political equality, (2) social equality, and (3) equalisation of circumstances. He explains equalization of circumstances as equal access to opportunities based on merit, equality of opportunity created by a relatively equal distribution of wealth, and economic sameness, that is, state ownership of all wealth. The concept of Equalisation of Circumstances, Sartori explains, means to all the same legal and political rights, the same social importance the same opportunities to rise, the same starting point, and zero-level (economic power to none).

Four Rights under Equality Embodie in the declaration of Rights of Man in France. French thinkers and jurists following *The Declaration of the Rights of Man* (1789) mentioned four rights under Equality: "the right to be treated equally with others, and on the same footing as others, in the eye of the law and in all legislative acts; the right to be treated equally with others in matters of justice and in courts of law; the right to be treated equally with others in matters of taxation so that each man pays the same proportion of his means as is paid by the others; and finally the right to be treated as equally admissible with others to public honours and officers of employment."

Universal Subjection to the Same Law in England. England has set an example in upholding equality. A.V. Dicey says on page 193 in *introduction to the Study of Law of the Constitution* (1956): "In England the idea of legal equality of or universal subjection of all classes to one law administered by the ordinary courts, has been pushed to its utmost limits. With us every official, from the Prime Minister down to a constable or a collector of taxes, is under the same responsibility for every act done without legal justification as an other citizen."

Adequate Opportunities, No Special Privileges and Equal Rights. Equality also stands for four principles: (1) All persons are provided with *adequate* (not equal) opportunities for the development of their personalities. (2) No class or caste or group is given special privileges which are denied to others. (3) Rights are equally distributed among all. (4) All have equal access to opportunities leading to authority.

Meaning of Inequality. While studying equality, the meaning of inequality also has to be understood. Inequality means that opportunities and privileges in a state may be given to a favoured few on the basis of birth, religion, class, caste, wealth, education and race. In almost all the countries of the world, at some stage of history, these were the passport to the realm of privileges and authority. In the *varnavyavastha* (caste system) in India, there was no equality, as the Brahmans and Kshatriyas enjoyed privileges not within the reach of Vaishyas and Shudras. There was no equality in France in the days of the Bourbon rulers, as the nobles and the higher clergy enjoyed special rights, which the common people did not have. In Nazi Germany, there was no equality, as Jews were treated as inferior to Germans, who according to the Nazi theory belonged to the superior Nordic race. In South Africa and Rhodesia today, there is no equality, as coloured people are not treated on a par with the whites.

Features of Equality

We may briefly refer here to the features of equality.

1. *Equality Not Given by Nature.* Men are not born equal, and absolute equality can never be realised. In fact, nature has

made men unequal; some men are endowed with great intellectual power, some with great physical strength, some with extremely handsome features and some with very rare gifts. Giovanni Sartori observes on page 327 in *Democratic Theory* (1965): "Physically some men are three or four times as strong as others, able to perform many times as much work. Intellectually the contrast is still greater, as may be realised when we compare an average person with a man like Sir Winston Churchill.....If intellectual inequality is more marked than physical inequality, moral inequality is still more so. The contrast between self-centred and cruel persons on the one hand, and saints and heroes on the other, is really incalculable." All these account for inequality given by nature. All men are not born in the same circumstances, and conditions of birth differ from child to child. Human beings are not like standardised commodities coming out of a factory. Every individual has his own points of strength and weakness peculiar to his personality. No two individuals even if they happen to be twins, are exactly like each other. "Factually men are not equal; and the more specific the investigation, the more apparent it is that men are unequal; unequal in strength, in spirit, in grace, in thought" (See page 439, *Encyclopedia Americana,* Vol. 10, 1959).

2. *Connected with Liberty.* Equality is closely connected with liberty, for without liberty people cannot have equality, and liberty will be poor in its content without the basis of equality. Equality came later than liberty. In our study, we take liberty and equality side by side. The formulation of the doctrine of equality took place in the eighteenth century. In a social order with want of harmony and imbalance, the principle of equality like the principle of liberty assumed great importance since the 19th century. The struggle for liberty could not be fully successful without eliminating the special rights and privileges of the few, that is, without removing inequality. Political social, economic and other types of inequality brought about great injustice to millions all over the world. When there is inequality, a few people

at the top enjoy special privileges and preferential treatment, and the masses of people suffer from handicaps. It becomes easy, for the former to develop their personality, while obstacles make it difficult for the latter to realize their potentialities fully.

3. *Essential for Social Justice.* Like liberty, equality is essential for social justice. All over the world, there have been movements aiming at social justice, and these have paid particular attention to the achievement of equality. In the Constitution of India (1950) the concepts of social justice and social welfare are upheld. In this connection, it should be stated that the principle of equality is enshrined in the Preamble, and that the Right to Equality is one of the justiciable Fundamental Rights.

4. *Positive and Negative Aspects of Levelling Process.* We observed while dealing with the meaning of equality that it is a levelling process; but this has its positive and negative aspects. Positively speaking, equality stands for the provision of adequate opportunities, and negatively it means absence of any type of unjust and meaningless discrimination or inequality based on class, status, caste, race, religion and other factors.

5. *Inspired Social Movements.* The principle of equality roused people everywhere and created an urge to launch social movements to pull down the old structure of society based on injustice and inequality. "Throughout the 19th century the concept of equality stood in the background of a great variety of social movements and proliferated into an increasing number of fields. A detailed history of its development would touch upon most aspects of modern life." (See page 576, *Encyclopaedia of Social Sciences,* Vol. 5, 1954.) The existence of glaring inequality between the privileged and the unprivileged led to the French Revolution (1789). The French Revolutionaries in their National Assembly adopted *The Declaration of the Rights of Man* (1789) according to which "men are born and always continue, free and equal

in respect of their rights." In other countries, too, people agitated for equality and justice. It is abused to refer to any movement against inequalities given by nature, as there have been no such movements. All movements were launched to fight against, unfair, unjust, meaningless and cruel inequalities artificially made by man. Sartori says on page 327 in *Democratic Theory* (1965): "Massimo Salvadori regards equality as a protest ideal, as men have protested and rebelled against man-made and undeserved equality."

6. *Equality not Absolute.* Equality cannot be absolute. Absolute equality is neither possible nor desirable. In no movement in the history of the world did men lay claim to absolute equality, as it would be ridiculous to do so. Equality does not mean uniformity and difference does not mean inequality. On page 157 in *Principles of Social and Political Theory,* Ernest Barker points out how efforts to introduce uniformity will be harmful to society. "Equality, in all its forms, must always be subject and instrumental to the free development of capacity; but if it be pressed to the length of uniformity and if uniformity be made to thwart the free development of capacity, the subject becomes the master, and the world is turned topsy-turvy." Though there are differences between man and man, there is something which is basically common between them "in the sense of possessing beneath the observed differences some more and universal attribute of manhood by virtue of which each should by right—and can with safety—be treated as the equal of every other in reference to certain functions and privileges in society." Burns and Peltason, *Government by the People,* 1953). Those who fought for equality did not demand absolute equal opportunities, but only adequate opportunities and the abolition of special privileges, which enabled a few to exploit the many. F.W. Coker says on page 308 in *Recent Political Thought* (1957): "By equality of rights the democrat does not mean as his critics sometimes imply that all men are equal in talents, virtues and capabilities. He does not mean that the claim of one individual to his life, liberty and

happiness must be treated equally with those of any other individual."

7. *A Condition of Good Life.* Equality side by side with liberty is a condition of good life. An individual finds that he enjoys good opportunities of developing his personality and having the fruits of a higher life, when the gap between those who are at the top and those who are at the bottom is not extremely wide. He feels satisfied that he does not suffer from any kind of legal and constitutional discrimination.

KINDS OF EQUALITY

Widening Scope of Equality. There was a time when the concept of equality was interpreted in a narrow way. But with the widening horizon of democracy, the concept came to have new dimensions. In democratic countries, the concept is understood very broadly, and there equality has gained entrance into many fields.

Difficulty of Analysing Equality. Owing to the difficulties of an exact connotation of equality, it is not possible to have one method of classifying various types of equality. All thinkers do not classify kinds of equality in the same manner.

Classification by Bryce. According to Bryce, there are four types of equality: (1) Civil, (2) Political, (3) Social, and (4) Natural.

Laski's *Classification.* Laski speaks of two types of equality: (1) Political, and (2) Economic.

Barker's Classification. Barker mentions two kinds of equality: (1) Legal, and (2) Social.

The study of each type of equality may be briefly made.

1. Civil Equality

Civil Equality Synonymous with Equal Civil Rights to All. Civil equality is synonymous with equal civil rights to all citizens. There is civil equality in a state when all citizens are subject to the same law (or there is equality before the law) and when law neither confers special privileges on some at the expense of others nor makes any individual suffer owing to his social status, religious beliefs, political views, race or caste. There can be no civil equality, when law makes invidious distinctions between one individual and another on any arbitrary basis and gives civil rights to some, while denying them, to others.

Civil Equality Emerged with Democracy. Civil equality emerged in modern times with democracy. Democracy will be barren if it does not give liberty and equality to the people.

Isonomia. The ancient Greeks, spoke of *isonomia* or equality before the law as we take it now. By this principle, all citizens are afforded equal protection of law, as all individuals (according to ethical principles) are equal to each other in intrinsic worth and dignity.

2. Political Equality

Political Equality Synonymous with Equal Political Rights. Political equality synonymous with equal political rights to all and equal access to seat of political power. All citizens enjoy the same political rights like the right to vote, the right to stand for election, the right to hold public office and the right to criticise government. Every citizen is given only one vote, as equality means that one man's vote is equivalent to that of another. Where all citizens enjoy full political rights, democracy prevails. It was only in present century that in various countries political equality was granted. In England, for example, till 1918 women did not have the right to vote. Throughout the 19th century only a minority had franchise. Uneducated people, those who paid no taxes and those who had no property were denied the right to vote. Universal franchise, ever in advanced Western countries, was introduced in the 20th century.

Political Equality in India. Under the Constitution of India (1950), there is political equality. All adult citizens have the right to vote and other political rights. During the British regime, Indians who were subjects and not citizens had no political equality, and franchise was restricted to a small minority of the population only.

3. Social Equality

Equality of Status and Absence of Social Discrimination in the Eyes of Law. Social equality stands for equality of status and absence of class or social barriers in the eyes of law. Social equality prevails when no individual is made to suffer on account of his race, colour, class, caste and creed.

Social Equality in India. Social equality is part of the Fundamental Right to Equality under the Constitutions of India (1950). No individual is made to suffer on account of his race, colour, class, caste, creed, sex and place of birth. Untouchability is an offence in the eyes of the Constitution and the law. But with all this even now untouchability prevails, as the masses of people are far behind the true spirit of the Constitution, and it will not be practically possible to punish all those who practise untouchability. Social equality is found only on paper, but not in actual society. The majority of people in India are Hindus. Hindu society is fragmented by a large number of castes and sub-castes. People do not mix freely and there are many restrictions on social intercourse, commensalisms and marriage alliances. Most of the people are conscious of their religious and caste status. Added to this is the social distinction based on wealth. The Constitution and law have put all on the same level, but in actual practice social equality is conspicuous by its absence. Normally, no Brahman will be friendly with a member of the lowest caste, and a rich man's son a rule will not normally fraternise with the son of a poor man. Unless education and literacy spread and people are freed from unemployment, poverty and want, glaring social inequality will continue. Social and economic uplift and other steps on a large scale will gradually eradicate wide social disparities; but this is not an easy task.

4. Natural Equality

Nature's Gifts Unequally Distributed: The concept of natural law of the 17th century says that all men have equal and inalienable rights. Though all men are born free and equal, a little thought will show that this is not true. Nature has not given the same gifts to all, and, in fact, she has made men unequal. The concept, however, has to be understood in the proper spirit.

Man-Made Inequality Resented. In modern times, the emphasis is on the egalitarian principle. Inequality given by nature has to be accepted as something inevitable, but man-made or artificial inequality is resented. In modern democratic states, law treats all in the same way irrespective of the gifts of nature with which some men are endowed or of the disabilities with which nature has handicapped men.

5. Economic Equality

Without Economic Equality Other Types of Equality Not Worth Much. In modern times, true democrats speak of the tremendous significance of economic equality. Political, social and civil equalities have little meaning, if the vast masses of people in a country are under great economic handicaps. Economic inequality is the result of differences in ownership of property and income. Great economic inequality is found between one who has much property and income, and one who has no property and very little income. Economic inequality does not mean that in a state all the property should be equally divided and all should have the same income. Such a type of equal distribution is neither possible nor desirable owing to vast difference between one individual and another in intelligence and ability. Economic equality stands for the availability of certain minimum property and income, and adequate opportunities to earn wealth. The principle of equality, however, is opposed to misdistribution of wealth and its concentration only in a few hands. Wealth, which is a source of great power and prestige, should be ustly and fairly distributed among the people. If it is concentrated in the hands of a few, who have the monopoly of power and high social rank, people will realize that other forms of equality are not worth much. Wealth provides all kinds of opportunities only to those who have it, and the poor are forced to suffer from serious disadvantages and frustration. A very poor or starving man, having no economic opportunities, has absolutely no use of the concept of equality. Therefore the concept of economic equality should be given the importance due to it in a state. H.J. Laski emphasizes on page 162 in *A Grammar of Politics* the tremendous importance of economic equality: "Political equality therefore is never real unless it is accompanied by virtual economic equality; political power, otherwise, is bound to be the handmaid of economic power."

Not Absolute Economic Equality, but Reasonable Economic Opportunities. Economic equality does not stand for the equal distribution of wealth; it only means equality to the margin of sufficiency. As regards the primary needs of life at least, there should be equality; but beyond a certain point, economic inequality may by allowed. Though literally economic equality is synonymous with equality in economic power, absolute economic equality is nowhere possible in the world, and it is absurd to claim such a type of equality. Economic equality prevails when all people have reasonable economic opportunities to develop themselves. Adequate scope for employment reasonable wages, adequate leisure and other economic rights create economic equality.

Increase of Economic Inequality after the Industrial Revolution. After the Industrial Revolution (1750-1850) wealth got concentrated in the hands of a few and the vast masses of people were exploited by the relentless industrial barons. All this resulted in the great increase of economic inequality. To combat the glaring economic inequality Marx and Engel's gave the principles of revolutionary socialism or communism. In Soviet Russia and the People's Republic of China (or Communist China) the communist revolutionaries tried to establish the Dictatorship of the Proletariat; but they could not succeed in introducing complete economic equality even after bringing all important means of production under state control and abolishing the institution of private property (except very limited property). Complete equality is something that can never be realised.

Political Equality Without Economic Equality Illusory. In the 19th century, or even earlier, many advocates of democracy and political equality propagated the idea that political equality (including universal franchise and one-man one-vote) would be the harbinger of a millennium. But this was found to be illusory, as the prospects of a golden age began to recede with the disastrous effects of the Industrial Revolution coming to the forefront. It was then fully realised that economic equality was as important as political equality. The right to vote and other political rights which bring political equality are a poor consolation to a man suffering from permanent poverty, want and degradation. To him life is a relentless struggle to keep the wolf away from the door. Most of his time is absorbed by the battle for dry bread without butter. He cannot have the leisure to take part in political activities, and the right to vote does not mean much to him. Unless he is given adequate economic opportunities to usher economic equality, political equality is not of much value to him.

Relationship between Liberty and Equality

Controversial Matter. The relationship between liberty and equality is a controversial matter, and diametrically opposing views have been expressed by political scientists.

View that Liberty and Equality Cannot Co-Exist. De Tocqueville and Lord Acton are of the opinion that liberty and equality cannot co-exist harmoniously, as they are antagonistic to each other. H.J. Laski, who criticizes their view, says on page 151 in *A Grammar of Politics* (1957): "To minds so ardent for liberty as Tocqueville and Lord Action, liberty and equality are anti-thetic things. It is a drastic conclusion. But it turns, in the case of both men, upon a misunderstanding of what equality implies." It is argued that the desire to have equality destroys the possibility of having full liberty. When the state passes laws to bring about equality, the liberty of some is restricted. This is because the liberty to produce more and more wealth for enjoying it as one likes is reduced by laws aiming at the introduction of equality. The state may pass laws severely restricting the ownership and use of private property, and this, it is said, acts as a curb on the liberty of private property-owners.

Mutual Dependence of Liberty and Equality. The view of Tocqueville and Acton is incorrect and cannot be accepted. Their interpretation of the meaning of liberty is wrong. Liberty can never mean the freedom to do anything one likes causing inconvenience or hardship to others or to earn money through industry and trade without any limitations whatsoever. The meaning of liberty has to be understood in a social context, and then it will be realised that true liberty implies reasonable restraints and responsibility for the good of all. The liberty enjoyed by an individual should never go against the larger interests of society. Unrestrained liberty or licence would enable cruel and selfish people to accumulate wealth unfairly for the exploitation of others under the cloak of *laissez faire* (free trade). This would ultimately lead to the destruction of the liberty of a vast majority in society. Therefore, the principle of equality should stand side by side with the principle of liberty. These two principles cannot be antagonistic, but mutually dependent. Elton Trueblood says on page 75 in *Declaration of Freedom* (Lectures delivered in 1954): "The paradox is that equality and freedom, which begin by being ideas in conflict and tension, turn out, upon anaysis, to be necessary to each other. The truth is that it is impossible to make a reasonable statement of the meaning of equality except in terms of freedom. Men are equal only because all men are intrinsically free, as nothing else in all creation is free." However, it may be emphasised that liberty should precede equality because equality will not be worthwhile without liberty. Men first demand freedom, and then equality. Slaves may be equal, but their lives are meaningless, as they have no freedom. Therefore in a way liberty is more important than equality.

Equality Provides Basis for Liberty. At the same time, the tremendous importance of equality is not to be minimised. It is the concept of equality that lay down the foundation of the concept of liberty. In a state, in which there is no equality, there can be no scope for liberty. It has to be emphasised that: (1) if there is no political equality, liberty will be barren, and large sections of population will have no share in government; (2) if there is no civil equality, those who suffer from civil disabilities will have no liberty; (3) if there is no social equality, liberty will be enjoyed only by a privileged few at the cost of many; and (4) if there is no economic equality wealth will get concentrated in the hands of a few, who alone will take advantage of the fruits of liberty, and the vast masses of people will suffer from poverty and degradation.

Liberty and Equality to be Reconciled. Both liberty and equality are conspicuously contributory to the same extent to the progress of mankind in all fields. When they are together making a happy pair, they enable the individual to gives his best to society.

Liberty and equality "are to be reconciled by remembering that both (liberty and equality) are subordinate means to the end of releasing the potentialities of individual personality on the widest possible scale. The development of a rich variety of personalities requires a large measure of liberty and forbids all attempts to impose a dead level of social and economic equality." (See Corry and Abraham, *Elements of Democratic Government*—1963,). Massimo Salvadori establishes on page 36 an intimate connection between liberty and equality in *Liberal Democracy* (1957). He says: "There is an intimate connection between the two because all individual liberties are related to the basic equality of all men, and because historically the aspiration for liberty became in practice the destruction of privilege or inequality."

Liberty and Equality Complementary. Though some value liberty more than equality, it is better to say that they complement each other. In a democratic state, the individual needs both; equality without liberty has little value, and without equality liberty cannot have a proper basis. Herbert A. Deane says on page 46 in *The Political Ideas of Harold J. Laski* (1955): "Liberty thus implies equality; liberty and equality are not in conflict nor even separate, but are different facts of the same ideal.....Indeed since they are identical, there can be no problem of how or to what extent they are or can be related; this is surely the nearest, if not, the most satisfactory, solution ever devised for a perennial problem in political philosophy."

Obstacles to Equality

Law Upholds but Practice Violates Equality. In modern times, the concept of equality came to be widely accepted all over the world, and different governments actually gave expression to it through comprehensive legislation or made constitutional provision to protect the principle of equality. Ernest Barker says on page 140 in *Principles of Social and Political Theory* (1935) that legally speaking, equality "means that the state treats all legal persons as equal in its presence, or as we say *in the eye of the law*. It will not assign higher and lower grades of legal personality." Legally, the road has been paved to equality; but law alone is not enough to realise the principle of equality in the realm of practical affairs. A wide gap prevails between law and actual practice.

Need of Tolerance and Broadmindedness. True realisation of quality needs the tolerance and broadminded spirit of the people, and there should be perfect reconciliation between what the law says and what the people actually do. Unfortunately people do not show the better part of their mind and are not prepared to be tolerant, considerate and fair to their fellow citizens. Therefore, we find the practice of inequality all over the world. In South Africa and Rhodesia coloured people are flagrantly denied quality by the whites. In the USA, in actual practice Negroes suffer from inequality. In Pakistan discrimination is practiced against Hindus. In India, the Right to Equality as a justiciable Fundamental Right is enshrined in the Constitution (1950). The right is quite comprehensive in its range; but there is a wide gulf between the written word in the Constitution and the deed in actual practice. We find in India today that is, 37 years since independence and 34 years since the commencement of the Constitution, glaring social and economic inequality. Untouchability is practised on a large scale. The Constitution and the laws have gone far ahead of the spirit of the people. It may take perhaps several decades to completely wipe out the stain of untouchability.

Full Equality a Paper Ideal. Outside the legal sphere, inequality exists among individuals in social status, in economic resources and in other respects. Ernest Barker says on page 141 in *Principles of Social and Political Theory* (1935): "How far the state can tolerate some of this inequality in the social or extra-legal sphere, and more especially how far it can tolerate inequality of economic resources, without offending against its own principle of the equality of legal persons within itself and its own sphere, is a grave question of our times which leads to a clash of conflicting arguments." Undoubtedly equality is a great democratic principle; but it has remained an ideal only on paper. The world moves but very slowly towards this ideal. It will take a long time for all countries, particularly the backward or developing countries to narrow down substantially the gap between the idealand the real. Rodee, Anderson and Christol say on page 88 in *Introduction to Political Science* (1957): "Current democratic thought views equality as less than an ideal, as a goal to be striven towards (yet never fully achieved) rather than as something actually possessed. Democratic policy tends increasingly to seek the removal of barriers to the attainment of equality but it does not today cling to the delusion that literal equality is either possible or desirable.

Obstacles to Equality

We may briefly refer here to political, social and economic obstacles to equality.

1. *Political Obstacle*. Monopoly of political power in the hands of a few persons even in democratic countries is the political obstacle to equality. When political power is practically vested in a few hands through the inevitable party system, there cannot be equality. Those who have political power enjoy privileges, which are against the principle of equality.

2. *Social Obstacle*. Long-standing evil social customs, tradition and usages, which cannot be eradicated easily by law, constitute the social obstacle.

3. *Economic Obstacle*._People enjoying political power also enjoy economic advantages, which most of the people do not secure. These people create the great obstacle to economic equality.

Results of Obstacles

The result of the three main obstacles mentioned above are seen all over the world. When a person goes to work or sets out of his house to the market place or travels by bus or train or sits in a park or dines in a hotel or enjoys a movie, he finds vast difference between himself and others. Some persons find themselves superior to others, whereas many find themselves far inferior to others. Many find that political, social and economic opportunities, which a few have, are far beyond their reach. This is the actual condition all over the world. As long as there is a wide gap in any field of opportunities, between one person and another, it cannot be said that equality prevails.

A slum-dweller's son suffers from disadvantages whereas a factory owner's son has many golden opportunities. The distance between the two is indeed very vast and unbridgeable. In the middle class, many youngsters feel that they have intelligence but limited opportunities. A landowner's son in a village has wealth, but perhaps no intelligence; all the same his life is comfortable. On the contrary the son of a landless labourer has intelligence but of opportunities of going to school. Wherever we go we find glaring inequalities with all the legal and constitutional rights conferring equality. There is much dissatisfaction and heart-burning among those who feel that they are the victims of actual inequality prevailing in society. There is no equality in a society in which a few families are of permanent rules, whereas the rest are in the ruled category. Some have fabulous incomes, while the vast masses of people with very limited means have to battle for survival. Some have jobs for the mere asking; but many able-bodied persons suffer from chronic unemployment or under-employment. To some life is a bed of roses, but to many it is a long spell of hopeless drudgery.

Books for Further Study

1. Barker, Enrest, *Principles of Social and Political Theory*—1953.
2. Burns and Peltason, *Government by the People*—1953.
3. Coker, F.W., *Recent Political Thought*—1957, The World Press Calcutta.
4. Corry, J.A., *Democratic Government and Politics*—1958.
5. Corry and Abraham, *Elements of Democratic Government*—1963.
6. Deane, H.A., *The Political Ideas of Harold Laski*—1955.
7. Dicey, A.V., *Introduction to the Law of the Constitution,* 1962.
8. Gettell, R.G., *Introduction to Political Science*—1956.
9. Joad, C.E.M., *Introduction to Modern Political Theory*—1951.

10. Laski, H.J., *A Grammar of Politics*—1957.

11. Rodee, Anderson and Christol, *An Introduction to Political Science*—1957.

12. Salvadori, Massimo, *Liberal Democracy* —1965.

13. Sartori, Giovanni, *Democratic Theory*—1962, Oxford and IBH Publishing House, Calcutta.

14. Tawny, R.H., *Equality.*

15. Trueblood, Elton, *Declaration of Freedom*—1954.

7

Individual and The State

It is easy, and perhaps even natural, to oppose the functions and powers of government to the rights and liberties of persons, as if they were mutually exclusive and each of them began at the point where the other ended. They may, indeed, be distinguished in thought, but they are inseparable in operation. Functions of government cannot be separated from rights of persons, except in the sense in which the reverse of a coin can be distinguished from the obverse.

On the one hand, the functions of government are a conditions of the rights of persons, because they are necessary to the enjoyment of those rights and because they exist in order to secure them. On the other hand, the rights of persons are a condition of the functions of government, because they are the source and the cause of the existence and action of government.

To claim, for example, a right to the enjoyment of personal security is also to claim a right to protection against any invasion of that security; to claim that right to protection is also to claim the exercise of a function of giving protection; and to claim the exercise of that function is also to claim an organ, possessing power or authority, by means of which it is exercised.

We may accordingly say that government is a service on behalf of rights, and not a power outside their range: 'servitium propter jura, non potestas praeter jura'. We may add that the service rendered by government to rights is both a consequence and a part of the general rights of persons. I have a right to the service, and the service is thus a part of my rights, because, and as a consequence, of the other and general rights belonging to me as a person.

The same view of the relation between functions of government and rights of persons may equally be attained if we follow another line of reflection. The State is, in its essence, a legal association. The mode of its action is law. The function of its organs of government is the declaration and enforcement of law.

What, then, is the nature of the relation of law to rights? Does it abridge them, or does it contain them? The answer, as we have already seen, is that law contains rights, and indeed *is* rights. Law and rights are simply two aspects of something which is essentially one: law is its 'objective' aspect or the thing as regarded from outside, and rights are its 'subjective' aspects, or the thing as regarded from inside, that is to say from the point of view of the 'subject' or persons concerned.

If we look at a sum or system of rights objectively, and regard it accordingly as an object projected outside ourselves or a fact confronting us, we think of it primarily as law; but we also think of it as apportioning both the rights which we ourselves own as persons and the consequent duties which we owe to others, as similar persons, in order that they may own similar rights.

Conversely, if we look at the same sum or system subjectively, and regard it accordingly as existing in us and ourselves as participating in it, we shall think of it primarily as rights; but we shall also think of these rights, with their consequent and correlative duties, as parts and portions of a sum or system which in the gross is law.

If law is thus rights, and rights are thus law, a conclusion necessarily follows in regard to the functions of government. The function of the organs of government, in declaring and enforcing law, is also and equally a function of recognizing and guaranteeing the rights of persons. To declare and enforce law is also, and indeed is the same as, to recognize and guarantee rights.

We are thus led once more to the conclusion that the function of government is the service of rights.

There is a corollary to this conclusion. If we think in terms of ownership, we shall say (as indeed we have already done) that the members of a political community are the owners of rights. We may also say, in addition, that along with their rights, and as a consequence and a part of those rights, they own the services required by their rights, and are therefore the owners of the functions of government which serve and secure the actual enjoyment of the rights which they own. The question may then be asked, 'What do the governors own, in their capacity of governors?' Shall we say that they own authority—the authority of declaring, interpreting, and enforcing the law? It is impossible to use such language. The members of the governing organs (legislative, judicial, and executive) certainly exercise authority; but they do not own what they exercise. They exercise authority as the appointees, direct or indirect, of the community which owns it, and which owns it as a consequence and part of its general ownership of rights. Authority in the sense of a function of government (or rather the sum of its functions) is not something *owned* by governing persons, but something which they *owe,* in virtue of their appointment, as a mode of service of rights. We may therefore conclude that governing persons own nothing as such (though as members of the political community they own rights equally and in common with other members): they owe rather than own. They owe the exercise of the authority which is necessary for the secure enjoyment of the rights of persons: they owe the service, remunerated by pay or prestige or both, of declaring, interpreting, and enforcing the law which is the objective side of rights of persons: we may even say, if we look only at immediate sovereignty, that they owe the service of sovereignty, in the sense of declaring, in the last resort, what the law is and is henceforth to be. All authority, and all the functions of government, including the function of immediate sovereignty, are services *owed* to rights.

The Classification of Rights

If rights are thus prior to functions of government, we shall do well to enumerate and classify rights before we examine the functions of government and the methods of their operation. It has already been noticed that there are three principles, or procedural rules, which regulate the distribution of rights among the members of an organised community: the principle of Liberty, the principle of Equality, and the principle of Fraternity or Co-operation. They preside together, and in common, over the whole of the distribution of rights; but we may none the less regard each of the three as having a particular connexion with a particular set or cluster of rights, and as regulating particularly the distribution of rights in that set or cluster. We may accordingly seek to classify rights under the three heads of Liberty, Equality, and Co-operation. In doing so we shall not only be concerned with the full legal rights which are already recognised and guaranteed by law: we shall also extend our view to include the nascent rights which are being convassed in the process of social thought, and which, as they become a part of common conviction of the political community, and come to be formally endorsed by the organs of that community, are ultimately turned into legal rights in the full sense of the term. The reason for this extension of view is that it is necessary to an understanding of that growth of the functions of government which is a feature of our times. It is the growing-pains of rights which cause the growing labours of government.

We may begin our classification under the head of Fraternity or Co-operation, reserving to the end the rights which come under the head of Liberty. It has already been noticed that the French jurist Duguit, using the term 'solidarity' or 'mutuality' in lieu of the older term, enumerates three particular rights with which the principle of fraternity is particularly connected—the right of education, the right of public assistance, and the right of employment—and that on this basis he would impose corresponding duties on 'governing persons' to provide these rights. The view of Duguit is suggestive, but it is also extreme. It is too narrowly economic—and too closely connected, at that, with a particular brand of economics—to offer any safe guidance. We shall do better to interpret fraternity in the sense of a general co-operation, which is not merely economic, but as wide as the general life of society; and on this basis we may proceed to argue, as indeed has already been argued, that there are two main rights which fall under this head, and two corresponding functions of government. The essence of both of the rights is that men need, and ought to enjoy, a common or public equipment of services and resources, which goes beyond the equipment that individual effort and the effort of voluntary groups are able to provide, and which can be provided only by the common co-operation of all. We may regard this equipment as twofold, or as being both material and mental; and this is why we may hold that it issues in two different rights. The one is the right of persons to enjoy collectively a common or public equipment of *material* necessities unattainable except by the co-operation of all, and ranging from means of public transport and methods of public sanitation to schemes of national insurance and plans for the national development of national economic resources. The other right is a similar right of persons of enjoy collectively a common or public equipment of what may be called *mental* necessities, ranging from schools and places of learning to galleries, museums, libraries, and the like, and thus including not only the facilities needed for public education but also those that are needed for the general national enjoyment of the accumulated treasures of culture.

Under the head of Equality the jurists and thinkers of France, basing themselves on the Declarations of 1789 and afterwards, have enumerated four rights—the right to be treated equally with others, and on the same footing as others, in the eye of the law and in all legislative acts; the right to be treated equally with others in matters or justice and in courts of law; the right to be treated equally with others in matters of taxation, so that each man pays the same proportion of his means as is paid by others; and, finally, the right to be treated as equally admissible with others to public honours and offices of employment. These four rights of the citizen in respect of the exercise of governing authority: they are claims, acknowledged and recognised by law or general custom, that governing authority should deal equally with all, alike in its legislation and its jurisdiction, its imposition of taxes and its distribution of honours and offices. But the progress of social thought has given a wider sweep to the notion of equality and to the nature of the rights which it involves. We have learned to think not only of what may be called political equality, in relation to the action of governing authority, but also of economic and culture equality, in relation to the general life of the whole of the organised community; and we have accordingly come to believe that there are further rights which ought to be added to the rights of political equality. These further rights are still, as it were, in process of construction: they are emerging from social thought, and beginning to pass into the common conviction of the political community; but the proper nature of their form, and the exact extent of their dimension, have still to be determined by the continuing process of social thought and by the method of tentative experiment. They are rights which men are beginning to claim, not in relation to governing authority and the distribution of its incidence, but in relation to one another: they are rights to a greater measure of general equality between man and man, partly in economic status and the distribution of economic possessions, and partly in educational opportunity and enjoyment of the general treasures of culture. These new and nascent rights of equality are obviously linked with the similar rights which have already been suggested under the head of co-operation. The greater the provision of material and mental necessities in the form of a common or public equipment in which all alike can share, the greater will be the achievement of equality on both the material and the mental plane. But in addition to common and equal sharing in the stock of common or public equipment there is also needed a greater measure of equality in the enjoyment of individual status, in the possession of individual equipment (or 'private property'), and in the opportunity of individual access to the benefits of education and general cultural development.

The rights which come under the head of Liberty are all the greater, and the more numerous, because Liberty is a multiple principle. Within the State, and apart from the area of Society (which has also a social liberty of its own), there are, it has been suggested, three divisions or regions of liberty. These three divisions are the political, the civil, and the economic. We may accordingly classify the rights which come under the head of Liberty according to these three divisions.

The rights of political liberty generally include the right of the citizen to participate in the election of the legislature, and thereby, indirectly, to share in the choice of the government. When the jury system exist, along with a system of unpaid magistrates drawn in large numbers from the general public, the rights of political liberty also include the rights of the citizen to participate in the administration of justice and to form, in a sense, a part of the judicature. The right to form political parties, and the right of such parties when formed, to play a part in the election of the legislature and thereby in the choice of the government, is a sort of border-land right, essentially connected with political liberty but formally a part of civil liberty and a product of the civil rights of freedom of the expression of opinion and freedom of association and meeting.

The rights of civil liberty have been divided by French thinkers into two different groups, distinguished from one another by the historical fact that the one group is earlier than the other. The first and earlier of these groups, already evident in the Declaration of 1789, includes the three rights of personal freedom, personal security, and personal or private property. The second group, gradually developed in the thought and expressed in the legislation of the century which followed the Revolution, includes some half-dozen rights; liberty in the choice and conditions of employment, and in the conduct of trade and industry; liberty of the press; liberty of assembly; liberty of association; liberty of teaching; and liberty of conscience and worship. This historical division of the rights of civil liberty into two different groups may square with the facts of French history, but it does not suit the history of England, where no such distinction can be traced, and it cannot be generally applied. Abandoning, therefore, any chronological scheme of division, we may suggest a logical classification of the rights of civil liberty into three different groups, based on the nature and character of the activity concerned. The first group will consist of the rights which come under the head of freedom of physical activity; it will include rights such as personal security (whether from arbitrary arrest and detention, or from torture and inhuman punishment, or from arbitrary interference with the privacy of home and domicile), and such, again, as freedom of movement and residence inside a country, along with the right to seek and enjoy an asylum in other countries. The second group will consist of rights which come under the head of freedom of the activity of the mind: this will include rights such as the right to freedom of conscience and religion, the right to freedom of opinion and its expression, and the right to freedom of meeting and association. The third group will consist of rights which come under the head of freedom of practical activity, or, as we may also say, freedom for the exercise of will and choice in the general field of contractual action; this group will include the right to the acquisition and disposal of property, the right to marry and found a family on the basis of full and free consent, and similar rights of that order. It may also be made to include a number or rights connected with the choice and conditions of employment and the conduct of trade and industry; but rights of this order, as has already been noted in an earlier part of the argument, are best treated as belonging to a separate class, and are most properly classified under the head of the rights of economic liberty.

The rights of economic liberty were already expressed in some detail in the part of the German Constitution of 1919 which dealt with 'Economic Life', and they have recently found their place in the Universal Declaration of Human Rights. If we seek to formulate them broadly, in terms of contemporary life and the growing demands of social thought, we may suggest that they fall into three main groups. We may regard them as extensions and expansions, into the economic sphere, of the old three rights of civil liberty already declared by Blackstone in England and by the revolutionary thinkers of France in the latter half of the eighteenth century—the right of personal freedom, the right of personal security, and the right of personal property. They are extensions and expansions entailed by the flood of economic development (often termed the industrial revolution', though the term is hardly adequate) which began to flow about 1750, and is still flowing swift and deep. The group of rights which is an extension of the old civil right of personal security includes the rights of workers under Factory Acts (the first of the rights of economic liberty to be formally acknowledged), their rights under Workmen's Compensation Acts, and their rights, under various acts, to insurance against the risks of sickness and unemployment and age. The group of rights which may be regarded as an extension of the old civil right of personal freedom includes already the right of workers freely to form trade unions and to bargain freely through such unions about the conditions and remuneration of their work: it may also come to include the further right, now beginning to be claimed, to the enjoyment of the status of free partners in the general control and conduct of industry. Finally, the group of rights which may be regarded as an extension of the old civil right of personal property may be held to include the right of workers to some share in the capital of the particular industry in which they are engaged. This means their right to acquire, by virtue of the rendering of permanent service, some permanent property in the undertaking for which they work, over the above their weekly remuneration: it means, again, the right to participate in a diffusion of ownership which makes personal property as general in its scope as personal freedom or personal security.

This attempt at a classification of rights may seem to be little more than an academic exercise. But it is, as has already been noted, something more than that. It is the necessary preliminary to any study of the functions of government, which are services owed to rights and can only be understood in the light of the rights they serve. On the other hand, classification is also the creation of compartments; and the creation of compartments, if it may be a help to clear thin king, can also be a danger to the breadth and sweep of thought which not only apprehends but can also comprehend. For one thing we have to remember that the movement of human life does not proceed in compartments. This same general problem recurs, if in different forms, under the different heads of our classification. The future of industry and the development of a fair system of economic rights is at one and the same time a matter of the rights which come under the head of liberty, of those which come under the head of equality, and of those which come under the head of fraternity or co-operation. We cannot think of the problem properly in the limits of one compartment; and we are driven back, in the issue, on that general and comprehensive idea of justice which seeks to reconcile the principle of liberty with that of equality, and both with the principle of co-operation, and which thus controls and co-ordinates the rights belonging to each. There is another thing also to be remembered, or rather there is another aspect of the same general truth. No right is absolute and inviolable, or entrenched by itself in its own inexpugnable iron compartment. The right of personal property is indeed a right; but it is a right which has to make terms, and to enter into combination, with a variety of other rights. Not only has my right to acquire property, as a condition of the development of the capacities of my personality, to be reconciled with the right of others to acquire it, as a condition of the development of the capacities of their personality: the right of each person to such acquisition has also to be reconciled with other rights in other spheres, such as the right of workers to enjoy the status of free partners in the general conduct and control of industry, a right which cannot be simply defeated or abrogated by the right of the owner of property to the free use and disposal of his acquisitions. Once more we are driven back on the general idea of justice by which one sort of right is 'mortised and adjoined' to another.

The Rights of Political Liberty and the Structure of Government

'Everyone has the right to take part in the government of his country.' The origin and basis of this right have already been suggested at a previous stage of the argument. We saw, at that stage, that discussion is the necessary and vital process of the life of an organised community, and that each and every member is entitled to contribute to this process. To be entitled to contribute to discussion is the same thing as to have 'the right to take part in the government'; for the process of political discussion is the essential activity of government in a politically organised community. The process of political discussion has evolved, in the course of time, a number of organs for its operation. These organs, distinct and yet connected, form a successive series, in which, as in a relay race, each of them hands to another the task of 'carrying on' from the point which it has reached itself. We may distinguish four of these organs, and proceed to trace their connexion.

The first of the organs of political discussion is party. Party, as we have already seen, is a social formation which also discharges a political function and has thus, as it were, one foot in Society and one in the State. Each party is a voluntary association; but each party also formulates a political programme for the consideration and choice of the political electorate, and each party submits to the vote of that electorate candidates for election to Parliament who offer themselves as symbols and exponents of its programme. At the first stage or lap in the process of discussion each party discusses in its own counsels the programme is which it process to formulate; and each, when the programme formulated, proceeds to discuss and debate it in public, before an attentive electorate, with the other party or parties.

The turn then comes for the second organ, the political electorate. That too is an organ of discussion, at any rate in periods of election (which is not to say that it is dead, or ceases to think and interrogate, in the intervals between such periods); it canvasses and considers the programmes, and examines and cross-examines the candidates, submitted to it for choice; and when it has made its choice, it hands over the further conduct of discussion to the representatives whom it has chosen, trusting them to carry it into far greater detail, and to carry it on with a far greater degree of continuity, than it can possibly do itself.

The third organ then succeeds in its turn to the same double task—the task of conducting discussion itself, and the task of preparing the way for further and later discussion. This organ is the representative body; the core and center of the whole system of representative democracy; the Parliament which, as its very name indicates, is peculiarly engaged in the activity of 'parley' and constant discussion. But the function of Parliament, like that of the electorate, is a twofold function. It is not only an organ of discussion itself, engaged in a process of constant debate intended to translate a general programme into legislative enactments: it also helps to create, and it continually serves to support, a government which it expects and trusts to carry discussion into even greater detail, and to conduct it even more continuously and intimately, than it is able to do itself.

We thus come to the fourth and last organ in the successive series; the responsible government or cabinet, which is the organ of government *par excellence* (though also, and at the same time, only *one* of a number of organs of government in the wider sense of the word), and which is therefore commonly called *'the* Government'. This government is 'responsible' in the sense that it must necessarily command the support of the representative body from which its members are drawn; but it may also be said to be responsible in another and even deeper sense. It is responsible for carrying the process of discussion to that crucial and final point at which it issues in decision. A responsible government, organised under its head, is at once the innermost core of discussion and the originating motor of action. Not that the decision at which it arrives, and the impulse which it accordingly gives, is necessarily final or absolutely conclusive. The decision, on any grave issue, will flow back, as it were, to the representative body for approval and confirmation; it may even flow back to the electorate, either for informal approval by what we call public opinion, or even for formal approval by an electoral vote in a general election at which a proposed decision is made the main or a dominant issue. The process of discussion may thus return on itself; and after flowing from the electorate to the representative body, and from that to the responsible government, it may in turn flow back from the government to the representatives, and then from them to the electors.

There is thus a general system of discussion which operates through a number of organs. The difficulty of this system is to reconcile two necessities: the necessity, on the one hand, that each organ should concentrate on its work with a free vigour and a fresh impetus, as if everything hung upon the conclusion at which it arrives; and the necessity, on the other, that each of the organs should also keep in touch and harmony with the rest, acknowledging that they too, as organs of the same general process, have the right and duty to do *their* work, in their place and at their time, and that their right and duty must always be respected. The peril of the system is that one or the other of the organs concerned should lay an exclusive emphasis on the first of these necessities, and arrogate to itself an exclusive and predominant importance. If that is done, the results will in any case by unhappy, because they will necessarily involve a disturbance of the whole system; but they will vary according to the nature of the organ on which an exclusive emphasis is laid as being the organ of discussion *par excellence* and therefore the dominant organ. If it is the organ of party which asserts its predominance, you may have the open tyranny of a single party (whether of the Right or the Left), or the secret tyranny of a cabal which unites the leaders of several parties in an interested coalition and controls behind the scenes both the representative body and the nominal government. If, on the other hand, it is the representative organ which is particularly conscious of its own importance, you may have a parliamentary autocracy, with the enthroned deputies installing and evicting governments as and when they think fit. The system of political discussion is a delicate as well as a difficult system. To remember, and to seek to observe, the two necessities which it imposes is to face the problem of doing simultaneously two different things which seem almost contradictory: on the one hand, leaving each organ free to act with an original vigour to the full stretch of its capacity; on the other hand, keeping each organ within the limits of its capacity (so that, in the Platonic phrase, it 'does its own business' and no more than its business), and thus keeping all the organs in harmony and co-operation. This is the general problem of representative democracy; and there is no way of avoiding the problem—except by substituting the dictatorship of one organ for a system of discussion divided among several. To do that is to abolish discussion, at any rate as a general process in which all, at some stage, have the right to participate. (There may be left some fragment or simulacrum of discussion within the organ which holds the dictatorship; not that a fragment or simulacrum is anything more than a travesty.) But if discussion be the vital process of the life of any organised community, to abolish discussion is suicide and the end of the common life.

Representative democracy, considered as a system for giving effect to the rights of political liberty, is often defined as a system of government by all, or of government by the people. It *is* that:

and yet is something more than that. The right of everyone to take part in the government of his country is not simple matter of all men saying, as a single aggregate, what is their will and what is the object of their volition. On the contrary it is a complex matter of all discussing, thorough a variety of organs which are necessary for the purpose of full and through discussion, what is their thought, what is the content of their common conviction, what is the idea which they consider right and ripe for realisation. Ideas have quality in them, as well as quality behind them; and while the quantity of wills assembled behind an idea matters, and matters greatly, the quality or value in an idea is also something that matters, and matters at least as much. That is a reason, a fundamental reason, for the time and the pains which we spend on the process of discussion, (It is not the only reason; for we also exercise and breathe our minds, and develop the capacities of our personality, in the course of the process). We want to get at the quality and value of the ideas presented to us, and we cannot do that without taking discussion through stage after stage, sifting and sifting at each new stage. The courts of law and the methods of justice offer an analogy: there, too, 'the rights of the matter', which are the object of search, are sifted and clarified by a process of inquiry which rises from instance to instance by a prograssive refinement. The short cut of an immediate decision is tempting; but the only sure way of arriving is the way of successive stages. The electorate is one stage; but it is only a stage, and a general election is neither the beginning nor the end of the matter. Government by all, in its true and full sense, takes time: it is not only a matter of the voting of all the electors: it is also, and even more, a matter of the deliberation of all the organs concerned and involved in the process of mature and considered discussion.

The Structure of Government in its Relation to the Rights of Civil and Economic Liberty

We have seen how the rights of political liberty affect the structure of government, and how they issue in government by all' in the sense which has just been defined. We have now to see how the structure of government, when it is true to the rights of political liberty, affects in its turn the rights of civil and economic liberty.

We have, in a word, to see what manner of fruits it produces: we have to inquire whether 'government by all' will not in its nature by 'government for all'.

It has already been argued that government by all has an intrinsic value, and is, of itself and in itself, something which is for the benefit of all and makes for the common good of all. Considered simply as a process, and apart from any results or product outside the process, it is a way of the development of the capacities of personality. But it has also an extrinsic value; it is also valuable for the results which it produces, and for the new rights—other than those of political liberty, and over and above them—which are added by its operation to the common fund of enjoyment. If we look at the matter historically, we are led at once to the conclusion that during the days of struggle men pressed for the political right of government by the people not as an end in itself, or not only as an end in itself, but because they wished to secure for themselves and their fellows, by the exercise of this right, the enjoyment of other rights hitherto denied, or at any rate confined to the few. The Chartists, for example, were vehement in urging the justice of their six political points; but the ultimate aims of their endeavour were economic aims. If that was true in the days of struggle, it is also true, as experience shows, that the actual achievement of political rights raises at once in the days of attainment two questions of economic rights: the question, first, of the economic rights which ought to follow on political rights by the logic of consistency, in order to secure more liberty for the worker in the course of his work and thus make the economic system correspond better with the political; and, secondly the question of the economic rights which will inevitably and in any case follow on the acquisition of political rights by the simple logic of fact; or, in other words, as a result of their fact that the mass of the people now have the vote and will tend to use it in order to secure economic rights which they regard as the necessary conditions of economic liberty.

It follows then, alike by the logic of consistency and by the logic of fact, that an extension of the rights of political liberty must involve a similar extension of the rights of economic liberty. When the structure of government is altered, by the extension of political rights, the altered structure of government will alter in turn the economic structure, and it will do so by means of the extension of economic rights. This extension of rights will take two forms. One of these forms is the extension to all of old rights, already recognised as belonging to the members of a section of the community, but not hitherto recognised as belonging to the members of the community as a whole, irrespective of section or class. The other form is a still further extension by the recognition of new rights, not hitherto recognised at all, and their general distribution to all the members of the community. In brief, we have both an extension of the number of those among whom rights are distributed and an extension of the number of the rights distributed.

For the present we may confine ourselves to the extension of the number of those among whom rights are distributed. That rights are for all, and not merely for the members of a single section, is a simple proposition which now seems self-evident; but the actual extension to all even of old and long-recognised rights has been a slow historical process. The width of vision which sees that 'a man is a man for all that', whatever the rank and the guinea's stamp, is a slow historical acquisition. There was a long defect of vision, honest and genuine in its own day, which made men as it were near-sighted, and prevented them from seeing beyond a small and limited circle. Privileged classes, accepting the idea of the general social necessity of different social functions arranged in an ordered hierarchy of ascending degrees or stations, proceeded from that idea to a firm conviction that the masses were confined by the nature of their functions—as ploughmen and artificers—to the one office of manual work, and were not intended, and indeed were not fit, either for the political right of the suffrage or for the civil and economic rights (full personal security, full personal freedom of movement, and the full ownership of personal property) which they themselves enjoyed. We may almost say that they naturally thought in terms of 'two nations', or even of two grades of humanity and two classes of human beings. Three movements of thought, two of them belonging to the eighteenth century, and the third emerging in the course of the nineteenth, have radically altered these terms.

The first is the movement of humanitarianism, mainly based (at any rate in England) on the foundations of the Christian Gospel, and inspired by a fervent conviction that the benefits of the Gospel belonged to all and must be extended to all—to the slave, the prisoner, the factory-worker, and whoever else needed the comfort of a recognition of his common humanity and his common human rights. Whether this Christian humanitarianism were Evangelical or Catholic, whether it proceeded from the Low Church or the High, it changed and widened men's view of the distribution of rights, and altered the narrow terms in which they had hitherto taught. The other two movements which have worked in the same direction, however, different they may be both from Christian humanitarianism and from one another, are the Benthamite utilitarianism which emerged at the end of the eighteenth century and the Marxian socialism which began to grow from the middle of the nineteenth. The Benthamites, going on the principle of the greatest happiness of the greatest number, and holding that all were capable of happiness and had therefore the right to enjoy it, attacked the limitation of this universal right by the sinister interests of a privileged few, and advocated a structure of government under which all alike had a voice and a vote and the majority could use their voice and their vote to counteract sinister interests and to enthrone general happiness. The Marxians, going on the assumption (not altogether unwarranted by the history of the past) that the existing structure of government was based on the domination of a small and interested social class, which made law to suit its own interest and thus limited rights to its own members, urged that the largest and the most numerous social class, the class of the workers, should acquire domination in its turn, and should then extend and generalize rights by instituting a workers' State in which all would be workers and all would enjoy the common rights belonging to workers. There is an obvious difference between the Benthamites and the Marxians. The Benthamits laid their primary emphasis on the rights of political liberty: they held that the extension of the suffrage was the key to a greater enjoyment of happiness by a greater number of individuals: they expected a peaceable extension of the rights of civil and economic liberty, following easily and naturally on a similar extension of the right of political liberty. The Marxians were primarily concerned with economic liberty: they held that its attainment demanded effort, and even violence: they respected less the rights of individuals than the rights and the status of a whole class. But great as is the difference between Benthamism and Marxianism, the effects of both have been so far similar, that both have tended towards the extension of rights to all, and both have helped to abolish the old assumption of a graded society marked by a graded enjoyment of rights.

The Extension of Rights in its Relation to the Extension of the Functions of Government

The argument has hitherto turned on the extension of existing rights to a greater number of persons. We may now turn to consider the extension of the number of rights, or in other words the creation and the general allocation of new and added rights, particularly in the sphere of economic liberty. The distinction between the two modes of extension is perhaps verbal rather than real. Actually the extension of rights to a greater number of persons is, *for them,* the creation of new and added rights. Actually, again, the creation of new and added rights is not so much a matter of the creation of something new as of the broader and more liberal interpretation of something old. The new and added rights in the sphere of economic liberty are really new and extended versions of old and recognised rights in the sphere of civil liberty—the right to personal security, the right to personal freedom, and the right to personal property.

We may begin with the extension of the right to personal security. That right had been recognised, however imperfectly, since the end of the sixteenth century, under the old system of poor relief: and a new recognition was added, from the beginning of the nineteenth century, under the system of factory legislation. Still another recognition has been added, in the course of the present century, under the system of joint or social insurance. There are thus three stages of recognition (first the poor law, than factory legislation, and then social insurance); but they are all stages of a continuous process, and though we may cherish a vivid sense of the value of the third stage, and associate it particular with a conception of the 'welfare' State, we have to remember that it is part of a process, and that the whole process has been inspired by the one fundamental idea of the right of personal security. It has become customary to apply the term 'social services' to the development of this third stage. But services are secondary and consequential things, entailed by the primary fact of rights, which are the cause and source of all services; and we shall do well to begin any study of the nature of these developments not from the services in which they end but from the rights in which they begin. From this point of view we may say that our century has been marked by a new and more social interpretation of the right of personal security. This new and more social interpretation has led us to regard the right of personal security as including (1) the right of the worker to be protected against the risks of sickness, unemployment, and age; (2) his right to be so protected by a method of joint or social insurance (producing a joint or social security, and thus broadening and strengthening personal security), under which he is linked with his employer in a partnership of contribution to the cost, and both are linked again in a similar partnership with the State; (3) his right to enjoy the necessary services of government, loosely called 'social services', which the method of social insurance demands. The general result is an extension of the rights of economic liberty under the head and rubric of the right to personal security. But it is also at the same time—necessarily, because an extension of rights is also an extension of services—an increase of the functions of government and an extension of governing authority.

The two results go together: they are indissolubly connected. It is here that we may possibly find a limit, or a principle of limit, to the extension of our rights to the enjoyment of personal security. There is always a cost involved; and it is wise to count the cost in advance. The cost is partly financial, or a simple matter of money: it is partly also spiritual, or a more serious matter of control. The financial cost is that involved in the payment of contributions by the workers, the employer, and the general taxpayer, to meat the expenses of a system of joint or social insurance. The spiritual cost is that involved in the extension of the area of compulsory uniformity and administrative control. The double cost may be well worth the while: what is certain is that it must always be paid. The extension of our rights to the enjoyment of personal security is thus subject to a double proviso: the proviso that the members of the community are ready and able to pay the cost of the benefits which they receive; and the proviso that they are willing to accept the extension of the functions of government, and the increase of administrative control, which are also the price of their receipt of benefits. In a word, new rights are new commodities which, like other commodities, have their price, and, like other commodities, must be bought. The commodity bought may be well worth the price; and the liberty gained by the greater enjoyment of personal security may be greater far than the liberty surrendered by the increased acceptance of administrative control. The fact remains that it is always wise to count the cost. Rights are not to be had for the asking, or as a matter of pure gift. There is always a sense in which they are bought; and they are only sure when they are fairly bought by an honest bargain.

We may now turn from considering the extension of the right to personal security, and proceed to consider the extension of the right to personal freedom and the right to personal property—two rights which in their nature are closely interconnected, and which come into question together as soon as we seek to examine the further and fuller extension of economic liberty. The extension of the right to personal security still leaves us with something which may be called *passive;* for though the new system of social security, attained by the method of social insurance, demands the contribution and co-operation of all, workers as well as others, it remains none the less, in its essential nature, a protective system of shelter in which the worker can find a refuge from the risks and changes of the economic process. The question then arises whether there is not also needed something which may be called *active:* some system of participation or partnership under which all workers can actively share in the conduct and management of the economic process; some extension of the right of personal freedom, and also of the right of personal property, which will give them a voice and a stake in the undertaking in which they serve. We have already seen that there are two general reasons for answering that question in the affirmative. The first is that you cannot well have, in the same community and at the same time, two separate worlds, one of political democracy and the other of economic autocracy. The second is that, if we assume the general principle that the ultimate purpose of all institutions is the greatest development of the capacities of personality in the greatest number of persons, we are bound to conclude that there must be room for such development in the working of the system of economic institutions which occupies so many hours of the daily life of so many persons, even though the immediate purpose of that system is simply the purpose of producing the maximum of material necessities at the minimum of cost. We may therefore admit, on these two grounds, that there is a presumption in favour of active economic rights; and we are then confronted by the question, 'What is the method, or methods, by which such rights may be secured and guaranteed to all the workers engaged in the general business of production?'

One method which has long been advocated, and partly put into practice, is the method of nationalisation. This means, in effect, that the capital resources of some particular branch of production are taken over by the State, and that the business of production, in that branch, is thenceforth handled, directly or indirectly, by the State which owns the resources. Such a method eliminates, in any range in which it is applied, the right of personal property in capital resources; and it eliminates, along with that right, such elements of value (initiative, variety, and personal responsibility) as are involved in its exercise. That is the price to be paid. On the other hand there may be argued to be corresponding gains which are even greater than the price. In the first place the nationalisation of capital resources makes each worker, in his capacity of a member of the nation, an owner of capital resources, vested as such with a right of property which he did not hitherto enjoy. In the second place it makes each worker, again in his capacity of a member of the nation, an active agent in the conduct of the business of production: indeed, it may even do more, and if there is devolution of the conduct of the business of production on the workers and technicians of each particular nationalised branch, it may make each worker an active agent in his capacity of a member of that particular branch. But it may also be argued that these gains are not so great as they seem to be, and are illusory rather than real. In the matter of ownership, or, more exactly, in the matter of a new and larger enjoyment of the right of property, we have to notice that the ownership is collective, and the right of property enjoyed is not a personal right vested in an individual person. The extension of collective ownership is *not* an extension of the right of personal property: it makes each man not an owner, but (in a State of fifty million members) a fifty-millionth part of an owner. Again in the matter of status, or the new enjoyment of the right of personal freedom arising from the new position of being an active agent in the conduct of production, we have equally to notice that the status is collective, and that the activity of each agent in the conduct of production is merely a fractional activity. When the business of production in the whole of a particular branch is undertaken by the State, directly or indirectly, through the length and breadth of the country, the scale of the undertaking is so vast that the personal activity of the individual worker in the conduct of business is necessarily infinitesimal; and experience appears to suggest that the result is a central mechanism, ponderous and impersonal, in which there is less play for the personality of the workr than there is in a smaller undertaking, even under the system of private ownership of capital. It may thus be argued that the method of nationalisation does not attain the end which alone can justify the means—the end of extending personal and individual enjoyment of rights, and thereby extending the area of the development of the capacities of individual personality.

We may therefore turn to inquire whether another and different method would not be better calculated to promote the attainment of this end. We may begin by assuming the existence, and the continuing right to exist, of personal property in capital resources vested in individual owners. That right, it is true, is not an absolute right of the *Noli me tangere* order. On the contrary, it is a relative right (as rights in general are) which has to be properly adjusted to the rights of other persons. The problem before us is accordingly a problem of the proper adjustment of the right of the capitalist to those other rights. The right of the owner of capital resources, if it is not an absolute right, is grounded on something more than the mere prescription of continuous possession in the previous course of history. In other words, it is something more than a mere historical right which can only plead the fact that it has been in favour of the claim that it should continue to be. The right of the owner of capital resources is grounded on permanent titles, which belong to the present and the future as well as to the past, and consist in the social and moral advantages which accrue from the possession and exercise of the right. These advantages are various; but they may be classified summarily under three heads. In the first place, the right of the individual owner of capital resources is favourable to the play of personal initiative. It encourages responsibility for taking a personal decision, immediately and directly, at the point where the problem arises; it prevents decision from being centralised in one focus, and therefore mechanised; it remits it to, or distributes it among, a number of separate and living centers, thus following a biological rather than a mechanical pattern. In the second place, the right of individual ownership of capital resources is favourable to variety of experiment and to the method of trial and error. It encourages competition between undertaking and undertaking, and serves, by encouraging such competition, to arise the level of all and to improve the service of each; so that here again it may be said in a metaphor, and in no ignoble sense, to follow a biological pattern. Finally, the right of individual ownership of capital resources, as we have already had reason to notice, is connected with and favourable to that *nisus* towards the development of the capacities of personality which is an essential element of our nature: it provides a way in which we try ourselves out, and become conscious of our capacities by seeing them externally expressed in results. It is easy to exaggerate the importance of such external expression, and to forget that the development of capacity, even if it is encouraged by being expressed in external results, matters infinitely more than any result by which it may be encouraged. But results matter none the less; and men do more, and develop more, when they are moved to action by the incentive of visible results.

We may therefore hold, on the ground of these various advantages, that individual ownership of capital resources has a continuing social and moral title over and above the title of prescription and vested interest. But there is another side to the matter, and it is a side which is still more important. Un-criticised and unadjusted, the right of the owner of capital resources at once does harm to *him* and depresses the workers whom he employs. It does harm to him, in so far as it gives him a power over the lives of others which corrupts, or tends to corrupt, the possessor, as uncriticised power always does: it does harm to him again, in so far as it makes him, or tends to make him, a member of a privileged and almost parasitic class, enjoying results which may not be the results of personal capacity or of personal effort, but of mere inheritance or of pure chance. Just as it does harm to the owner, so too an uncriticised and unadjusted right of private ownership of a capital resources also depresses the worker. It depress him to the almost servile status of 'hand' (or, in Aristotle's phrase, 'a living tool') in the undertaking for which he works. It depresses him also to a 'propertyless being, with no share in the right of personal property, when by the same title of effort and output of personal capacity which the capitalists pleads he too should have his share in the capital of his undertaking. It follows that both in the interest of the capitalist and in that of the worker the State is forced to undertake the function of adjusting and reconciling the right of the owner of capital resources to the worker's rights of personal freedom of status and the enjoyment of personal property. This is a matter, once more, of the general task of the State: the task of achieving a right order of human relations, and thereby realizing the reign of justice, by adjusting the rights of one set of its members to the rights of another. Here the particular task is that of adjusting the old rights of the owners of capital resources. long recognised in positive law, to the worker's new rights, or more exactly his new claims to rights, which are now being recognised in social thought and are moving forwards to the further stage of legal recognition.

The method by which the State will seek to perform this task, if it remains true to its own proper nature and continues to follow the line of action which it has hitherto followed, will not be the method of 'nationalisation,' but the method of 'supervision'. It will not assume the new form of the socialist State, annexing the means and administering the business of general production: it will keep its old form of the supervisory State, still watching and easing the play of rights, as it has always done, but extending the range of its vision and increasing its work of adjustment. Recognizing the right of individuals who are owners of capital resources as a necessary part of the process of production, it will at the same time supervise the whole of the process of production with a view to co-ordinating this right, belonging to these individuals, with the other rights of other individuals which are also a necessary part of the process. It will see with the eye of its vision individual persons and personal rights, and it will think in terms of such persons and rights; but at the same time it will 'over-see' them and think them over together (which is the true sense of 'supervision'), and it will seek to adjust them accordingly. If we can imagine the State engaged in reflection, and expressing its reflections in speech, it might address itself and its members in words such as these:

'I am by my nature, and I must remain if I am to be true to my nature, a legal association. As such, I am not an agent of production, except where the principle of co-operation compels me to produce some system of public or common equipment (a postal system, or a system of fuel and power, or a transport system) which is needed by all and must be provided by the cooperation of all; but even here I think it best, as a general rule, to delegate the actual work of management to some economic body or board which will manage it simply and separately as a pure matter of business, and thus prevent it from being entangled in my own legal machinery. On the other hand, if I am not an agent of production, I am by my nature the supervisor of the whole process of production; and though it is not my business to manage the work of production, it certainly is my business to lay down the general rules to which such management must conform. That is the line of action which I have long been following. It is now a century and a half since I began to lay down the rules of factory legislation, in order to protect the right of every factory worker to the enjoyment of personal security. My rules have grown and grown. They are based on my two great principles of liberty and equality: they are intended to protect and secure the rights which are involved in the application of those principles; and as the social interpretation of those principles grows, my rules must continue to grow in order to keep in step with that interpretation. Today the interpretation of these principles is beginning to demand from me an adjustment of the right of the owner of capital to the double right of the worker: his right to enjoy a status of personal freedom, by virtue of being treated not as an instrument but as a collaborator; and his further right to enjoy the permanent possession of some personal property, by virtue of being made a partner or 'share-holder' in the ownership of capital. The beginnings of that adjustment have already been made in the course of the last fifty years; I started, for example, as long ago as 1909, a system of Trade Boards which gave to workers in unorganised industries an active right of helping to fix the rate of their wages, and thus enabled them to enjoy a status of greater personal freedom. Much has been done since 1909; but there is more to be done in order to improve the status of the worker, and far more to be done in order to increase the diffusion of ownership. It is ali a mater for tentative experiment and progressive movement from stage to stage. It is a matter of keeping a constant watch on the whole of the process of production: a matter of noting emergent claims for new rights, and how they affect and impinge on the existing scheme of rights; a matter of observing the tentative efforts made by the parties concerned to secure some form of voluntary adjustment between new claims and old rights, until finally, at the end of the watch and the noting and the observing, the time comes for my making of a uniform rule of compulsory adjustment, in the light of all the data collected and all the experience gained. If this is the way in which I act, I shall be acting strictly within my sphere as a legal association: I shall be simply adjusting one right to another—the right of the owner of capital resources to the worker's rights both of status and property—as it always is my duty to adjust rights and to serve thereby as the organ of justice.'

There is a gloss or corollary which follows naturally on this view of the economic function of the State. Whatever the State may do in the way of securing an involuntary adjustment of rights by the method of legal compulsion and in the form of statutory rules, there also exists, and there will always exist, the way of voluntary adjustment by the method of spontaneous agreement between the parties concerned. This way of voluntary adjustment has had a long if chequered history. It has meant the formation of associations of workers, trade by trade: it has meant the long struggle of these associations, or trade unions, for recognition and for the right of bargaining and making agreements with the similar associations formed by employers. At first thwarted by the State, and repressed by Combination Acts, but afterwards recognised and even encouraged, these associations have gradually established themselves as permanent social organs, seeking to achieve by social methods a social accommodation between conflicting claims. In themselves, and by the mere fact of their existence and action, they have already given the worker a new and added enjoyment of freedom of personal status which he derives from their collective strength. They have their defects as well as their qualities. The collective strength which can give to the worker a new enjoyment of personal freedom can also be used to insist that each worker shall merge himself and his personality in the collective mass; and the adhesion of these associations of workers, in the mass and in their collective capacity, to a particular political party wedded to policies of nationalisation, has had the disadvantage, whatever its gains may have been, of distracting them from that policy of the voluntary social adjustment of rights which belongs to their essential nature, and of turning their attention to the method of compulsory legal regulation through the agency of the State. Yet these may not be the permanent trends; and it is possible to hope, as has already been suggested, that the future may have in store not only negotiation and voluntary adjustment between the associated workers and the associated employers in each industry, but also negotiation and voluntary adjustment, in some form of voluntary 'social parliament', between representatives of the whole body of associated workers and the whole body of associated employers over the whole of the field of production.

This is not to say that the State will tend to become less active in its own work of legal adjustment by general rules. On the contrary it may well become even more active. A country which follows simultaneously the two ways of adjustment between conflicting claims of right—the way of voluntary adjustment by social agreement, and the way of legal adjustment by means of general rules—may become increasingly busy in pursuing *both* of these ways. True, the State will normally wait for the exploration of the way of self-help and voluntary social agreement before it begins to follow the way of public help and legal adjustment. True, again, the State, when it follows that way, will often, and perhaps even mainly, find itself concerned with generalizing, and making compulsory for all, what has already been tried and has already approved itself experimentally in the field of self-help and voluntary social agreement. But that only goes to prove that an increase of activity and experimentation in the social field, far from discouraging, will tend to encourage and foster an increase of activity in the legal field and the area of State-adjustment. The busier the effort of voluntary adjustment the greater will be the amount of material and the volume of suggestion on which the State can act.

The general method of advance which emerges from these considerations is a method which may be called by the name of 'experimentalism'. It is a method which begins with the ventilation of new claims to rights in the field of social thought and the forum of social discussion; with the pitting of these new claims against the old rights which they challenge; and with the demand for an adjustment between the old and the new. It is a method which then proceeds to the stage of social and voluntary adjustment, along a variety of lines and by a variety of experiments which tentatively compete with one another, and are tentatively pitted against one another, in the course of a process of social selection. It is a method which finally arrives at the stage of a legal and general adjustment, ultimately achieved by the State (through the action of its various organs of political discussion), as it works on the data before it and selects for endorsement and registration the solution which commands the adherence of general or common conviction. The whole method is a dialectical method, though it is far from being the method of 'dialectical materialism': it also is a method which has in its favour biological analogy, though it is far from being a method of natural selection of the fittest, and may rather be called a method of spiritual selection of the best—so far as the spirit of man is able to discover the best. If we call it by the name of experimentalism, which is only a shorthand name with the necessary defects of shorthand, we may plead that we mean by that name the process of gradually feeling a way, through time, by means of discussion, with the aid of the method of trial and error.

This experimentalism, if it may be so-called, is something different from 'gradualism'. Gradualism means that you start from, and stick to, a preconceived plan, though you move slowly and with a Fabian cunctation towards its achievement. Experimentalism means that you start from the postulate of the sanctity of human rights—but also from the postulate of the constant growth of new rights (or the constant reinterpretation and extension of old rights) and the consequent need of adjustment between the new and the old—and that you are always seeking to discover, by fresh thought and experiment as you come to each new problem in each new generation, how you can meet the demands of your double postulate. But just as experimentalism is not gradualism, so neither is it opportunism; and just as it is not a plan or 'blue-print,' inherited from some past prophet, for the methodical shaping of the future, so neither is it a matter of immediate and extemporised expedients intended merely to meet an immediate contingency. Its essence is indeed the freedom of the present to shape and determine itself by its own motion, in the light of the situation immediately presented for decision. But it is also the essence of experimentalism that the situation so presented has itself been prepared by thought, experiment, and debate, and is thus, as it were, a 'planned situation', which as such suggests and invites a planned and deliberate decision. There is thus, after all, a plan in the method of experimentalism. But the plan is not a transcendent scheme, preconceived before the beginning of action: it is immanent in the process of action, and conceived by and during that process. To proceed by experiment is to proceed by constant planning, but not to proceed 'according to plan'.

The Functions of Government and their Organs

The word 'function', in its political application, may be said to have two senses. It has the sense of purpose or aim, as when we say that the function of government is the maintenance of a scheme of law, or the service of rights, or some other such purpose or aim. It has also the sense of a particular mode of action, or a special kind of activity, by means of which a government seeks to fulfil its general purpose; and from this point of view we speak of the legislative, the judicial, and the executive function.

In the first of these senses, that of purpose, the course of the argument has led to the conclusion that the fundamental function of government is that of the service of Right. If we look at Right as 'objective', and as expressed in the external form of a body of general rules, we shall say that it is the function of government to render service to Right by translating social thought about the right order of human relations into a system of recognised and enforced law. If we look at Right as 'subjective', and as expressed in the form of rights which belong to persons or 'subjects' as their shares in objective Right, we shall say that it is the function of government to render service to rights by adjusting them to one another and removing obstacles to their enjoyment. In either case, and whether we regard the function of government as the service of Right or the service of rights, we shall say that the function of government is limited; limited by, and to, a service which it cannot transcend, a service which is the cause of its existence and the justification of all its action. On the other hand, just because it is service, and limited to being service, the function of government is also constantly growing. Since social thought about the right order of human relations is growing thought; since, in consequence of that growth, the system of Right and the rights of persons necessarily grown; since, in consequence of *that* growth, the service owed by government to securing the enjoyment of rights also necessarily grows; it follows that the function of government, even while it is limited to service, must be a growing function. All that has hitherto been said, in the previous course of the argument, about the extension of rights of persons involves a consequent and connected extension of the function of government.

Turning now to the second of the senses of the word 'function' in its political application, the sense of a mode of action or a kind of activity, we may begin by laying it down that there is always one great and general mode of action which government is bound to follow. It is the mode of proceeding by general rules of declared law backed by enforcement. Here again we may notice in passing that government is limited; limited by its general mode of action as well as by its general purpose; limited to acting by the one method of enforceable general rules, and limited therefore to acting in that sphere of acts of external conduct in which alone it is possible to enforce a general rule by means of an act of external compulsion. But within this great and general mode of action, to which government is limited, and by which it is limited, we may now proceed to distinguish particular modes of action, or special kinds of activity. They are commonly held to be three: the legislative, the judicial, and the executive. At this point, however, there emerges something of a confusion of terms. Sometimes the three are described as 'functions'; sometimes they are described as 'powers' (*pouvoirs*); sometimes they are regarded and described as 'organs'. Before we attempt to consider them, or to discuss in what sense and to what extent they are or ought to be separate, and in what sense, and to what extent, they merge or should merge into one another, we shall do well to clarify our terms. What do we mean when we speak of the legislative, the judicial, and the executive, and what is the noun we imply when we use these adjectives?

We may identify, for our purposes, the term 'function' and the term 'power'. A mode of acting, which is the specific sense of 'function', is nothing very different from a faculty of acting, which is the specific sense of 'power'. But we must distinguish both of these terms from the term 'organ'. A function or power, such as vision, is one thing: an organ, such as the eye, is another. On this basis we may proceed to argue that while we may sometimes, or even generally, use one organ for one function and one function only, yet there is nothing to prevent us from using one organ for a number of functions, provided that it can perform them, and provided again that they are best performed by being held together and interconnected in that one organ. This May seem to be an abstract and even irrelevant argument. In fact it has a definite and practical bearing on the political doctrine and practice which goes by the name of 'separation of powers' (*la séparation des pouvoirs*). This was a doctrine expounded by Montesquieu: it was also an axiom incorporated in the French Declaration of Rights of 1789, which lays it down that 'a society in which the separation of powers is not fixed has no constitution'. But what is this 'separation of powers'? Does it only mean and involve a distinction of *modes* of action, and is that its essence? Or does it also mean and involve a distinction of *organs* of action; and, if so, is each of the different organs confined and limited to one mode of action, so that none of them can possibly act except in a single mode, and each of them is entirely debarred from acting in the mode or entering the province of the others?

Separation of powers must certainly mean a distinction of modes of action. There is a mode of action for legislation, which is a distinctive mode with its own technique; a mode at once deliberate and deliberative; a mode which proceeds slowly and proceeds by debate, with 'reading' succeeding to 'reading' and one chamber succeeding to another. There is a mode of action for jurisdiction, which again is a distinctive mode, with its own peculiar technique and its own particular rules of procedure; a mode which is critical rather than deliberative; a mode which mainly depends on a critical appreciation of the relevant rules of law, a critical sifting of evidence, and a critical weighing of the arguments tendered by the rival advocates. Finally there is the executive mode, which is similarly a distinctive mode; a mode which proceeds with rapidity (at any rate in comparison with both the legislative and the judicial mode) and proceeds by way of decisions and instructions intended to follow out (*exsequi*) and give effect to the results of the legislative and judicial modes. This distinction of modes is clear; and whether each mode has its own separate and special organ, assigned to it and confined to it, or whether there is less separation of the organs and less confining of each to a single mode, the distinction of modes remains. The legislative mode, with its separate technique, is one thing: the judicial is another: the executive another still. But even if there is thus plurality of modes, there is also, we have to remember, a great and general mode of action which is common to the whole of government, and which blends the different modes in a unity of operation. Whatever the government does, and in whatever particular mode it acts, it always follows the general mode of acting by general rules of law formally declared and regularly enforced. The fact of this unity stands behind the difference of particular modes; and it is obvious that this unity may affect and qualify the extent to which difference and specialisation can properly be carried in the general conduct of government.

If 'separation of powers' thus means a distinction of modes of action, it also means, in any modern system of government, some sort of distinction of the organs of government. In early communities there may exist a single undifferentiated organ (the Anglo-Norman *Curia Regis* was of that order), acting in all the different modes, and simultaneously serving as a legislature, a judicature, and an executive. But in any developed community there will be a plurality of organs. There will be a legislative organ, which may not, indeed, be wholly and solely confined to the legislative mode of action, but will certainly be primarily and mainly concerned with that mode; there will equally be a judicial organ, primarily and mainly concerned with the judicial mode of action, but not necessarily confined to that mode; and there will similarly be an executive organ, which may, however, be concerned with other modes of action beside the executive. In a word we shall find three organs corresponding to the three different modes of action; but we may find none of the organs so absolutely specialised in its mode of action, or so entirely separate in its province, that it cannot also act in the mode and enter the province of the others.

It may be urged that the system just described, which combines a separation of modes of action (or 'functions' or 'powers') with a competence of each organ to act in more than one mode, is simply an inheritance from the past which is destined to disappear. On this view there has been an evolution from a primitive homogeneity, with little differentiation of modes and none of organs, towards heterogeneity and differentiation. That evolution has brought an increasingly clear differentiation of modes; but it has still left, as a sort of historical relic, a considerable confusion of organs, with each organ still showing signs of an old undifferentiated past. There may be some truth in this view; but it may also be urged, with even more justice, that a system in which each organ proceeds by more than one mode, and is concerned with more than one function, is inherent in the general unity of the operation of government, and is thus far more than a relic. In any case it is certain that such a system is still embedded in modern government; and it is also certain that, far from diminishing, it is constantly tending to increase. Instead of moving towards greater heterogeneity we are actually moving in the reverse direction. The more complicated government becomes, and the greater the service which it has to render, the greater becomes the trend to a unity of operation, and the more each organ of government tends to proceed by more than one mode of action.

The judicial organ perhaps shows this tendency less than the other two. Indeed it may be said that the judicial organ is a critic rather than an example of the tendency; in particular it is a critic of what some of its members regard as the encroachments and 'the new despotism' of the executive organ, now reverting, in their view, to the antiquated practice of medieval monarchy, by which the King in Council was a judicial and even a legislative as well as an executive organ. It is natural that a professional feeling should animate the legal profession, and should lead its members to vindicate the principle that a specific function is specifically reserved for the judicature and should not be exercised by other organs. 'The Law', in the sense of the Bar and the Bench, thus becomes the peculiar custodian of the doctrine of separation of powers, at any rate against executive encroachment. But we have already had reason to notice that the judicature itself is an organ which is something more than judicial in the strict sense of that word. In addition to interpreting the law it also in some measure declares it: it has acted in the past, and it still acts in the present, by the legislative mode.

Just as the judicature may thus be saia to exercise more than one function, so too may the legislature. The legislative organ in England was originally a body of mixed legislative and judicial competence, proceeding indifferently by both modes; and either House of Parliament is still a Court, if in different ways and different degrees. Moreover, though the legislature does not act as an executive, or by the executive mode, it is everywhere brought into intimate contact with the executive, and it affects, if it does not control or determine, the action of the executive organ. This is not only true—though it is true to a greater extent—in countries which have adopted and follow the cabinet system of responsible government, under which the executive organ is generally answerable to the legislature and dependent on its confidence; it is also true, if in a less measure, in countries in which the executive is independent of the legislature.

Finally, just as the legislature has been increasingly brought into contact with the executive by the modern evolution of government, and has come increasingly to exercise an influence on executive policy and action, so, conversely, the executive has also increased its scope, and has moved, or been drawn, into action proceeding not only by the executive, but also by the legislative and even by the judicial mode. The development of the executive into what may be called a multi-functioning organ (or, in other words, an organ proceeding by all the three modes) is one of the most notable features of modern government. If the growth of the legislative organ, in consequence of the development of the cabinet system, was the notable feature of the eighteenth century, it may be said that the growth of the executive organ, in consequence of the extension of rights and the corresponding extensions of services which mostly fall to the lot of the executive, is the notable feature of the twentieth. Today the executive is not only an executive: it is also, at the same time, a legislature, and that in a double sense. On the one hand it suggests and guides the process of law-making by the legislative organ. It does so even under the American system of division of functions between the executive President and the legislative Congress; and it does so even more under cabinet systems such as the British. On the other hand, the executive, apart from and in addition to its work of suggesting and guiding the process of law-making by the legislative organ, also acts itself as a legislature, when it issues supplementary rules of law in the form of 'regulations' and 'orders'. This power of the executive organ to issue supplementary rules of law is particularly evident in the sphere of the social services, and in matters such as housing and insurance; and it is to be noted that the power is often, and indeed mainly, exercised in virtue of a delegation of legislative power, made by the legislature itself, in a law which specifically authorizes an executive minister or ministers to supplement in detail its own more general prescriptions.

The same extension of services (and particularly social services), which has largely caused the growth of this executive legislation, in order to cope with all the detail necessarily involved, has also caused the growth of executive jurisdiction. But such executive jurisdiction, while it is similar to, is also different from, executive legislation. It is similar, in so far as it owes its origin to a similar act of legislative authorisation. A law about housing, for instance, which orders the clearing of slums, and therefore entails a decision, in any case of dispute, whether a given property belongs to the category of a slum and is therefore liable to clearance, may authorize an executive minister, as the person most likely to be familiar with the nature of the problem, to act judicially and give a decision. On the other hand, executive jurisdiction is different, in one respect, from executive legislation. When the legislative organ confers a measure of legislative power upon the executive, it takes something away from itself; but when it confers upon the executive a measure of judicial power, it is diminishing not itself, but an organ other than itself. That is one reason, though not the only reason, why the growth of executive jurisdiction is a more serious matter than is the growth of executive legislation.

The notable tendency of the executive organ to become more and more multi-functioning is itself sufficient to disprove the idea that the evolution of government is in the direction of a greater heterogeneity and an increasing differentiation of the various organs of government. On the contrary, the modern tendency would rather appear to be setting in the reverse direction. But though this tendency is a fact, it is also a problem, or a cause of problems. If the various organs overlap, and if some of them may enter the province and proceed by the modes of action which, primarily at any rate, belong to other organs, how is it possible for them to act amicably, without incessant disputes about boundaries and spheres? Again, if the executive takes to itself, or induces the legislative to allow it to take, both legislative and judicial powers in addition to its primary executive power, will not the rights of persons suffer from an authority so triply armed, and will not the principle of liberty be endangered by an overgrown and over-mighty executive?

It may be argued that the system works, and that the overlapping organs are able to act in unison, because one of these organs, the organ which is primarily concerned with the primary function of law-making, is the dominant and therefore the co-ordinating organ. In other words the legislature, as being the immediate sovereign under the constitution and therefore possessing the sovereign power of making final adjustments, is able to determine boundaries and spheres between the executive and the judicature, and between them both and itself. It may thus be said to secure a unity of operation in a system of different overlapping organs. But there is another factor which must also be present, in addition to the co-ordinating and adjusting activity of the legislature, if a system of multi-functioning organs is to work without friction and without detriment to liberty. Each of the organs, when performing a function or proceeding by a mode additional to its own specific function or mode, should act in the way and according to the technique appropriate to the function or mode thus added. If the executive, for example, is vested with judicial power, and accordingly performs the judicial function and proceeds by the judicial mode, it must really and actually proceed by that mode; and discarding the technique of executive action it must adopt and follow, as far as possible, the proper and peculiar technique of judicial action. It must accept the procedure of a public hearing, with a proper confrontation of witnesses according to the regular rules of evidence: it must publish its decision and the reasons for its decision: it must also admit, if it possibly can, the possibility of appeal. The result will be that the distinction of modes will still be observed, even if there is not a separation of organs; and the executive organ, when acting judicially, will cease to follow the executive mode and adopt instead the judicial.

Granted these two conditions—the co-ordinating and adjusting activity of the sovereign legislature, and the observance of the distinction of separate modes even when the distinction of separate organs ceases to be observed—we may accept the contemporary tendency towards the confusion or overlap of multi-functioning organs. But this is not to deny the justice and the propriety, for its time and under its conditions, of the eighteenth-century doctrine of the separation of powers. That doctrine was developed by Montesquieu in reference to French conditions. It was relative to the contemporary French facts of an over-grown royal executive organ; of the suspension of any legislative organ, and the substitution of executive decrees for legislative enactments; of the subordination of the judicial organ (the *parlement* of Paris) to the sovereign appearance of the King in person when he sat in a *lit de justice*. Under these conditions Montesquieu could argue, fairly enough, that with the executive claiming to do all things, confusing all the modes, and making its will the canon of Right and controller of rights, it was only possible to clarify confusion and to vindicate rights by asserting the titles to two other organs, the legislative and the judicial, to a separate existence and a separate power of acting independently by their own proper modes. In favour of such an assertion he could also plead, fairly enough (even if he was necessarily unaware of the nascent English system of responsible or cabinet government, and of the close connexion thereby established between the executive and the legislature), that the government of England was an example of the principle of separation of powers. The case is altered today; but if the facts are different, the principle, in its essence, remains. There is bound to be confusion, and there is bound to be a menace to rights, if it is not, in some way, observed. But that way, under our conditions, is now a different way.

Today we have in all countries, at any rate formally if not always in fact, the three separate organs which Montesquieu desired. But we have also something more than, and something different from, what he desired. There is in Britain (and there is also in other countries, in various ways and different degrees) an overlapping and an interlacing of the separate organs of government. The legislature does something more than legislation; the judicature does something more than adjudication; and the executive, in particular, does something more than executive action. But we get a co-ordination of what might seem to be confusion by the action of a dominant and sovereign legislature; we preserve a distinction of modes even if we do not maintain a clear separation of organs, and by that distinction of modes we preserve liberty and the rights of persons; and, finally, lest it succumb to the corruption of absolute power, we set bounds which it cannot overpass even to the sovereign legislature.

These bounds of the sovereign legislature are many and various. Some of them have already been traced in the previous course of the argument, and need only be summarised here. In the first place, the legislature, by its nature, is simply an organ of the legal association, or in other words the State; but besides the State and its legislature there is also Society and its social organs, with all the general play of voluntary social activity which proceeds, in the main, independently of the State. Secondly, the legislature, like the whole of government, is limited both by the purpose it fulfils and by the mode of action it follows: the purpose of serving Right and the rights which issue from Right, and the mode of action which consists in proceeding by general rules of law relative to and enforceable in the sphere of external conduct. Thirdly, the legislature is an organ of government acting in and under a general system of democracy, which proceeds by the method of discussion and thus reflects and repeats, at the political level, a process of debate which is already at work in the social area. Being an organ in such a system it may be said to be doubly limited, first by the play of social debate and the growth of common conviction which are precedent to its own action, and secondly by the existence of other forces and foci of discussion (party and the electorate on the one hand, and the cabinet on the other) which are concurrent with its action, and to which its action must be adjusted in some sort of balance and with some measure of mutual respect.

But there is a still further limit on the legislature which demands our consideration. This is the limit imposed by the development and the activity of political parties. The legislature has not only to respect the system of political parties as a force and focus of discussion parallel to and concurrent with itself. It has also to respect the system as something *within* itself; something by which its motion is *internally* affected and qualified. In an earlier passage of the arguments it has already been suggested that the democratic method of government, being as it is in its essence a method of government by discussion, necessarily requires a plurality of parties as a condition and *sine qua non* of discussion. We may now go on to suggest that the legislature, as a representative body reflecting in its own composition the plurality of parties in the national community, is inherently limited by the fact of that plurality, and is bound by the necessity, which arises from it, of attaining such measure of common agreement as is required for any united action proceeding from the whole body. It may be objected that no common agreement is required; that the majority party, or combination of parties, can simply overbear the minority and force it to acquiesce; and that a majority-vote is thus sufficient to ensure the united action of the legislative body. The objection does not hold; and the operation of a representative legislative based on a plurality of parties is more than a matter of counting votes and then doing a sum in subtraction.

Whether the parties are only two, or more than two, they generally arrange themselves in two sides (there may be many *parties*, but there can be only two *sides*)—the side of the party or combination of parties which supports the executive government or cabinet, and the side of the party or combination of parties which opposes that government. The government side, under normal conditions, does not simply outvote and overbear the opposition side; nor is the opposition side always waging a war in which it is always defeated. The two sides are indeed engaged in the conflict of debate; but they are also engaged in to co-operation of managing the nation's business together. The conflict is public: the co-operation, which is unacknowledged and may even be unconscious, is hidden in the background. But its always there. The two sides must, at the least, attain some agreement about the conduct of the current business of legislation. They must, in a grave emergency, whether of peace or of war, attain some agreement about the conduct of the general business of the nation. But even without an emergency, and even in normal conditions, they must always attain some agreement which goes beyond the conduct of current business and the routine of daily procedure. They must, in regard to all major measures of proposed legislation, endeavour to achieve some sort of compromise which is likely to command the general consent and to be endorsed by the common conviction of the whole community, and which is therefore likely to last even after a change of government, and even when the government side has been succeeded in office by the side now in opposition. This is the price of continuity, and continuity, in its turn, is the price of peaceful progress.

We may accordingly say that the legislature is two as well as one, and that it is inherently limited by the fact that the two have to act as one. In other words a joint effort—an effort of construction on the one side and of constructive criticism on the other; and effort which combines contradiction with co-operation—is involved in the double nature of the legislative body. The necessity of this joint effort is an internal limit; and the separation of the two sides of the legislature, thus at once opposed and conjoined, is the return in a new and different form of the old eighteenth-century system of *séparation des pouvoirs.* We do not indeed now separate, or seek to oppose and balance, the executive and legislative organ: on the contrary we unite them together in a system of responsible government which beings the executive into the legislature and enables either to affect the other in a constant interaction. But within this union and interaction we retain separation and maintain a balance. We retain a separation of two sides and the leaders of the twosides (the head of the Government and the leader of the Oppostioin): we maintain a balance in the sense that we require both sides and their leaders to adjust their claims and accommodate their policies in a compromise which eventually may command our general consent. Thus the end of the argument on the functions of government is at once in favour of union and in faovur of separation. You may unite the executive with the legislature; but when you have done so you must provide some element of separation and balance within that union. Again, and from another point of view, you may set your executive organ to act not only by the executive mode of action, but also by the judicial (in the exercise of executive jurisdiction) and in addition by the legislative (in the shape of executive legislation); but again when you have done so, and when you have thus united three modes in a single organ, you must ensure that there is also separation, and that the one organ uniting the modes nevertheless acts separately, and acts by a separate procedure, in each of the different modes. Union, but also separation—such is the rule which, in this way or that, is always imperative in the discharge of the functions of government.

Collectivism and Individualism

We may now return, in conclusion, to the theme of the relation between the functions of government and the rights of individuals. However government may discharge its functions, and however those functions may be distributed among its different organs, they are always, in their nature, functions of service rendered to rights and therefore rendered to persons, *individual* persons, who own these rights as the necessary conditions of the development in action of their individual personality. From this point of view the current antithesis between collectivism and individualism is verbal rather than real. If by individualism we mean a belief in the rights of individual persons, and by collectivism we mean a belief in the collective service owned and rendered to such rights by government, we shall see no opposition, but rather a necessary connexion. It is possible, indeed, to draw a distinction, as some thinkers have done, between a period of individualism, dominated by the influence of Bentham and his followers and marked by the idea of liberation, which lasted in the third quarter of the nineteenth century, and a period of collectivism, marked by the extension of the idea of protection, which succeeded the period of individualism from 1870 onwards. But the distinction is a distinction of the study; and it may even be said to show a class or professional bias. Some classes or professions might mourn a loss of individual rights after 1870: others, and those were numerous, began to enjoy an increase. Generally the whole of the nineteenth century, far from being divided into two different parts, was a century of a single and homogenous process; a process of the extension of personal rights, which may be called individualism, but a process entailing, at the same time, an extension of the service of government on behalf of those rights, an extension which may be called by the name of collectivism, but is really and in fact the consequence and the other side of the extension of personal rights which is called by the name of individualism.

Individualism is a word which is easily used in different and even conflicting sense. It can be used, and is often used, to denote a doctrine that the State leaves the individual alone, 'letting him do and letting him go' (*laissez faire et laisez passer*) as he himself thinks best. The phrase is a phrase of the French Free Trade economists of the eighteeth century: it originally belonged only to economics, and only to one part of that—the part concerned with commerce. It was a good enough phrase in its day, and it has its value still, in its own restricted field. But it cannot be properly applied to economics generally, or made to include the field of industry as well as the field of commerce: still less can it be applied to the whole broad field of politics. Individualism of the *laissez-faire* order in *that* field, individualism which meant that the State should leave each individual alone in the general business and whole conduct of life, would not only mean dereliction of its duty by the State; it would also mean the destruction of the individual's power to do anything freely or to go anywhere freely. A true individualism, in the field of politics, involves a recognition of the State's liberating power, coupled with a recognition of its duty to use that power according to its nature, and therefore for liberation and the removal of obstacles.

Individualism so conceived starts, indeed, from individual personality, and from the inherent title of each individual person to enjoy the conditions necessary to the development of his capacities. But just because it starts from that basis, it cannot end in any conclusion of *laissez faire,* or issue in any doctrine that it is the duty of the State of leave individuals alone. The conditions necessary for the development of each individual person are not to be had for the whistling, and they do not come of themselves in obedience to each person's call. They have to be assembled by a collective effort which is only possible to an organised State. They are assembled for the sake of the individual; but he cannot assemble them himself, or be left alone to shift for himself by his own unaided devices. On the contrary, he must be surrounded with service; a collective service which, in union with others, he himself helps to provide for others as well as himself: a service which becomes all the greater, the more fully the conditions necessary for his development are recognised and the more his rights are thereby extended. The State which is based on regard and respect for the worth of individual persons is not a 'let-alone' State: it is a State which follows and attends, 'with unperturbed pace', and with a constant office of service. To argue for individuality is not to argue for the unserved and unattended individual. It is rather the opposite: it is to argue for the general legal framework, and the whole system of collective service, which individuality needs for its development: it is to argue for the rights it requires, for the system of Right which is the other side of these rights, and for the service of the State in declaring and enforcing the common conviction about that system.

The argument seems to result in a paradox: 'the greater the liberty of the individual, the greater the interposition of government: the more rights, the more law, and therefore the more the activity of the State in declaring and enforcing law'. The statement of the paradox suggests a reflection. There is always a price to be paid for rights. That price, as has already been noted, is partly financial, or a matter of payment in money; partly spiritual, or a mater of payment in the acceptance of control. We need not pause to discuss the nature and the implications of the financial price. That is a matter of economics: of national finance and the balancing of national income and national expenditure. It is the spiritual price which matters most: and the crucial balance to be struck is the balance between the spiritual profit gained in the increased enjoyment of rights and the spiritual loss incurred or involved in the increased acceptance of control. When we seek to strike this balance, we have two calculations to make. The first is a calculation of the gain and loss in the private account of each individual: it is a matter, as it were, of the private bank-book of each; it is a business of reckoning individual gain of liberty against individual loss. The second is a calculation of the gain and loss in what may be called the common account of the whole community; it is a matter of reckoning between classes or sections of the community it is a business of computing the gain of one class or section, in liberty and personal rights, against the loss of another.

The necessity of reckoning spiritual gain and spiritual loss in the private account of each individual is a necessity which may easily be forgotten; but it still remains a necessity. Men readily accept new rights and the enlargement which they immediately bring: they are less ready to remember the price and the restrictions which may be entailed. The rights comprised in a system of social security are precious; but they are necessarily accompanied by administrative control and regulation, and they necessarily involve the performance of prescribed and compulsory acts in the channels of regular routine. There is at once an increase of liberty and an increase of automatism; and the question is whether the increase of liberty is more than enough to offset the increase of automatism. To enjoy the rights of social security is to be liberated from fears and dangers; to be more of a freeman, and to have more freedom for the development of personal capacity. If the freedom is grasped and used, and if the development is actually achieved, the game is well worth the candle, and the commodity is worth far more than the price. On the other hand there *is* a price. To be liberated from a set of risks is also to be liberated from the responsibility of facing those risks: indeed it is even more, under a system of collective insurance; it is also to be subjected to the control involved in the system. Only if the liberty gained is actively grasped and used; only if it is something more than a passive acceptance of benefits; only then will there be a net gain on the whole of the transaction. The man who is formally made more free by a system of social security must actively use his freedom to make something more of himself if he is to be really and actually more free.

The necessity of reckoning gain and loss between different classes or sections is a still more obvious necessity, daily forced upon our attention by the process of class-debate. The extension of rights for one class may mean the limitation of rights for another; and it is possible that the one class may lose even more than the other gains. But that, in itself, does not necessarily mean that the bargain is bad. The previous distribution of rights between classes may have been unfair and inequitable: one class may have been entrenched in the possession of superfluity, and the other depressed below the level of bare necessity. If the greatest number are to enjoy the greatest possible development of the capacities of personality, correction is inevitable, and it may be as just (in terms of the sovereign justice which assigns rights equally to each and all) as it is inevitable. The distribution of rights among classes is not a thing fixed for ever. It is a matter for constant adjustment and readjustment, as social thought about justice grows and as the interpretation of the principles of liberty and equality broadens with its growth. But there is still a limit to the process of adjustment and readjustment. It may be fair to ask one class, particularly when in numbers it is a small and limited class, to surrender old rights and responsibilities for the sake of another and larger class, and in order that the members of that class may enjoy new rights and responsibilities. But it will only be really fair if two conditions are satisfied

The first of these conditions is that the rights and responsibilities surrendered should be used by those who receive them for their own higher development, and not merely accepted as prizes or trophies. Otherwise there may be no gain, and there may even be loss, in terms of that development of personality which is the financial criterion. The other condition is that the class surrendering rights (such as the right to ownership of capital resources and the management of those resources on the basis of personal responsibility) should not be made to surrender so much that it becomes impotent to contribute any energy of initiative or originality of experiment to the development of the national economy and the general national culture or type of civilisation. Under any system of organisation a national community will always need an initiatory and experimental class which can generate and distribute the electricity of ideas. The recruiting of that class should be broad and generous; and every talent should have an open way into its ranks. But however recruited, and however broad, this class will always require the conditions necessary for the discharge of its electric work; and there will always remain a modicum of rights and responsibility which it must necessarily retain if it is to be itself and to contribute its own gifts to the cause of general development. The days of hereditary aristocracy are gone; but there is no numbering of the days of what may be called the professional aristocracy, in he widest sense of the word 'professional'. The more a national community moves towards the greatest possible development of the capacities of personality in the greatest possible number of persons, the more it needs the stimulus which professional skill and managing capacity can give to the whole development of the whole community.

It has been argued that there is no antithesis between individualism, in the sense of a belief in the development of individual personality, and collectivism in the sense of a belief in the collective service necessary for individual development. On the other hand, it has also been argued that though there is no antithesis there is or may be tension—a tension between the 'pull' of individual development and the 'pull' of a collective service which must always be in some measure also a collective control. The two may be complements to one another; but they are complements which need a nice and delicate adjustment. There is a principle of polarity in the political nature of man, as there is in human nature generally: a 'quality of exhibiting opposite or contrasted properties', a 'tendency to develop in two opposite directions'. In his general nature man has the contrasted properties of privacy and sociability; and though he is one being, and though he needs them both, he is also divided between them, and he also feels the tension between their different pulls. Similarly in his political nature he has the contrasted and yet complementary properties of the individualists who would fain be himself and the collectivist who would merge himself in a fellowship of service; and though he is one being and needs both these properties, he is also divided between them and feels in himself the tension of a 'tendency to develop in two opposite directions'. Individualism and collectivism are not the banners of two separate armies, composed of two separate bodies of men. All of us fly them both, and we all serve under both. There is a polarity in each of us, as well as in the whole community to which we all belong. We need not dread the resultant tension. That would simply be to dread life; for life is tension, as tension is life. We have to accept it as it exists, both within ourselves and within the community; and we have constantly to find, in each new conjuncture, the new adjustment which the new conjuncture demands, surrendering neither individual development nor collective service, but endeavouring to find an adjustment which preserves them both and may even make them both mutually serviceable to one another.

There is another polarity, and another tension, besides the tension within the State between the call of individual development and the call of collective service. This is the polarity or tension between the State and Society; between the community permanently organised in a single legal association for the one legal purpose of declaring and enforcing universal and uniform rules, and the community organised, or rather constantly organizing itself, in a number of voluntary associations for a variety of purposes (religious, cultural, recreational, charitable, economic, and whatever else may be comprehended under the general designation of 'social') which adorn and supplement, and may even stimulate or anticipate, the activity proper to the purpose of the legal organisation. The question which thus emerges, and the tension thus presented, bring us back at the end to the theme from which the argument originally started. What is the province of the State, and what is the province of Society? Is there any definite boundary, or how shall we conceive their relations?

In attempting to answer this question we may begin by asking ourselves whether the goal which is set before us—the securing of the greatest amount of rights for the greatest number of persons; the providing of the conditions of the highest possible development of the capacities of personality over the widest possible range—is a goal which can be simultaneously attained by two parallel lines of action, or a goal to be attained by one and only one. Can the extension and spread of rights 'in widest commonalty' be partly secured by voluntary action in the social area, or must it be altogether secured by uniform and compulsory action in the legal area, with a large consequential growth of State-action and a large increase of the functions of government in the necessary service of rights? There is a good case to be made in favour of the first of these alternatives. Voluntary action in the social area is needed as well as, and no less than, the uniform and compulsory action of the organised State in its own legal area. Both are necessary, but the first comes first; and the prior thing, in the order of time (though not necessarily in order of importance) is the voluntary action of Society. We do our best if we do what we can for ourselves, by voluntary social co-operation, before we invoke the action of the State—which indeed is also ourselves, wherever it is democratically organised, but is ourselves engaged in the making and enforcing of compulsory rules. There is a time for voluntary and varied experiment as well as for the uniform obligatory rule. Indeed the distinction between social action and the legal action of the State is perhaps rather a distinction of time than a distinction of space or area. It is not always the case that one sort of action is concerned with one area or set of subjects, and the other with another area or set; on the contrary, both sorts of action may well be concerned with the same areas or sets of subjects. Rather it is often the case that the one sort of action belongs to one time or conjuncture, the time of the laboratory and the experiment, and the other to another time or conjuncture—let us say, in a metaphor, that of mass-production, when a result of the laboratory is being put on the market as a standardised uniform commodity.

If we follow this line of thought, we shall be led to believe that a reorganisation of the economic process, such as will introduce the principles of liberty and equality into this process, and will therefore secure to all who are concerned in it the rights involved by these principles, may well begin, and may even sometimes remain, as the level of voluntary agreement between voluntary associations (those of the workers and those of the employers), an agreement based on voluntary consultation and issuing in voluntary co-operation. But often the matter will not end there, and there will come a time and conjuncture for acting in a different way and by a different mode. Voluntary social effort, feeling its way, making its experiments, proceeding by trial and error, may discover a best which is so obviously best that it deserves to be made the general rule. In that case the State, which is not the enemy of Society, but rather stands to it in something of the relation in which a solicitor may stand to a family, will register and endorse this best as a rule for general application and enforcement. But just as it is wise to avoid going to a solicitor unless or until you have a case to submit, so it may also be wise to avoid recourse to the State (to which we are perhaps too prone to carry our problems instantly) until social thought and experiment have done their preparatory work. The issue between Society and the State, if we can speak at all of an issue, is not an issue between opposites. How indeed can it be so, when the State is just Society writ legally—Society organised in the form and for the purposes of a legal association? It is either an issue between two alternatives, either of which may serve, but one of which, at a given moment, may serve better than the other, or an issue between two complements, both of which are needed, but one of which is needed as the forerunner of the other.

The conclusion to which we are thus led is not a conclusion in favour of the individualism which means leaving individuals alone, to shift for themselves by their own devices: nor again, on the other hand, is it a conclusion in favour of the form of collectivism under which the State serves individuals so much that they have little or nothing to do for themselves, and thus lose much of their liberty in the very act of their own liberation. It is rather a conclusion in favour of the maximum of voluntary self-help by groups of individuals, voluntarily acting for themselves in the social area; thinking out for themselves, in their own sphere of interest, the requirements and conditions of their own development; and, when they have thought them out *for* themselves, going on to achieve them *by* themselves, and by their own efforts, so far as in their own sphere they can. In one sense this may be called individualism; for it involves a belief in the value of the spontaneous activity of individuals, freely associated for the purpose of shifting for themselves, by their own devices, in a scheme of voluntary self-help. In another sense, however, it may also be called collectivism; for it involves a belief in the value of the concerted activity of collective groups, each knit together by a common interest of all the members in a common object, and each seeking to achieve its object by means of common effort. But on a broad view the method of voluntary self-help by the concentrated effort of a voluntary association is neither individualism nor collectivism, in the ordinary sense of those terms; it is a happy bridge between them. The essence of the method is a spirit of 'voluntary community', which marries *voluntas* to *communitas;* and the essence in trun of that spirit is the power not of force but of persuasion.

The power of persuasion, issuing in the spirit of voluntary community, has studded that world in which we live with a profusion of social institutions. Professor Whitehead, in one of the most suggestive of his essays, has spoken of the transformation wrought in the problem of liberty by 'a profusion of corporations originated by explicit thought'. In his view the development of these autonomous institutions, limited to special purposes, places the problem of liberty at a new angle: and he holds accordingly that the novelty of our days, and the modern method of solving the problem of liberty, 'consists in the deliberate formation of institutions, embodying purposes of special groups, and unconcerned with the general purposes of any political state'. His authority and his persuasive power reinforce the argument here advanced. The future will largely lie with the development and the activity of a variety of social institutions. What such institutions can do, and what they may ultimately achieve, in the economic field, is a matter already touched upon in the previous course of the argument. But there are other fields besides the economic in which the development of social institutions may contribute greatly to the solution of the ancient problem of liberty. There is, for example, the field of education, which is not, and never can be, a monopoly of the Sate. Educational associations—of parents, of teachers, of workers, and of members of religious confessions—are all concerned in the development of educational experiments, and in offering that liberty of choice among types of school and forms of instruction which is essential to the growth of personal and individual capacity. Indeed on a general view, and looking beyond particular fields to the general field of the way of life and the type of civilisation common to the whole community, we cannot but notice that social institutions are active in all its range and over all its extent. 'Our lives are passed from the first not in a monistic, homogenous circle, but in a number of circles.... we live in various social complexes which are in the last resort concentric and each of which has its own intellectual content.' These circles and social complexes, each with its intellectual content, and all with their moral aim of mutual aid and common service, are essentially personal unions, enlisting personal interest and eliciting fully the initiative of their leading personalities. The greater the part which they play, on that basis and in that form, the greater their contribution to the development of the capacities of individual personality in the community at large, and thereby to the growth of a better way of life and a higher type of civilisation. But they must be true to their personal basis, and retain their personal form, if they are to contribute effectively. Social institutions can easily become ossified, no less than political: they can become official organisations, in lieu of personal associations: they can dictate to their members, instead of responding to the lift and surge of their minds. They must constantly be renewed and reviewed: sometimes, when they have served and outlived their purposes, they may even have to be destroyed, in order that something new and better may be able to take their place. It might be a motto for a community: 'Never rest content with your institutions, whether social or political—but least of all with the social: there is a virtue in continuity, but there is no less virtue in change.'

All in all, the question before us is not a question of 'the man *versus* the State', or of individualism *versus* collectivism. There is no point in the question: there is no such antithesis; there is, at the most, a tension, which is as healthy as it is necessary. Nor is the question before us a question of 'Society *versus* the

State', or of the voluntary principle *versus* the principle of legal control and regulation. There may be more point in that question; but again there is no antithesis, for both of the things thus opposed are needed, and both may be needed equally. Here, however, the tension is greater; and here, as we have already seen, there is a reasonable ground for debating, not so much *what* the State should do and *what* Society should do (both handle equally a number of matters, and few matters can be said to belong exclusively either to the one or to the other), as *when* and in what conjuncture Society should be the agent, and *when* and in what conjuncture the agent should be the State.

Each mind has a drawing bias, which makes it naturally run in some particular direction. The bias of the writer has always inclined his thought—the more, the older he grows—towards a belief in the value of the social mode of action. With all its imperfections and its possible inefficiencies, it is none the less a mode of action which permits and even demands the free energy of the mind. The movement of the State is the regular revolution of steady and unfailing machinery. The movement of social institutions is a varied and irregular movement, like the movement of trees and plants as they spring from the seed in the ground: here one group, and there another, thrusts up its fresh particular idea into the varied field of social life and experiment. The humming automatism of the State is about us and all our doings, engaged in constant service and constantly intending our good. The varied field is untidy, irregular, unregulated: it has many gaps: it has even more redundancies. But may the time never come when all our life spins round on the revolving wheel of legal regulation.

E. Baker

8

The Welfare State

The Individual or the ordinary citizen or the common man came into his own when Rousseau rang the bell which reverberated through every country in the world. Respect for the human personality and dignity of the human soul gradually began to be understood. The idea that every individual had a value and was entitled to consideration, irrespective of his ability or capacity, opened up a new chapter in political science and made a new and revolutionary contribution to the history of human freedom.

Before Rousseau Christianity had preached the equality of all human souls in the eye of God. But although that religion undermined the majestic edifice of the Roman Empire, the Catholic Church became as authoritarian as the Empire it had destroyed. The dogma of papal infallibility and the hierarchy of clergy could not be reconciled with individual freedom. Even in the Greek City States and in Rome during her palmy days of sturdy independence there was only a democratic superstructure. But it was built upon the putrid foundation of slavery. Even in England it was the barons who wrenched the Magna Carta out of the unwilling hands of King John, and even though slowly the monarchy became constitutional and Parliamentary institutions were established, power remained securely vested in a few aristocratic or rich families. The first real assault upon privilege was made by Rousseau and the right of every man to his own individuality was for the first time accepted as a political principle.

It must be remembered that for centuries before Rousseau the world was more interested in security than in liberty. The breakup of the Roman empire and the invasion of the barbarian hordes turned the thoughts of men more to the question of setting up a stable State than to individual freedom. And even when ultimately the stable State emerged from the political chaos of the Middle Ages it was the Nation State which glorified the nation in the person of the Ruler. Thought the nation was accepted as a political concept as a conglomeration of men having certain racial and cultural affinities, no consideration was paid to the individuals who went to constitute that nation.

In India the position has been no different. In recent times both the Mogul and the Mahratha Empires were wholly authoritarian. The wars which were fought were largely dynastic. Indian history hardly records the life, thoughts or aspirations of an average Indian. He tilled the land, paid taxes and sometimes joined the army on one side or other. His religion taught him to think of his soul and to look upon the world as Maya. He turned a philosophic eye upon the march of history and ignored it. With the break-up of these two Empires and the advent of the British, security assumed considerable importance. It is only when the British Empire became a settled fact and the administrative unity of the country has been established that people's minds began to turn to the question of liberty.

It is a cardinal article in the democratic faith that the State exists for the individual. He is the pivot round which society revolves, and the main function of the state is to help the individual to develop this personality to the full. The State has no personality or existence independently of its citizens. The prosperity or power of the State is the prosperity or power of all its citizens combined. But from this it does not follow that the individual is free to do what he likes and the State has no right to control his actions or fetter his freedom. The most important and pressing problem in political science today is to draw the line between State-control and individual freedom. In this connection certain basic principles must be borne in mind. The individual, if I might so put it, has both a moral and a civic personality. The moral personality expresses itself in the free choice between doing right and wrong.

It also expresses itself in its upliftment towards something higher, nobler, more sublime than itself. In this sense the individual is a religious personality. The individual also forms and holds opinions on various subjects, without these opinions necessarily leading to action.

The primary duty of the State is to create an atmosphere of security in which the individual can develop himself. But it would be a very poor view of the Modern State which would confine its activities to the maintenance of law order The State has to strike a proper balance between the liberty of each and the liberty of all. The State is not responsible merely for security of the life and limb of its citizens. It is also responsible for their economic security. It is not sufficient that legal justice should be dispensed by the Courts and the State should provide for the means of its enforcement. The State must do what the courts cannont do—provide economic justice by its laws and administrative acts.

It is in this respect that the civic personality of the individual assumes importance. The individual does not and cannot live in anarchic isolation. He is essentially a social animal. He is affected and influenced by his social environments and he in his turn helps to make and create the society of which he is a member. It an individual has social rights he has equally and perhaps more so social duties and obligations. Even the greatest individualist must now accept as axiomatic that social duties and obligations must have precedence over individual rights. The Real problem is to draw the line of demarcation between social control and the rights of the individual.

In this connection it is necessary to bear in mind the Aristotelian principle that the State exists for the good life—in order that the individual citizen should achieve the good life. There are many definitions of the good life and students of ethics have debated for ages between the various shades of good and evil. But there is general agreement that the greatest good that an individual can aspire to is the full and complete realisation of his own personality. Therefore every compulsion that impedes or prevents this consummation is to be deprecated. Unless we look upon the

State as having an existence independent of its citizens and put it upon the pedestal of a mighty and semi-divine corporation, the quality of the State must ultimately depend upon the qualities of its individual citizens. Therefore the State should itself be interested in preserving and safeguarding individuality. The State should recognize that every law which prevents the individual from experimenting with his own life and giving effect to his own ideals and aspiration not only undermines the freedom of the individual but in the long run goes to make the State less powerful. For the greatness of a State depends upon the manifold variety of the opinions held by its citizens and the rich diversity of the aims and objects pursued by them.

We must recognize that there are many ways that lead to God and every individual must find his own salvation. There is common agreement that the State should be secular and there should be complete religious freedom. But the difficulty arises when we approach the realm not of religion but of morality. Has the State the right to impose by compulsion its own standards of morality? Can it prevent a citizen from experimenting with his own life and seeking happiness in his own way?

To reduce life to one pattern is to deny the uniqueness of individuality. The State cannot judge what is good for every citizen. Its opinion of what is moral and what is immoral can only be formed by the experience of those who form that opinion. That experience would not necessarily be the same with regard to those upon whom the moral standard is being imposed. It is the essence of morality that it should be based upon individual experience and individual judgment. While the State cannot prevent individual experience, it would be depriving the individual of the right to form his own judgment based upon his own experience. The name of morality cannot be conferred upon any action which is not the result of free will and free choice. Virtue must develop in a free atmosphere and to be virtuous by compulsion is infinitely worse than to be immoral by free choice. This must be so because if the object of good government is the development of human personality then moral compulsion can only produce a twisted, dwarfed and frustrated individual and not an individual who gathers his own experience and applies to it his own touchstone and his own standards and will.

There is a striking passage in Bakunin's God and the State quoted by Bertrand Russell in his *Roads to Freedom.*

"The State is authority; it is force; it is the ostentation and infatuation of force; it does not insinuate itself; it does not seek to convert......Even when it commands what is good it hinders and spoils it. Just because it commands it, and because every command provokes and excites the legitimate revolts of liberty; and because the good, from the moment it is commanded, becomes evil from the point of view of true morality, of human morality (doubtless not of divine), from the point of view of human respect and of liberty. Liberty, morality and the human dignity of man consist precisely in this, that he does good, not because it is commanded, but because he conceives it, wills it and loves it."

But there may be individual actions which though falling within the sphere of morality may yet impinge upon society. A man may get drunk and in doing so he is only harming himself. He must be allowed to benefit by his own experience and to form his own moral judgment. But he may be drunk and disorderly in a public place. He may waste money on drink which he should use to support and maintain his family. He would then be acting in an anti-social manner which would justify the State in controlling his conduct. Therefore the restraint upon individual freedom must be justified not by condemning an act as being wrong or immoral but as being against the interest of society. Society has a right to claim from the individual that he should conform to certain social standards and the State in its turn has an equal right to lay down these standards for the welfare of society as a whole.

A clear distinction must be drawn between opinion and action. Opinion, in order to have any significance, must be entirely free and untrammelled. The State has no right to demand from the citizen that he shall hold the same view as it itself propounds or propagates. All progress depends upon men holding heterodox views and adhering to them in the teeth of opposition and even contumely. Even the correctness of the policy put forward by the State depends upon its being tested by discussion and debate. Power is so all-absorbing that those who wield it expect complete obedience and conformity. Even a difference of opinion seems to suggest intransigence and a possibility of revolt. But it is apt to be forgotten that it is better to look hostile opinion in the face rather than drive it underground and thus make it more powerful and more dangerous.

The State is rarely if ever justified in persecuting opinion even in times of national crisis. When mass hysteria overtakes a country the first victim is likely to be free opinion. In this connection it is well to remember the wise words of Holmes, the famous Judge of the American Supreme Court, uttered in *Abrams* v. *United States,* 250 U.S. 616. "It is only the present danger of immediate evil or an intent to bring it about that warrants Congress in setting a limit to the expression of opinion where private rights are not concerned.....We should be eternally vigilant against attempts to check the expression of opinions that we loathe and believe to be fraught with death, unless they so imminently threaten immediate interference with the lawful and pressing purpose of the law that an immediate check is needed to serve the country."

But what is true of opinion is not necessarily true of the action that is the result of the formation of an opinion. However heated the berate and discussion may be, however strongly various shades of opinion may express themselves, when the policy of the State takes shape in the form of legislative action, the duty of the citizen is to conform his action to the law of the land. Respect for law is the very basis of democratic institutions—and inherent in this is the acquiescence of the minority in the decisions arrived at by the majority. No citizen has the right to say that he will disobey a law because he disapproves of it. His only democratic right is to agitate for its repeal. He is free to hold the opinion that the law is abhorrent—he is not free to defy it or commit a breach of it.

This may raise the larger question as to the right of the citizen to refuse obedience to a law which he thinks morally unjustifiable. It is true that Mahatma Gandhi raised a whole political philosophy and won freedom for a whole nation on the doctrine of passive resistance to laws, which were degrading to our national self-respect. But it must be borne in mind that Gandhiji was fighting against a foreign Government for national emancipation. A weapon which may be a proper one against an alien ruler is not necessarily a justifiable one against one's own Government democratically elected by the people. Therefore political fasts and Satyagrah make no meaning in a democratic setting.

Philosophically the right cannot be denied to an individual to disobey a law which asks him to do something which goes against his conscience. But the individual must always remember that he is pitting his own individual conscience against the social conscience. And it is very rarely that the individual should permit his own conscience to prevail over that of Society. If he does allow its to prevail he is a rebel and in effect he is withdrawing his allegiance to the State of which he is a member. Theoretically no citizen has entered into a slave bond with the State and the right of rebellion is the ultimate manifestation of liberty which the individual can exercise and which every State must fear as limiting it power and jurisdiction.

In the history of freedom there has been one great advance—and that is that there is now general agreement as to what are the fundamental and inalienable rights of an individual, even though in practice very few of these are really enjoyed by men all the world over.

On 10 December 1948 the General Assembly of the United Nations adopted and proclaimed the Universal Declaration of Human Rights. The Rights which are so proclaimed are the fundamental and inalienable rights of every human being, whatever his caste or community, Whatever the country he may be living in.

The Declaration of Human Rights, to use the language of Roosevelt, constitutes "the international Magna Carta of all mankind" in which full effect is given to Roosevelt's four freedoms—freedom of speech, freedom of worship and freedom from want and fear. I attach greater importance to the freedom from want and fear than to the first two freedoms. It is rather ironic to speak of the right of a starving man who fears for his own security and for that of his dependents and who does not know what the morrow will bring, to give expression to his opinion and to practise his religion. There are rights which only a well-fed man who has a comfortable job has time to think of. Therefore freedom from want and fear is the very basis of human rights and from which all other freedoms flow. It is no freedom to be free in poverty and destitution. It is for this reason that the Declaration emphasizes that every one as a member of society has a right to social security, that every one has the right to work, that every one has the right to a standard of living adequate for the health and well-being of himself and of his family, the right to security in the event of unemployment, sickness, disability, widowhood, old age or other lack of livelihood in circumstances beyond his control and the right to rest and leisure.

The Declaration of Human Rights has no legal validity, nor has it any legal sanction behind it, but it supplies a moral standard and a sure touchstone by which all legislation and social conditions in different countries can be judged. No country can be legally hauled up for passing a law which deviates from the principles enunciated in the Declaration, but it can be put in the dock and condemned by international opinion. The Declaration has undoubtedly awakened the social conscience of every Government in the world. The Declaration is like a brave banner flying from the highest tower in the world which no one can ignore.

In our own Constitution we have made a striking departure from past precedents and English precedents by guaranteeing the fundamental rights of the citizen and providing the judicial machinery for securing those rights. Most of the human rights which we find enshrined in the Declaration find a proud place in the Chapter on Fundamental Rights in our Constitution. We have equality before the law and equality of opportunity in matters of public employment. Right to freedom of speech and expression, right to form associations, right to freedom of conscience and the right freely to profess, practice and propagate religion are all guaranteed. No person shall be deprived of his life or personal liberty except according to procedure established by law and no person shall be deprived of his property save by authority of law. Our Constitution establishes the rule of law and sets up an independent judiciary to act as the custodian of human rights. Even Parliament cannot deprive the citizen of his fundamental rights. The Constitution is supreme and sovereign and all the organs of the State function under the Constitution and are subject to the Constitution.

There is a difference of opinion among political thinkers as to whether it is wise to limit and control Parliamentary sovereignty by what might be called a Bill of Rights. "A Bill of Rights," says Laski, "so to say, canonizes the safeguards of freedom; and, thereby it persuades men to worship at the alter who might not otherwise note its existence." On the other hand it is argued that in a democracy the chosen representatives of the people should have full and untrammelled power and should be trusted with that power. Parliament should have the power to undertake any legislation which is in the interest of the community and which is necessary for the creation of a Welfare State. Fundamental Rights, it is said, delay and impede social legislation and further it is often left to the Judges to determine the pace of legislation rather than to Parliament. It is therefore felt by some that we committed a grievous error in not following the British model of complete Parliamentary sovereignty and in pursuing the will-of-the-wisp of the supremacy of the Constitution after the American fashion.

As against this we must not forget that we are new to democratic institutions and new to power. Power has a tendency to be all-embracing and to remove from its path all impediments and obstacles. Therefore it is the course of wisdom to circumscribe power as much as possible. There is a further danger in India. We still lack the great democratic corrective of an opposition. Our Parliamentary institutions, although based on those of England, lack the one salutary check which England provides to dictatorship. We have here the rule of one party with very little possibility of that party being replaced by any other. There is no more dangerous dictatorship than the dictatorship which wears the garb of democratic institutions. A dictatorship which has been raised to power by a popular vote has nothing to fear and need suffer no qualms of conscience. It is therefore a tribute to the wisdom of our Constitution-makers that they provided a powerful safeguard against the possible tyranny of a legislature dominated by a powerful party which in the first flush of freedom might have swept away all individual freedoms in order to create a monolithic State. Cardozo in his *Nature of the Judicial Process* has a striking passage which will bear quotation: "The great ideals of liberty and equality are preserved against the assaults of opportunism, the exigency of the passing hour, the erosion of small encroachments, the scorn and derision of those who have no patience with general principles by enshrining them in Constitution and consecrating to the task of their protection a body of defenders. By conscious or sub-conscious influence the presence of this restraining power aloof in the background but nonetheless always in reserve tends to stabilize and rationalize the legislative judgment, to infuse it with the glow of principle, to hold the standard aloft and visible for those who must run the race and keep the faith."

Fundamentally the State exits to do social justice. It must redress the balance where the balance has been tilted by privilege or unfair competition. The State can never bring about complete equality—because that is against the order of nature—men being so unequal in their capacities and aptitudes. But it can remove inequality where that prevents every citizen from realizing the full results of his own personality. It was said long ago that too much wealth on the one side and too much poverty on the other does great harm to a State. Even Plato in his *Laws* would not permit any citizen to possess more than four times what the poorest citizen possessed. Wealth is the main source of all inequalities. It does not make a man wiser or more intelligent or endow him with qualities which he does not possess. But in the struggle for existence it gives a flying start to the one who possesses it and imposes an intolerable handicap upon those who do not possess it. The Welfare State has to remove this glaring inequality from our country. Much has been done and much is being done to see that the race should be run on equal and fair terms. Taxation and estate duty are gradually but inevitably bringing about a state of affairs where very soon no one in India will be rich—as indeed has already happened in England.

But the mere abolition of inequality and privilege is the negative aspect of the welfare State. It positive aspect is to provide social security to every citizen. Every citizen has a right to a certain standard of living. He cannot obtain this by merely doing nothing. He must be prepared to work and indeed he has a right to work. But whatever the nature of his work he is entitled to be compensated in a manner which would permit him to maintain the dignity of his human personality. In India especially it is essential to emphasizes the dignity of labour. All work is necessary for the welfare of society—and in whatever capacity a man may be working he is discharging his obligation to society. It may be difficult to reach the socialist millennium of equal pay for all workers, but there has been more and more approximation between the lowest paid and the highest paid worker in the land and there is a growing compulsion by the State that no worker shall be paid less than a certain minimum.

Social security always requires that a citizen should be supported in his old age and illness. Today many a worker is just thrown on the scrap heap when he is superannuated. He may receive a pension which may just be sufficient to put off starvation or he may even receive no pension at all. It is now recognised that it is the fundamental and inalienable right of a human being not merely to exist but to live. And it is for the Welfare State to build the bridge which will enable the citizen to cross over from a state of degrading existence to a state of life which is ennobling and purposeful.

In removing the inequality of wealth and in insisting upon certain standards being maintained by employers and industrialists the State is, undoubtedly in a sense, interfering with the liberty of the individual. In the days of laissez-faire this liberty was elevated to such a high pedestal that in its sacred name workers were sweated and starved and the State looked on while the poor had the freedom to remain poor and the rich had the freedom to become richer. Liberty has no meaning unless it is a monument erected on the edifice of equality. To vary the metaphor, it is only in the setting of equality that true liberty can ever be enjoyed. And the real function of the Welfare State is to make possible the enjoyment by the citizen of real freedom.

But the difficulty arises when the State launches upon measures of social reform. The distinction between social good and individual morality must always be borne in mind. Social good is a relative term and it is relative to time and place. What may not be a social good at a particular time and in a particular place may be so at a different time and in a different place. Social good consists in satisfaction of demands and attention must be paid to the nature and intensity of the demands and also to the sacrifice of other interests. There are certain social matters where the State must be in advance of public opinion—it cannot wait for public opinion before legislating. In other matters public opinion must be in advance of the State and the State must satisfy public opinion by putting social measures upon the statute book.

Proper timing is essential in all social legislation and it is also a question of priorities. The State cannot undertake all social legislation at the same time—the funds at its disposal are limited and they have to be allocated to various head in the best interest of the community. Our own Constitution contains an almost complete and exhaustive list in Part IV entitled Directive Principles of State Policy of what a Welfare State should do. But this Part does not lay down in what priority these various principles should be given effect to. The paramount duty of the State is to determine what are the immediate needs of the people and satisfy those in preference to others which may be less pressing and which may bring in a lesser return of social good.

One aspect of social legislation which is apt to be overlooked is that it should be capable of being enforced. May desirable ends cannot be achieved by legal compulsion. If a fairly influential section of the community does not acquiesce in the law, the law does not merely become a dead letter but it engenders a dangerous frame of mind in the community, a disrespect for law in general and a desire to break an obnoxious law without bringing upon itself popular opprobrium. A law can always be attempted to be enforced by the coercive agency of the State. But there always is a natural and practical limit to the sovereignty of the State—and that limit is the failure to get the acquiescence of the community as a whole to the law that has been passed. Social legislation which produces "the spy, the sneak and the informer" ultimately does more harm than good.

There is one danger that the Welfare State must guard against—a sense of complacency and lock of initiative that may be instilled in the people by their relying upon the State to do everything for them and to get them out of every difficulty. In India particularly this tendency is very strong. In the old Indian States where there was a ruler he was looked upon as the father of the people. Now that we have a democratic Government—the Government is invested with the same parental qualities. If anything goes wrong Government is to be blamed and if anything is to be done Government is to do it. It is therefore necessary to emphasizes even in a Welfare State the desirability of having voluntary organisation doing welfare work. The present system of Government tends to over-centralisation. Except at the time of elections the ordinary man has no part in the Government of his country. He is too remote from the administrative machine and he accepts the orders of Government in the same spirit as he would accept the firmans of an absolute ruler. The main task of democracy therefore is to associate as far as possible and as much as possible the people with the Government. It is only then that the expression Government by the people comes to acquire some significance. What we need therefore is decentralisation in welfare work—setting up of autonomous bodies in various localities to carry out work which can best be done in its own local setting and in which the people of the locality can co-operate.

The function of the Welfare State in the realm of education raises an important question. Education is as great a necessity for the people as bread and it is as much the duty of the State to see that the facilities are provided for education as it is to see that every citizen obtains the bare necessities of life. It is no longer open to a parent to say that he will deny his child the benefits of education and keep him in intellectual darkness. The State can and does exercise compulsion against the parent and rightly insists upon education being imparted to the child. But has the State the right to determine what is the nature of the education that the child shall receive? To concede this right to the State is to undermine the very basis of the liberty of the mind. By controlling education the State can indoctrinate the mind of the child, can instill into him a particular ideology and can regiment him into a particular pattern. Every Totalitarian State—whether it be Hitler's Germany or Lenin's Russia—builds up its strength by capturing the minds of the youth. Whatever else may be free, idea is not free. The critical faculty is dulled and deadened by the State alone being in charge of the mind of the child and the State alone deciding what should be put into that mind and what should be excluded from it. It is precisely because of this that the Declaration of Human Rights lays down that education of the child is the *prior* concern of the parent. The parent must give education to the child, but it is he and not the State which must determine what the nature of the education will be. Therefore, while it is the duty of the State to provide facilities for education, and for that purpose to set up educational institutions of its own, it should not frown upon parallel educational institutions set up by private agencies. The more experimentation there is in education the richer and more varied will be the culture of the people.

As Bertrand Russell has pointed out we cannot be content merely to be alive, rather than dead. We should wish to live happily, vigorously and creatively. And the function of the Welfare State is to provide a part of the necessary conditions. But he sounds a note of warning that the State should not in the pursuit of security stifle the largely unregulated impulses which give life its savour and its value.

There is a feeling that because the modern State is a Welfare State the question of the liberty of the individual has lost much of its importance. It is said that the power of the State is now used not for the aggrandizement of any individual or individuals but for the good of the society as a whole. And if the result of social legislation is the curtailment of individual liberty, the individual must be prepared to make this sacrifice. This is a sound argument so long as the distinction between social good and morality is constantly borne in mind. What Mill said long also in his *Liberty* is equally true today if not more so. "To extend the bounds of what may be called moral police until it encroaches on the most unquestionably legitimate liberty of the individual is one of the most universal of human propensities."

Allen in his *Democracy and the Individual* points out the disastrous consequences of the State exceeding the reasonable controls of personal liberty.

"Go beyond the reasonable controls of personal liberty, and the reaction of excess, depredation and disrepute of law are truly appalling. There is a savage part of man which when under the censorship of decent social behaviour can hold itself in check, but when caged and whipped becomes a roaring beast. A little too much law, and you turn the moderate drinker into a dipsomaniac, the agnostic into a blasphemer, the enlightened employer into a Gradgrind and a flirt into a prostitute." These words should be inscribed at the entrance of every legislative chamber to warn the enthusiastic legislators who are in a hurry to change human nature and improve individual morality.

There is one final and rather important aspect of the subject with which I must deal before I finish. What part are the Judges called upon to play in the building up of a Welfare State, in giving effect to social legislation and in the removal of inequalities upon which our present State is based? The obvious answer would seem to be that a Judge should take no sides, should have no politics and should decide matters that come up before him without any bias and strictly according to the letter of the law. But this answer would ignore the basic facts of human nature, and even a Judge, however judicial he may want to be, is not quite free from the taint of human nature.

All social legislation, to a very large extent, must operate as restraints upon the various freedoms guaranteed to the citizens under our Constitution. And social legislation can only be upheld by the Courts provided the Judge considers the restraint as reasonable. What yard-stick is the Judge going to employ in order to decide the reasonableness of the restraint upon individual freedom? It is here that the Judge's training, background and political and social leanings assume the greatest importance. Holmes used to say that he could decide a case either way on mere general propositions of law. What ultimately decide the case in a particular way was "the inarticulate major premise", the intellectual bias of the Judge. "In the long run there is no guarantee of justice except the personality of the Judge", says Ehritch as quoted by Cardozo in *The Nature of the Judicial Process.*

At one time a Judge in interpreting a statute had only to consider the mischief that was aimed at and the remedy prescribed by the legislature. The canon of judicial interpretation was simple. Today the Judge has to consider the social or economic policy of the State and to consider the law in the light of this policy. To quote the classic phrase of Holmes, the Judge has to be conscious of "the felt necessities of the times". It is absurd to suggest that the Judge must sit on the bench ignoring the social and economic needs of the people and of the desire on the part of the Legislature to satisfy these needs. That is a standards of judicial detachment which is both unattainable and in my opinion entirely undesirable. In my opinion the duty of the Judge is to help the Legislature to satisfy the felt necessities of the times. He should not set himself up as a brake against social progress—he should not justify the criticism one often hear that the judiciary in India is a third chamber which exercises the power of the veto over legislation passed by the elected representatives of the people. While resisting unjustifiable encroachments of the executive upon freedom of the individual, the Judge should not forget that he is also a citizen of the country as interested as any one else in the great social and economic adventure upon which we are launched—and that it is not enough that he should do legal justice which he must; but he must also try and do social and economic justice if he can without hurt to his judicial conscience.

9

Sovereignty and Pluralists

Pluralist Criticism of Monistic Sovereignty. The monistic or traditional theory of sovereignty came in for scathing criticism at the hands of Harold Laski, J. Neville Figgis, Ernest Barker, G.D.H. Cole, A. D Lindsay, Miss M.P. Follet, R.M. MacIver and other pluralists. Pluralists say that the traditional, legal or monistic sovereignty which emerged when European countries were plagued by disorder and strife in the feudal structure and when there was struggle between the church and the state, lost its relevance in modern times, when the importance of national welfare came to be fully realised. The legal theory of sovereignty is based on power and not on service, and hence it does not fit in a world where the emphasis is on welfare and service.

Different Angles of Pluralists. Pluralism has been explained through different angles by philosophical writers, jurists like Leon Duguit, guild socialists like G. D. H. Cole and sociologists. R. N. Gilchrist says on page 104 of *Principles of Political Science* (1961): "Not an unusual feature of pluralist criticisms of sovereignty is that the individual writers wish to lay stress on some particular type of autonomous organisation or support some special type of social organisation such as socialism."

THE THEORY OF PLURALISTS

Need of State without Sovereignty The State like other associations is essential for the life of the individual. Hence it should continue to serve human beings; but it should be deprived of its sovereignty. The state should only have the power to co-ordinate and adjust the activities of various associations. R.G.

Gettell says: 'The pluralists deny that the state is a unique organisation; they hold that other associations are equally important and natural; they argue that such associations for their purpose are as sovereign as the state is for its purpose. They emphasize the inability of the state to enforce its will in practice against the opposition of certain groups within it." The role of the state should be distributive and not collective. Associations, which are parts of the state, are as real as the whole, and therefore the state should not be given supreme power to dominate over them.

State should Share Sovereignty with Associations. Pluralists are opposed to the monistic principle that supreme power is to be located in the state alone. The state cannot be regarded as "all-inclusive, all-mighty, or all-comprehensive." F.W. Coker say on page 497 in *Recent Political Thought* (1966): "Man's social nature, they maintain, finds expression in numerous groupings, pursuing various ends—religious, social, economic professional, political; no one of the groups is superior, morally or practically, to the others." All groups or associations, through which man realizes his political, social, economic and other aspirations are of equal importance to the individual, and it is wrong for the State to claim absolutism and omnipotence. Associations have a will of their own, and they need not depend on the state for their existence and continuation. Society is a huge network of groups and associations through which the individual expresses himself. Many associations arose in a natural and spontaneous manner to meet the needs of the individual. They are not created by the state and do not depend upon the state for their progress. J.N. Figgis significantly says: "The state did not create the family nor did it create the churches, nor even in any real sense can it be said to have created the club or trade unions, nor in the Middle Ages, the guild or the religious order, hardly even the universities or the colleges within the universities; they have all arisen out of the natural associative instincts of mankind......" The definition of the pluralist state is given by Hsiao on page 1 in *Political Pluralism*: "The pluralistic state is simply a state in which there exists no single source of authority—it is divisible into part and should be divided."

Vital Role of Medieval Guilds. During the middle ages, when there was the feudal state and central governments all over Europe were weak, the smooth and successful functioning of guilds, particularly in rich towns and cities, revealed the great importance of social groups or associations in serving the individual and meeting his needs.

Origin of Pluralist Thought. Otto von Gierke (1844-1921) in Germany and F.W. Maitland in England were pioneers in pluralist thinking. They espoused the cause of groups and associations, which according to them had a consciousness and will of their own, and that each of the groups having a personality of its own made a contribution to the framing of laws. The origin of pluralist thought can be seen in the writings of Gierke. Three causes explain the background of pluralist thought: (1) Originally the concept of the police state prevailed, and the state was regarded as an instrument of domination. But this concept had to yield place to the new concept of the welfare state. This made the state an agency of service and weakened the sovereignty of state in the internal sphere. (2) Statesmen realised that for the good of mankind and international peace there should be international co-operation and understanding. This tended to weaken sovereignty in the external sphere. States, which had to depend more and more on one another, had to dilute to a little extent at least their external sovereignty. (3) The increasing importance of various social groups and associations to cater to the needs of the individual came to be realised. Many of these associations grew independently without state help and could stand on their own feet. Pluralists pleaded on behalf of these associations for greater autonomy.

Need of Autonomy and Freedom for Associations. Each association, which has a specified field of functioning and serving the needs of society, should have the maximum scope for its functional freedom and autonomy. Freedom for associations to function efficiently and effectively is of different types: social, cultural, educational, artistic, economic and religious. Figgis speaks of various fields in which different social groups can function usefully. He cites the example of the church, whose functions and services were of paramount importance to society in the middle ages. Other writers like Paul Boncour and Emile Durkheim also thought along similar lines. In order to enable these groups to work smoothly and with full autonomy, the state should not be given indivisible sovereignty and should not be allowed to assert its omnipotence.

State of Co-ordinate Activities of Associations with Superior Legal Status. Though the pluralists are against giving indivisible sovereignty of the state, they are prepared to concede to the state a superior legal status, which is required to bring about a co-ordination in the activities of various associations.

Different Opinions of Pluralists. The opinions of all pluralists are not the same; some believe that the state is *unus inter pares,* that is, one among equals, while others regard it as *primus inter pares,* the first among equals.

Relentless Attack on Monistic Sovereignty by Laski. As a pluralist, H.J. Laski's attack on the monist theory of sovereignty is relentless and vehement. He says that the state should be shorn off its absolute sovereignty and lowered from its superior status to a co-ordinate status with other associations. Laski, who wants associations to be given complete autonomy, is confident that a time will come, when the concept of absolute sovereignty will be discredited and rejected like the Divine Right Theory of Kings. Further, Laski goes to be extent of saying that the legal theory of sovereignty cannot the made valid for political philosophy, and it would be good, if the whole concept of sovereignty is surrendered. Krabbe, who is more vehement than Laski in criticizing monism, says that "the notion of sovereignty must be expunged from political theory."

Laski's views on sovereignty can be summarised as follows:

1. Sovereignty is not monistic, but pluralistic. It can be divided among the state and various associations.

2. Sovereignty is not absolute and unrestrained, but constitutional, limited and responsible.

3. The state is one of the many associations, which play an important part in social life. It cannot lay claim to a supreme position. It can only be *primus inter pares,* that is, first among equals.

4. Associations must be completely free and autonomous so that they can play a meaningful part in social life.

5. Society is federal, and therefore authority has to be federal and not unitary.

6. The state as the first among equals can act only as a coordinating authority among associations.

7. The coercive power of the state should be reduced. The decrees of the state should be directive rather than dominating.

Cole calls for Co-Sovereign Groups of Consumers and Producers. G.D.H. Cole, another staunch advocate of pluralism, calls for the formation of consumers' groups and producer's groups for which he wants co-sovereign status to be given. Further he says that national producers' guild should be given legislative authority besides administrative power. Here Cole's suggestion is sweeping and revolutionary, as this would put guilds on a par with the state. He also pleads for the formation of consumer's parliament and producers' parliament.

MacIver's Onslaughts on Absolute Sovereignty. Robert M. MacIver, who condemns the legal concept of sovereignty as false and regards the state as one of the many associations, makes bitter attacks on monistic sovereignty. He says that like the state the various associations work for the welfare of the people and the only power the state should have is to bring about co-ordination and unity in the activities of the various associations. The concept of absolute sovereignty should be given up as "dangerously false".

Evaluation of Pluralist Ideas

The political thought of pluralist rebels on sovereignty needs close scrutiny. A brief reference to the merits and drawbacks is made here.

Merits

There is much truth in what pluralists say. The following are the merits of pluralist thought on sovereignty:

1. *Undue glorification of State.* Pluralists deserve credit for exposing the undue glorification of the state and the exaggerated importance given to the legal and monistic view of sovereignty. Their protest against the over-interference of the state is timely. They emphasizes that several associations render various types of services to the individual, and therefore, it would be unfair to give undue importance to the state and sidetrack the significant role of associations. J.N. Figgis complains that the state unnecessarily interferes in the activities of the church, trade union and other associations, though the state has not created them. It is only when the state sovereignty is removed, these associations can function better in complete freedom and serve the individual and the community in a better manner.

2. *State Not All-Inclusive and Omnipotent.* The pluralists wish to recognize the importance of the state, but they refuse to concede that the state is everything, that is all-inclusive, omnipotent and absolutely supreme. They wish to fully bring out the useful part played by various associations, whose importance has been ignored by the protagonists of the monistic theory of sovereignty. Pluralists argue that a too narrow and legal view of sovereignty is harmful to the interests of the people. If the wishes of the people are to be realised, the state should give proper representation in the legislature, to various groups and associations.

3. *Life Rendered Rich and Colourful by Associations.* The numerous groups and associations give much scope to people to realize their aims and aspirations and develop their personality. They render several services which are beyond the scope of the state activity. Undoubtedly associations make life rich and colourful.

4. *Need of Decentralisation of Power.* The greatest merit of pluralists is the case that they make out for decentralizing

power and giving as much autonomy as passible to associations.

Drawbacks

Pluralism, which has serious drawbacks, is untenable and has to be rejected. The infirmities from which it suffers may be summarised as follows:

1. *More Destructive than Constructive.* Pluralists enthusiastically seek to destroy more than what they are capable of constructing, and their doctrine of revolt against monism in the ultimate analysis falls flat. Pluralist philosophy is arm-chair philosophy, which will miserably fail in the practical field. Theoretically, pluralist principles may appear sound or even grandiose, but a scrutiny of their ideas will reveal the great dangers to which society will be exposed, if pluralism is actually implemented, and associations are given a co-ordinate position with the state. J.W. Garner says on page 159 in *Political Science and Government*: "The existence of several supreme will each equally capable of issuing commands and exacting obedience would obviously result in conflicts and an ultimate paralysis of state.

2. *No Pluralism without Monistic Sovereignty.* A close examination of pluralism shows that pluralism cannot survive without monistic sovereignty, which it seeks to annihilate. It has to be emphasised that associations, whose cause the pluralists are championing cannot exist without the sovereignty of the state. Each association will function as it likes disregarding the interests of other associations, and in the absence of a coercive authority many associations will clash with one another. Without a sovereign authority, a state will present a dismal picture of complete chaos and anarchy. It seems pluralists have not exercised adequate seriousness and caution while putting forward their principle of division or destruction of sovereignty. Undoubtedly pluralism is hollow and cannot go beyond the frontier of theory into the domain of realities. J.D. Mabbott says on page 124 in *The State and the Citizen* "Every association in its corporate

capacity must keep the peace, be subject to criminal law, submit disputes to the civil, law, obey such regulations as are necessary for the achievement of those aims which only the state can secure, and contribute to the taxation which makes all the above state actions possible."

3. *Destruction of Divisible Sovereignty.* Pluralists commit the serous mistake of trying to destroy sovereignty by dividing it. Sovereignty cannot survive, if it is disintegrated. It is indeed fantastic that after depriving the state of legal supremacy and putting it on a footing of equality with other associations, pluralists desire to give it the responsibility of bringing about co-ordination and adjustment in the activities of associations. It is difficult to understand how the state can be asked to shoulder the responsibility of bringing about coordinating and adjusting the activities of associations without arming it with supreme power to order, coerce and punish individuals and associations defying it. No supervision of the activities of associations is possible without indivisible sovereignty. If the state is on a par with associations, the former cannot order the latter. The very fact that the state is not superior to associations will embolden associations to challenge state authority and bring the state into contempt when it issues orders without having sovereignty to enforce them.

4. *Possibility of Disintegration of State.* Pluralist thought creates the distinct possibility of the disintegration of the state. The picture of a state dominated by pluralist ideas is most confusing. The pluralist assurance that the various associations would run on parallel lines, and that there would be no overlapping of functions or conflicting claims will deceive nobody. Even now, when sovereignty is monistic, states find it difficult to maintain peace and order owing to the activities of refractory elements. Then, what would be the conditions in such state if sovereignty is divisible and a hundred associations are given co-sovereign status, one can easily imagine. If the state is not armed with indivisible sovereignty the members of one or more associations may

withdraw their membership of state. This will ultimately result in bringing about the complete disintegration of the state. R.N. Gilchrist says on page 106 in *Principles of Political Science* (1961): "if a large trade union were to have powers independent of the state, a similar claim could be put forward for a village debating society, or perhaps even for a criminal organisation. Further, pluralism is a doctrine of disruption and revolution, for it implies that international groups may have powers superior to those of national states."

5. *Danger of State Despotism Generally Not True.* It cannot be denied that there are states like Nazi Germany, Fascist Italy and Communist Russia, where state despotism is true. But taking into consideration the whole world we have to conclude that the pluralists give a totally misleading picture, when they say that state sovereignty leads to despotism. A study of the actual working of constitutions show that except in states run on the basis of totalitarian principles or Hegelian ideas, individuals and associations are given adequate rights. In democratic countries the dignity of human personality is upheld, and subject to the sovereignty of the state the individual enjoys fundamental rights to develop his personality. If at any time, these rights are abridged, say during extraordinary times or national emergency, it is all in the best interests of the individual and social groups. The pluralist presumption of the dangers of sovereignty has no basis; it has a place only in pluralist imagination.

6. *Unrealistic and Confusing Approach.* The approach of pluralists is unrealistic and impractical. They do not know how exactly their principles are to be put into practice when the state is deprived of its sovereignty. The precise position of the state and state-association relations are not unambiguously and clearly defined. There is much confused thinking on their part, and sometimes, perhaps unwittingly, pluralists admit the supreme power of the state. Eddy Asirvatham quoting Miss M.P. Follett, a pluralist, says on page 288 in *Political Theory* (1957): "The state is a unifying

agency. My citizenship is something bigger than my membership in the vocational group......The true state must gather up every interest within itself." Though the pluralists do not want the associations to be quite independent of the state they are not prepared to give the state a sovereign status. They wish to have the cake and eat it also. The pluralist argument, which is a contradiction in terms tries to reconcile two irreconcilable principles: complete freedom or autonomy for associations and coordinating function for state. "While most pluralists have sought to drive sovereignty out of the front door of their new society, they quietly smuggle it again through the back door, more or less disguised, but nevertheless a sovereignty."

SETBACK FOR PLURALISM

Factors Unfavourable to Pluralism. In recent times, several factors have been unfavourable to pluralism, which has suffered a serous setback. The duties and responsibility of state all over the world have increased enormously owing to the acceptance of the concept of the welfare state. Planning on a large scale is done in every state for bettering the lot of the masses of people. Planning compels states to shoulder very heavy burdens and they have to be armed with wide controlling and regulating powers. In the new circumstances in every state there is very little scope for the free play of pluralism.

Shift in Stand of Pluralists. Pluralists themselves have realised that times have changed and it will not be possible for them to stick to their rigid principles and therefore revision of their attitude towards monism has become obligatory. Leslie Lipson says on page 427 in *The Great Issues of Politics* (1973): "Because a society in rapid flux requires a central focus for organisation, the latter-day advocates of pluralism have been placed on the defensive and forced into retreat. Some like G.D.H. Cole, who was a pluralist in the days when he argued for guild socialism, or Harold J. Laski, who wrote from a pluralist standpoint until the depression of the 1930's reversed their positions and accepted the logic of monism. Others have maintained their view, but with increasing difficulty."

Regarding the shifting of their stand F.W. Coker says on page 51 in *Recent Political Thought* (1966): "Miss Follett criticizes the pluralists' conception of the state as "competing" for citizen's loyalty; and she explains so fully the state's unifying functions, and its direct contract with individuals, that she is hardly to be closed properly among the pluralists."

Conclusion. The following conclusions can be drawn about pluralists.

1. Pluralists have done well in aptly upholding the importance of associations, for which they claim autonomy.

2. However, as regards the relationship between the state and associations, they have betrayed confused thinking.

3. They attack and undermine the very basis of the state by dividing and breaking sovereignty.

4. They indirectly admit the need of sovereign state, which can coerce all individuals and associations into submission for maintaining peace and order and for promoting the happiness and welfare of the people.

5. It is true that pluralists begin their argument by asking for the abolition of sovereignty but end in admitting the need of sovereignty. This, however does not mean that the pluralist thought is totally meaningless and worthless. As stated above, pluralism does have merits. The greatest merit is to emphasise that sovereignty should not be exercised in too narrowly political or legal manner. It has to represent and serve the different social purposes—cultural, social, economic and religious.

Book for Further Study

1. Agarwal Bhushan and Bhagwan, *Principles of Political Science*—1971, Ramchand & Co., Delhi.

2. Asirvatham, Eddy, *Political Theory*—1957.

3. Coker, F.W., *Recent Political Thought*—1957, The World Press, Calcutta.

4. Figgis, J.N., *Churches in the Modern State.*

5. Finer, Herman, *The Theory and Practice of Modern Government*—1961, Asia Publishing House, Bombay.

6. Follett, M.P., *The New State.*

7. Garner, J.W., *Political Science and Government*—1955, The World Press, Calcutta.

8. Gilchrist, R.N., *Principles of Political Science*—1961, Orient Longman.

9. Hsiao, Kung Chun, *Political Pluralism*—1927, Harcourt Brace.

10. Laski, H. J., *A Grammar of Politics*—1957.

11. Laski, H. J., *The Problem of Sovereignty.*

12. Lipson, Leslie, *The Great Issues of Politics*—1967, Jaico, Bombay.

13. Mabbott, P. J., *The State and the Citizen*—1948, Hutchinson,.

14. MacIver, R. M., *The Modern State.*

15. Ray and Battacharya, *Political Theory*—1962, The World Press, Calcutta.

16. Ray, Dasgupta and Ray, *Principles of Political Science*—1963, Macmillan.

17. Ward P.W., *Sovereignty*—1928, George Routledge.

10

Anarchism

Extreme Type of Communism. Anarchism is one of the theories dealing with the sphere of the state activity. It is an extreme theory challenging the very existence of the state and disparaging all forms of authority. There have been anarchists in countries like Britain, the USA and France; but it was in Russia, where communists, nihilists and terrorists rose that anarchist thought found a favourable climate for development. Anarchism may be regarded as an extreme type of communism.

Hoary Beginning. Some form of anarchist thought prevailed in ancient Greece among the Stoics and the Cynics. In the middle ages in Europe several poets and philosophers strongly expressed themselves against state authority. J. H. Hallowell says on page 476 in *Main Currents in Modern Political Thought:* "Anarchism has a long intellectual lineage extending to the earliest beginning of Western political thought, but it acquired a special point of view in the nineteenth century that puts many anarchists in the camp of socialists."

Need of Total Abolition of State. Anarchist philosophy, which emerged in the 19th century, went to the extreme end of saying that the state should be abolished altogether. Its is a revolutionary doctrine that all government restraints should be removed for realizing the ideal milieu for social and political freedom. Hence it is diametrically opposed to the idealist philosophy. While the idealists on the one hand lay emphasis on the importance of the state, with the help of which alone the individual can develop his personality, anarchists on the other hand regard the state as an evil coming in the way on the individuals' development. In ancient Greece, Aristotle said with great emphasis that the state in indispensable for human beings; but in modern times anarchists said with equal emphasis that the state should be scrapped unceremoniously. "The essential features of anarchism are the abolition of all constituted authority and the complete emancipation of the individual from every form of control, political, social or religious. Oscar Jaszi defines it as an attempt to establish justice (that is, equality and reciprocity) in all human relations by the complete elimination of the state (or by the greatest possible minimisation of its activity), and its replacement by an entirely free and spontaneous co-operation among individuals, groups, regions and nations." (See J.S. Roucek and Others, *Introduction to Political Science*—(1954, page 98.) *Webster's Unified Dictionary and Encyclopedia* says that anarchism is a "political theory advocating the abolition of the state and all central law, substitution of free will agreements between local and occupational groups. Based on the concept of Zeno (4th century B.C.) the idea of anarchism has appealed to many thinkers such as Thoreau, who have believed in the fullest possible individual freedom." *The Random House Dictionary of the English Language* says that anarchism is "a doctrine urging the abolition of government or governmental restraint as the indispensable condition for full social and political liberty."

Against Government by Coercion. E.M. Burns who says that basically anarchism is against *government based on force* observes on *Ideas in Conflict* (1960): "Correctly defined, anarchism means opposition to government based upon force. No anarchist with pretensions to philosophical understanding has ever proposed to dispense entirely with government. He condemns the state conceived as an agency of coercion with armies, jails and police, but he regards government as at least potentially a beneficent institution."

Opposition to Private Property and Hostility to Religious Authority. F.W. Coker mentions on *Recent Political Thought* (1957) that anarchism is against the state, private property and all kinds of religious control. "Anarchism is the doctrine that political authority, in any of its forms, is unnecessary and undesirable. In recent anarchism, theoretical opposition to the state has usually been associated with opposition to the institution of private property and also with hostility to organised religious authority." On page 49 in *Roads to Freedom* Indian Edition, Allahabad, 1946), Bertrand Russell says that anarchism is "the theory which is opposed to every kind of government. It is opposed to the state as the embodiment of the force employed in the government of the community. Such government as anarchism can tolerate must be free government, not merely in the sense that it is that of a majority, but in the sense that it is assented to by all. Anarchists objects to such institutions as the police, and the criminal law by means of which the will of one part of the community is enforced upon another part."

Natural Impulse of Human Beings to Co-operate. Anarchists lay great emphasis on the natural impulse among human beings to co-operate. They firmly believe that human nature is essentially good. They say that established artificial authorities like the state and the church prevent human beings from being naturally good and co-operating in a spontaneous way. The gist of an anarchist thought is that human beings can live better without a government than with it. A government is not all at necessary; in fact it is a positive evil, which should be completely dispense with. W.F. Willoughby says on page 47 in *The Government of Modern States* (1936): "The anarchist school represents the extreme school of individual rights. To its adherents, liberty, individual liberty is the important thing. All coercion or compulsion such as implicit in government is inherently and fundamentally wrong and not to be justified."

Importance of Natural Law and Voluntary Agreements. The anarchist appeals from the state law to what he deems to be a higher law, the natural law. The needs of the individual and society can be met by voluntary agreements among territorial and professional groups. Anarchists speak in terms of free agreements, and are against the individuals' submission to the state, whose authority is based on force and not on human volition.

Supreme Place Given to Liberty. Liberty is given the highest place in anarchist thought. Bakunin says "The liberty of man consists solely in this that he obeys the laws of nature, because he has himself recognised them as such, and not because they have been imposed upon him externally by any foreign will whatsoever, human or divine, collective or individual."

All Anarchists Anti-Authoritarian. All anarchist leaders agree on the common points that state authority is harmful to the individual and should be done away with.

Two Schools of Anarchists. All anarchists leaders do not fully agree with one another, but all of them are anti-authoritarian. E.M. Burns says that modern anarchists fall into two schools: (1) those like William Godwin who are economic individuals, and (2) those like Bakunin who are collectivists and revolutionists.

Godwin and Proudhon mixed anarchism with individualism, whereas Bakunin, Kropotkin and others combined anarchism with collectivism.

Basic Principles of Anarchism

We may briefly refer to the basic principles of anarchism.

1. *State Upholds Inequality and Injustice.* Anarchists say that the state is an unmixed evil against which people should fight and get it abolished. State authority serves no rational purpose and is unnecessary, and undesirable; it is a hindrance in the way of society, and it upholds a system, which makes society miserable. The state, which upholds inequality and injustice, gives full scope for all kinds of evils. People, who were originally good by nature, become bad under state authority. They lose their innocence and become unhappy. The state brings about degeneration in people, makes people criminals, and then exercises its authority to punish them in different ways. Law, the instrument of the state, is an evil, and people obey it, as they are compelled to do so. Bakunin says in *God and the State:* "The state is authority; it is force; it is the ostentation and infatuation of force. It does not

insinuate itself; it does not seek to convert....Even when it commands what is good, it hinders and spoils it, just because it commands and because even command provokes and excites the legitimate revolt of liberty; and because the good, from the moment that it is commanded, becomes evil from the point of view of true morality..."

2. *Need of Destroying Capitalism and Private Property.* Anarchism condemns the institution of private property, which flourishes under capitalism. Capitalism has produced evils like the degradation of those who work, the enjoyment of the few who exploit others without doing any work, poverty and suffering to millions, extravagance and ostentation of the rich, colossal waste in society, immorality and unemployment. Therefore capitalism should be destroyed along with the state. Kropotkin relentlessly criticizes private property which leads to "want and misery, millions unemployed, children of retarded growth, constant debts for the farmers; among the wealthy few—prodigality, ostentation, idleness leading to the pursuit of the coarsest pleasures, debasing the press, and inciting war."

3. *Church another Great Evil.* The church, the friend and collaborator of capitalists and of those in authority in the state misleads the poor and the needy, who are called upon to reconcile their lot with a system, which brings about their suffering sorrow and degradation. Religion thus is force of evil, and an obstacle to social progress. Hence the authority of the church also should be over-thrown. Kropotkin says that religion is a primitive myth and a crude attempt of explaining the working of nature; "it is an ethical system which, through its appeals to the ignorance and superstitions of the masses, cultivates among them a tolerance of the injustices they suffer under the existing political and economic arrangements."

4. *Anarchist Society Based on Decentralisation, Fraternity and Freedom.* State authority is based on compulsion, fear, egoism and exclusion. In the evil conditions created by the

state, good people turn bad and suffer. The state is therefore a curse. The remedy lies in the establishment of anarchist society, which is based on fraternity, freedom, union and love. Anarchists put great faith in the worth of the individual, who they think will give his best when he is emancipated from state coercion and when he is able to function freely as a member of a voluntary organisation. "A complex interweaving of associations with order everywhere and compulsions nowhere forms the stuff of which an anarchist society will be made. For anarchy, as Lowes Dickinson's speaker puts it "is not the absence of order; it is the absence of force." (See C.E.M. Joad, *Modern Political Theory*). The state should be abolished to make room for voluntary associations functioning on a co-operative basis. Anarchist society is stateless and classless, and it is free from the evils of competition and conflict. The soul of anarchism is decentralisation.

5. *Criticism of Representative Institutions*. Anarchists criticize even democracy and representative institutions, which they say function very badly. They have no faith in representative bodies, which are in charge of persons who know very little and who do everything badly. Anarchists say that it is not possible for a person (who is a member of the legislature) to represent other for all matters.

Methods of Anarchist

Evolutionary and Revolutionary Anarchism. There are two forms of anarchism: Evolutionary and Revolutionary. Anarchists like Tolstoy desire to employ evolutionary and peaceful methods. They believe in ends and good means too and they intend to establish an anarchist society through love and persuasion. But there are anarchists, who are wedded to revolutionary ideas and violence. They think that violent and distructive methods should be employed to establish anarchist society. They firmly believe that non-violent and persuasive methods are useless in dealing with those who uphold the state, the church, capitalism and private property. Levine points out on *Syndicaliasm in France:* "The anarchists saw only one way of bringing about the emancipation of the working class: namely, to organize groups, and at an opportune moment to raise the people in revolt against the state and the propertied classes; then destroy the state, expropriate the capitalist class and reorganize society on communist and federalist principles. This was the social revolution they preached." Kropotkin says that anarchist society can be established by Acts of Parliament, but by taking possession of granaries, cloth shops and dwelling houses. He believes in a total and violent war far the emancipation of society.

Violent and Destructive Tactics of Anarchists Communists and Syndicalists. Like nihilists, communists and syndicalists anarchists employ violent and destructive tactics. Nihilists, who were against all existing institutions, developed the cult of violence and were behind many activities of violence, outrage and murder. They believed that the end justified the means, fair or foul. Nihilists in Czarist Russia were the authors of several atrocious deeds like poisoning, shooting and bomb-throwing.

Like communists, anarchists spread bitterness, hatred, fanaticism, and class prejudice. Communists, unlike anarchists, desire to make use of state authority to introduce revolutionary socialism; but in the long run, like anarchists, they want the state to wither away.

Similarly, comparison can be drawn between syndicalism and anarchism. Syndicalists wish to employ violence to get rid of the state to establish a federation of workers' associations.

Syndicalism, communism and anarchism are against peaceful and evolutionary methods, and are the deadliest enemies of capitalism. It should be noted however that there is some difference between syndicalism and anarchism. While anarchists speak for all and different kinds of interests, syndicalists speak for workers' associations only.

Anarchist Literature. Anarchist principles were propagated among the workers of Europe through a large number of magazines. Some of them could not last long owing to government action or financial difficulties. Several anarchist clubs with strange and frightening names like. "The Bomb Throwers" were established. In Russia more revolutionary type of philosophy known as nihilist was developed to wipe out traditional institutions, ideas and values.

Views of Great Anarchist Thinkers

We may briefly discuss the views of prominent anarchist thinkers like William Godwin, Thomas Hodgskin, Pierre Joseph Proudhon, Henry Thoreau, Count Tolstoy, Michael Bakunin and Prince Peter Kropotkin.

William Godwin (1755-1836)

First Modern Anarchist. It seems the first modern anarchist was William Godwin, an Englishman who was Shelley's father-in-law. He expressed his extraordinary views in his book: *An Enquiry Concerning Political Justice and its Influence on General Welfare and Happiness.*

State Upholding Injustice. Godwin say that the state upholds injustice inequity with the help of its authority. This prevents the individual from acting in a just and reasonable way. The individual is suppressed, and there is no scope for his free development and self-expression.

Evils of Government and Property. Government is an evil, as it is based on violence; and property is an evil, as it creates vanity and depravity among the propertied people, and servility and immorality among the poor. When man is born, he is neither virtuous nor vicious. It is the environment that makes him good or bad. Evils arose in society owning to government and property, which should be abolished.

Word Anarchism not Used. It is significant to not that Godwin did not employ the term Anarchism in his books, and technically speaking, it may not be quite correct to regard his philosophy as fully anarchist.

Thomas Hodgskin (1787-1860)

Utopian Anarchist. F.W. Coker regards Thomas Hodgskin,

an Englishman who lived in the post-Napoleonic war, as a utopian anarchist. The individualistic doctrine of Adam Smith had a profound impact on his mind. He says that there is no need for law and planning, as man is a part of the universe, which "is regulated by permanent and invariable laws." He says that human beings have a natural property right of securing all the fruit of their labour, and nature stands as a guarantee to this right.

Pierre Joseph Proudhon (1809-65)

Father of Anarchism. Pierre Joseph Proudhon, who championed the cause of liberty which he regarded as the mother of order, condemned the government of man by man. Expressing himself strongly against government, he said: "I am, in the full sense of the word, an Anarchist." Proudhon, who was the first person to regard himself as an anarchist and use the term anarchy in the technical sense is regarded as the Father of Anarchism.

Government Stands for Oppression and Injustice. Proudhon says that government is synonymous with oppression and it upholds injustice. Therefore it is better to get rid of government, the instrument of oppression and injustice. He regards government as "the scourage of God."

Need of Voluntary Groups. The state is against reason, justice and understanding. Instead of having the state, voluntary groups should be formed and they should engage themselves in productive enterprise. State authority should make way to the rise of mutualism in voluntary associations.

Bank of People to Eliminate Private Capital. Proudhon advocated the establishment of a Bank of the People, which would eliminate all private capital ultimately. The free credit supplied by the Bank of the People to various voluntary associations would make it possible to have positive and meaningful anarchy. Cooperative banking alone would enable people to get rid of the evil of private capital.

Property as Theft Promoting Injustice. Proudhon condemned private property as theft and advocated equal property rights for all. It is incorrect to think that he was completely opposed to the institution of private property. What he exposed and attacked was the system of property distribution existing under capitalism, which upheld and nursed social injustice. There is nothing wrong, if individuals own property. But it should be limited and should not become an instrument of exploitation and suffering. Each person who should be permitted to enjoy the right of inheritance may be given three acres of land and a cow.

Society to Seek the Highest Perfection. Proudhon, who stood against authority, privileges and private property as a tool of exploitation, was in favour of forming a society seeking the highest perfection "in the union of order and anarchy." Though Proudhon regarded himself as a socialist, he was against communism, which he criticised as utopian. Karl Marx ridiculed Proudhon as a petit-bourgeois.

Henry Thoreau (1817-62)

State as Hurdle. Henry David Thoreau was an American anarchist, who strongly opposed the very existence of the state. He said that Americans would have achieved much, has the state hot acted as a hurdle.

Against Tax Payment. Thoreau did not approve of the authority of the state and was against the payment of taxes. He made non-payment of taxes as a matter of strong conviction and refused to pay taxes. It was others who paid his taxes for saving him from embarrassment and trouble. In 1846 he was given a jail sentence for his refusal to pay taxes to the state of Massachusetts.

Against Slavery. Thoreau condemned the maintenance of slaves in the state of Massachusetts as something abominable and sinful.

Against Rule of the Majority. Thoreau criticised the rule of the majority prevailing in modern state as unfair and unjust. Government exercises authority wrongly and unjustly, causing injustice and suffering to good men. Therefore men cannot have true respect for law. Thoreau emphasised that human conscience is above the law.

Inspired Mahatma Gandhi. Thoreau was in favour of offering active and passive resistance to the American government. Mahatma Gandhi (1869-1948) about 50 years later was deeply influenced by Thoreau's thought, and actually followed the principles of non-payment of taxes and of active and passive resistance to the imperialist British Government in India.

Count Tolstoy (1828-1910)

Philosophical Anarchist. We may regard Leo Tolstoy who belonged to an aristocratic Russian family as a philosophical type of anarchist. He shunned a life of luxury and sophistication and wished to lead an honest, unostentatious and simple life. Mahatma Gandhi felt the impact of his noble anarchist principles. The anarchist books of Tolstoy include *The Kingdom of God within You* and *What Shall We Do?* Tolstoy says that anarchists should disobey laws, resort to non-cooperation with state authorities, resist payment of taxes and offer passive resistance to establish an anarchist state. Such methods found favour with Mahatma Gandhi, who followed the precepts of Tolstoy, when he launched his movement for *swaraj* in India. Tolstoy read widely, and tried to put into practice whatever great philosophical and anarchist ideas he picked up from books. He condemned the state strongly without mincing words and promoted the cause of anarchism.

Synthesis of Anarchism and Christian Socialism. Tolstoy brought about a blending of anarchism and Christian socialism. This was possible, as he stood for peaceful methods and establishment of justice.

State an Evil Superstition. Tolstoy says that the state arose and exists as an evil superstition. "So-called science supports the superstition with all its power and with the utmost zeal. This superstition resembles exactly the religious one and consists in affirming that besides the duties towards an imaginary being which theologians call God and political science the state."

Criticism of State and Private Property. Tolstoy believes that private property and state are against the teachings of Jesus Christ, as the former violates the principles of charity and brotherhood, and the latter is based on coercion.

Principles of Christian Anarchism. Tolstoy's principles, which are labelled as Christian Anarchism, are governed by the ethical code of Christianity. He feels that the Christian Principle of love is conspicuous by its absence in the state. He upheld Christ's principle: "Resist not evil, but overcome evil by good." The state, which functions on the basis of force, is contrary to Christ's teaching. F.W. Coker says on page 223 in *Recent Political Thought:* "Tolstoy's doctrine has been called Christian Anarchism. He rejected many of the traditional dogmas of Christianity—particularly, the trinity, the divinity of Christ and personal immorality—but he was a thorough Christian in his ethics. He scorned the Russian Church because he believed that it had, by supporting the tyranny of the Russian state and condoning the idle and selfish lives of the Russian upper classes, forsaken entirely the teachings of Christ."

Need of Liberation from State Control. Tolstoy argued that the authority of the state prevented people from doing good and desirable work. The state compelled men to do what they did not like and prevented them from doing what they liked. Moreover people were forced to pay taxes to support the authority which stood for evil. Therefore liberation of people from state control would be beneficial to all.

Michael Bakunin (1814-76)

How Bakunin Became Anarchist. Another anarchist upholding anti-authoritarian philosophy was Count Michael Bakunin, who belonged to a distinguished noble family in Czarist Russia. He underwent military training and served as an officer in the army. It was at that time that he got opportunities to know the high-handed and despotic ways of Czarist officers. He came in contact with Proudhon, Marx and Engels, who influenced him much. He visited countries like Germany, England, France, the U.S.A. and Japan. He is regarded as the founder of scientific anarchism.

Narrowly Escaped Death. As a communist and anarchist, Bakunin criticised the Russian Government strongly. E.M. Burns observes on page 38 in *Ideas in Conflict* (1960): "Born a member of the Russian aristocracy, Bakunin dedicated his life to the cause of revolutionary anarchism, spent twelve years in prison and was twice sentenced to death. For a time he was associated with Marx...but Marx repudiated him when he realised the significance of Bakunin's belief that the state could be abolished overnight." He was condemned to death repeatedly by the Czarist regime, but was not executed. He was exited to Siberia; but here again he was lucky to effect his escape.

Establishment of Social Democratic Alliance. In 1869 Bakunin established the Social Democratic Alliance to disseminate his ideas, which were clearly anti-political, anti-national and anti-authoritarian.

Rulers and Ruled Corrupted in State. Bakunin says that the state is an evil, as it degrades and demoralizes people. The state functions with the help of force, and its activities are not based on persuasion and enlightenment. Whatever may be the garb of government, it is an evil. Even a democratic form of government is an evil, as it cannot change the nature of state. Power acts as a corrupting influence on all the rulers as well as the ruled. Therefore the state should be eliminated. Bakunin vehemently condemns the state in this book *God and the State*: "The state is not society, it is only an historical form of it, as brutal as it is abstruct. It was born historically in all countries of the marriages of violence, rapine pillage, in a world war and conquest with gods successively created by the theological fantasy of nations. It has been from its origin, and it still remains at present, the divine sanction of brutal force and triumphant inequality." He also explains the evil effects of the exercises of power in a state. "Among those who exercise power, natural sentiments of co-operation and fraternity are supplemented by traditions of prerogative, class differentiation, and sacrifice of individual welfare to the interest of the public office. Thus the state makes tyrants or egoists out of the few and servants and dependents out of the many."

God and Czar Uphold Tyranny. Bakunin vehemently criticised the church on which he proured his wrath. He complained: "Of all despotisms that of the doctrinaires or inspired religionists is the worst. They are so jealous of the glory of their God and of the triumph of their idea that they have no heart left for liberty or the dignity or even the suffering of living men, of real men." Bakunin put God on a level with the Czar of Russia, as both stood for tyranny and oppression.

Private Property used for Exploitation. Bakunin also attacked the institution of private property, which is used for exploitation. Religion and private property are the instruments with which the rich enrich themselves further and impoverish the poor further. Though Bakunin was not against an evolutionary method to realize his goal, he favoured the revolutionary method as people shall have to wait long to be liberated from the state, religion and private property, the institutions which subject men to suffering. Bakunin made a devastating comment on the institution of private property. He regards it "both the ground of existence and the consequence of the state. To millions of workers, it brings economic dependence laborious toil, ignorance and social and spiritual immobility; for the few wealthy, it provides superfluous luxury and special opportunity for physical and artistic and intellectual enjoyment." As he wanted quick action, he said: "Our task is terrible, total, inexorable and universal destruction."

Formation of Anarchist Society and World Community. In preaching a type of proletarian anarchism, Bakunin spoke not of Russia only but of the entire world. He spoke in terms of forming an anarchist society, in which there would be no distinctions of nationality, race colour and belief. Ultimately, this would lead to the abolition of state frontiers and the formation of a world community.

Prince Peter Kropotkin (1842-1921)

Dynamic Leader Fighting for Justice Through Anarchism. Kropotkin was a dynamic leader fighting for justice through anarchism. He was a Russian, who was the most distinguished among Bakunin's anarchist disciples. Like Bakunin, he belonged to a reputed noble family and had opportunities to know fully the despotic and cruel ways of the Czarist officers, when he served as a military officer. In 1872 he went to Switzerland and became a member of the International Workingmen's Association at Geneva, which he had to leave, as his views were very radical.

Participation in Nihilist Movement. For participating in the nihilist movement based on terrorism is Russia, he was arrested in 1874 and put in prison. He escaped from prison in 1876 and visited Foreign countries like England, France and Switzerland.

Author of Several, Books. Kropotkin lived in London for a long time and wrote several books like *Modern Science and Anarchism.*

Condemnation of State, Religion and Private Property. Like Bakunin, Kropotkin was against state, religion and private property. He says that there was a time, when people worked through natural institutions, which gave liberty to the people. But when the state emerged, it imposed its authority on the people, who forfeited their liberty. People obeyed laws not because laws were good, but because authority forced them to do so.

Reasons for Eliminating State. Kropotkin, who is regarded as the scientific interpreter of new anarchism, advanced valid reasons for making out a case for anarchism and elimination of state. (1) The state is not only useless, but is a positive hindrance to liberty. The state, which is an evil, should be eliminated, and other associations should be entrusted with the work, as they can function better than the state; (2) The state and other forms of authority make the lives of the people miserable. In the state, people work in bad and unhealthy surroundings, and they have no interest in doing the type of work, which is forced on them. There is too much of injustice in society, and hunger drives people to work like slaves. People under the tyranny of state need emancipation. This is possible by the elimination of private property for which many work, but few enjoy at the cost of many.

Production Serves Public Need in Anarchist Society. Under state authority and within the framework of private property, people do not produce, what the community needs, but what is dictated by directors and shareholders of companies. Therefore progress is not possible under the conditions created and upheld by the state. But in anarchist society, production will cater to the real needs of the people. Progress is registered only through the collective efforts of the people in workshops and factories, which provide workers with the types of jobs they like. People will find in these factories opportunities to engage themselves in useful tasks, which would give them true pleasure. Work in anarchist society will not be treated as slavery, but as something that is purposeful and gratifying to the individual.

Society Served by Communes. In anarchist society envisaged by Kropotkin, communes will serve the needs of the people. E.M. Burns says on page 42 in *Ideas in Conflict* (1960): "With the overthrow of the state, Kroptkin would set up an association of free communes composed of individuals banded together for a definite economic purpose. The original communes, in turn, would federate with others in neighbouring localities until eventually a large area would be covered by voluntary organisations seeking mutual advantages...... Manual work would no longer be performed by a degraded class nor would intellectual labours be the monopoly of a few."

Other Anarchists

Other Anarchists were Josiah Warren (1799-1874), Johann Kasper Schmidt (1806-1856), Stephen Pearl Andrews (1812-86), Benjamin R. Tucker and Lysander Spooner (1808-87). Among these anarchists, Schmidt, the German, advocated a dangerous type of anarchism similar to that of Russian nihilists.

EVALUATION OF ANARCHISM

We may briefly refer to the merits and defects of anarchism.

Merits

Some of the arguments advanced by anarchists are correct. The following merits of anarchist views may be enumerated:

1. Tolstoy and other anarchists sincerely draw the attention of people to the unhappy conditions prevailing in states, and

offer solid arguments in support of anarchism. No one can gainsay that in capitalist society, there is misery and unemployment, and people are forced to do the type of work, in which they have no interest at all or have very little interest. There is no real joy in work, and people work only because hunger goads them to exert themselves.

2. People have no true liberty, whatever may be the form of government. It is a fact that in several countries, in which the form of government is democracy, people suffer from degradation, misery and unemployment, and real liberty is enjoyed is enjoyed only by those in power and their friends.

3. Few people are in power in a state, and they misuse this in their own selfish interests.

4. Religion is used side by side with private property for exploitation.

5. The individual in anarchist society will be able to live freely work spontaneously and with joy contributing his best to society. He will be entirely free from state control, capitalist restraint and religious tyranny. "There is to be no compulsion, now law, no government exercising force; there will still be acts of the community, but these are spring from universal consent, not from any enforced submission of even the smallest minority."

Drawbacks

The following drawbacks of anarchist views may be mentioned:

1. *State not Responsible for Destruction of Moral Values.* Anarchists want the state to be abolished. But this is neither desirable nor feasible. It is not correct to say that the state is responsible for the decline and destruction of moral values and for the degeneration of human beings. The record of various states all over the world shows that the state has more than justified its existence and has indirectly let to the moral development of man. As Aristotle correctly said 2,300 years

ago, the state came into being for life, and it continues for the sake of good life. Anarchists desire to have voluntary associations working on a co-operative basis. But these associations too have to wield authority without which they cannot function. The hope that authority can be got rid of altogether can never be realised. If government in the existing form is abolished, authority will have to manifest in some other form. State authority, which anarchists push out, will stage a come-back through the so-called voluntary associations. Authority in some form or the other to regulate and control human activities is indispensable.

2. *State Authority not Against Liberty.* The anarchist argument that liberty and authority are antagonistic to each other does not hold water. In fact legislative authority acts as a supporting pillar to individual liberty instead of going against it. If the state is abolished, there will be disorder and confusion. In such an atmosphere, no progress will be possible, and the individual will lose whatever freedom he originally had under a well-organised government. Democratic states like Britain, the U.S.A., France and India uphold the liberty of the individual and try to promote the welfare of the people. Hence, it is not true to say that in all states the individual has no liberty. It is also not true that the state promotes misery and unhappiness. It fact in modern times, states are wedded to the concept of the welfare of the people, and in many states people have gained much through the services rendered by the state.

3. *Realisation of Anarchist Dream Impossible.* It is impossible to realize the anarchist dream of having a completely happy and coercion-free society. It seems that in the paradise the anarchists seek to create, there will be no immorality, exploitation, misery and compulsion. In a stateless, classless and churchless society, all will be happy. Such a state is too good to be true. Unless human beings become gods or saints, it is not possible to free society absolutely from vices and weaknesses. While it is quite true that human misery can be reduced, a classless, stateless and churchless paradise can never be realised.

4. *Anarchist Remedy worse than Disease.* Like syndicalists, nihilists and communists, anarchists spread fanaticism and hatred, and depend upon brute force for the realisation of their aims. By resorting to revolt, destruction and murder, anarchists desire to have anarchist society based on love and co-operation. The entire anarchist concept seems ridiculous and fantastic. Anarchists suggest a remedy which is worse than the disease.

5. *Too much Faith in Human Nature.* Anarchists put too much faith in human nature. They believe that there will be a paradise once human beings are entirely freed from state control. It is hard to believe that when there is no state, human beings will live freely, co-operate whole-heatedly and express nothing but understanding and goodwill. Had this been true, there would have been no need for the state at all. The very fact that human beings came to live in peace and order only after the state was formed is enough to debunk anarchist thought.

6. *Utopian Ideals.* Anarchists entertain sweet and grand ideals, which cannot be realised anywhere in the world. There is a vast difference between the real conditions in the world and the conditions anarchists would love to have. Their ideals are utopian and too good to be true and real.

7. *Confusing Picture.* Anarchist thought is not very clear and consistent. The picture presented by them is confusing.

Books for Further Study

1. Agarwal, Bhushan and Bhagwan, *Principles of Political Science*—1971, Ramchand & Co., Delhi.

2. Asirvatham, Eddy, *Political Theory*—1968, Upper India Publishing House, Lucknow.

3. Burns, E. M., *Ideas in Conflict*—1960.

4. Coker, F.W., *Recent Political Thought*—1966, The World Press, Calcutta.

5. Cole, G. D. H., *Socialist Thought, Marxism and Anarchism*—1850-90.

6. Ebenstein, William, *Today's Isms*—1958.

7. Hallowell, J. H., *Main Currents in Modern Political Thought.*

8. Harmon, Judd M., *Political Thought from Plato to the Present.*

9. Joad, C.E.M., *Modern Political Theory*—1951.

10. Levine, L., *Syndicalism in France*—1974.

11. Ray and Bhattacharya, *Political Theory*—1964, The World Press Calcutta.

12. Russell, Bertrand, *Roads to Freedom*—1946, Indian Edn., Allhahabad.

13. Singh, Sukhbir, *A History of Political Thought,* Vol. II-1974, Rastogi & Co., Meerut.

14. Spahr, *Reading is recent Political Philosophy.*

15. Wilson, *C., Anarchism.*

Fascism

Definition and Meaning of Fascism

An Authoritarian Theory and Movement. One of the authoritarian theories and movements that arose in the inter-war period (1919-39) in the 20th century was Fascism. It is a doctrine explaining the functions of the state and sphere of state activity. A movement based on the Fascist doctrine was launched by Benito Mussolini, the Italian dictator (1922-43). The period was very gloomy for Italy. Governments were unstable; demobilised war-weary soldiers were discontented; inflation had assumed monstrous proportions; merchants were shamelessly profiteering; the ranks of the unemployed were dangerously swelling; prices were sky-rocketing; people were in deep frustration; and there was a plethora of strikes. Mussolini was determined to tackle all these problems speedily under his Fascist banner; but it was all for getting power for selfish purposes. He showed no eagerness to follow the ideals and noble objectives of Mazzini or Garibaldi. His ultimate objective was dictatorial power.

Militant Movement against Liberalism, Democracy, Capitalism and Communism. The term Fascism is derived from the Latin word Fasces, which means bundle. (In ancient Rome, a bundle of rods with an axe was the symbol of authority, which included the power of life and death.) Mussolini vigorously started the movement as a reaction against liberalism, democracy, capitalism and communism. "Mussolini had declared that Fascism was an ideology compounded of the teaching of Machiavelli's doctrine of opportunism, Hegel's political absolutism, Sorel's doctrine of violence and William James's pragmatism. Fascism did not have a dogmatic ideology and adapted its doctrine as the exigencies of the moment required.": (See J.S. Roucek and Others, *Introduction to Political Science*—1954.) The Fascist theory is not precise, and it is difficult to give clearly the ideas and principles it covers. But one thing is certain. Fascism is dead against the ideologies of democracy, individualism, capitalism and communism. It stands for absolute state control in all fields. The individual has hardly any margin for his liberty. The state is placed on a high pedestal and the individual is called upon to worship it.

Fascist Movements Everywhere. The term Fascism also applies to similar movements, which broke out in the nineteen-twenties and thirties with the Italian Fascist movement as their model. Nazi (National Socialist) movement in Hitlerite Germany, Felange in Spain, Iron Guard in Rumania, Arrow Cross in Hungary, Heimwehr in Austria and Ustachi in Croatia are described as Fascist. These movements were directed against what Fascists called corrupt influences, which included parliamentary democracy, capitalism, socialism and particularly communism. Scores of Fascist and semi-Fascist movements were started on a small scale all over the world.

Mussolini's Attack on Toothless Democracies and League of Nations. Italy, the disgruntled victor of World War I, was not in an enviable position in the twenties of this century, and Fascists under Mussolini's leadership exploited the problems of their country to further their own selfish ends. Maxey observes on page 676 in his *Political Philosophies* (1959): "Italy, bitter over her treatment at the Versailles treasure-hunt and rent with internal discord, had forgotten the ideals of Mazzini and Garibaldi and surrendered to a Fascist dictatorship that was rabidly anti-democratic." Mussolini Discovered at the end of World War I that the leading democracies and the League of Nations were absolutely toothless, and would do nothing to prevent him from building up his ruthless totalitarian dictatorship according to Fascist principles.

Prominent Fascist Philosophers. The prominent Fascist Philosophers were Giovanni Gentile (1875-1944), a disciple of

Hegel and Giuseppe Prezzolini, a great admirer of Benito Mussolini. E. M. Burns says on page 217 in *Ideas in Conflict* (1960): "The original forerunners of Italian Fascist political theory were a group of intellectuals who had adopted with weird modifications the philosophy of Hegel. Taking as their fundamental position the Hegelian idea that the state is the supreme manifestation of God on earth, they demanded that Italians should submerge their individual and class interests in a united endeavour to revive the greatness of their nation."

Racialist, Militarist and Imperialist Single Party Totalitarian Dictatorship. Fascism is "a government system led by a dictator having complete power, forcibly suppressing opposition and criticism, regimenting all industry, commerce etc. and emphasizing an aggressive nationalism and often racism." (See *The Random House Dictionary of the English Language.*) In Italy Mussolini established his single party dictatorship, crushed all opposition, wiped out all democratic institutions imposed militarism and brought all aspects of the individual's life under totalitarian control. William Ebenstein observes, on page 85 in *Today's Isms* (1958): "Stripped to its essentials, Fascism is the totalitarian organisation of government and society by a single party dictatorship, intensely nationalist, racialist, militarist and imperialist. In Europe, Italy (1922) was the first to go Fascist, followed by Germany (1933). In Asia, Japan went Fascist in the nineteen-thirties; gradually evolving totalitarian institutions out of its own native heritage."

Not Easy to Define. It is not easy to say what precisely Fascism is, as it is the product of a synthesis of several ideas and principles. C. C. Maxey observes on page 938 in *Political Philosophies* (1959): "To trace all of the sources of the political philosophy now known as Fascism is not easy. It is compound of many ingredients, which have been blended together with great ingenuity. We may perceive, among others, borrowings from Machiavelli, Hobbes, Fichte, Hegel, Treitschke, Nietzsche, Marx, Sorel, Mosca, Schopanhauer, Bergson, James and Pareto." Mussolini himself proudly admitted that it was not possible to be precise about Fascism, as it locked consistency, logic and coherence. Regarding he and his Fascists, Mussolini declared: "We permit ourselves the luxury of being aristocrats and democrats, conservatives and progressives, reactionaries and revolutionaries, legalitarians and illegalitarians according to the circumstances, time place and environment."

Origin, Growth and Decline of Fascism

Fascism as a Mighty Authoritarian Force in Italy. Fascism strongly manifested itself after World War I (1914-18) under the leadership of Benito Mussolini in Italy. Mussolini whose father was a blacksmith and village inn-keeper and mother a school teacher was born in 1883. He took full advantage of the chaotic conditions in Italy and tried to win public support by placating the various sections of society. With Fascism as his instrument, Mussolini was able to capture power and become Italy's Prime Minster in 1922. As Duce (Leader or dictator) he remained in power till July 24, 1943, when he was overthrown.

Fascism in Other Countries. After establishing itself in 1922, Fascism spread in other countries. Mussolini boasted that Fascism would be a world movement, and Italy would be the leader of the world. Though Fascism did not spread all over the world, it made rapid progress in European countries in the third and fourth decades of the twentieth century. Governments of Austria, Hungary, Bulgaria, Greece, Rumania and Poland accepted Fascist principles by 1936.

Aggression of Italy, Germany and Japan as Axis Powers. The spread of Fascism brought the world to the cataclysm of World War II (1939-45). Nazi Germany under Hitler and Fascist Italy under Mussolini shared certain common principles and objectives. Hence it was possible for them to enter into a defensive and offensive alliance in May 1939, barely three months before the Second World War began. In the Far East, Japan was also eager to participate in a Global War, and in December 1940 Japan made a Fascist Alliance with Germany and Italy with the grand objective of setting up a *new order* in Europe, Asia and Africa, During the Second World War, Italy, Germany and Japan were called Axis

Powers; Berlin-Rome-Tokyo Alliance or Axis had been formed by them in 1937.

Surrender of Fascist Italy. In the early stages of the war, the Powers did well, and Fascism became a real menace to the world. In June 1940, when France surrendered to Germany, democracy was abolished and a Fascist type of government was established in that country. In the later stages of the war, Fascism and Nazism (which was also a type of Fascism) got a setback, and ultimately with the fall of Italy and the death of Mussolini, Fascist hopes were shattered. Fascism played a vital role in the holocaust of World War II.

Fascism in Action

Emphasis on Action. Mussolini had contempt for theory and discussion. He was all for action. He said his programme was action, not talk. He claimed that Fascism was based on reality in contrast to Bolsevism, which was based on theory. He declared that he wanted to be definite and real and come out of the cloud of discussion and theory. He made it clear that he wanted to govern Italy for the future well-being of people. Italy had too many programmes, but what was needed was action. He cared little for plans and formal principles, which he regarded as iron and tin fetters.

Mussolini's Programme of Aggressive Expansion. Mussolini, the high priest of Fascism, did not given elaborate philosophy of Fascism. Taking inspiration from Eurico Corradini and Gabriel D. Annunzio, who advocated aggressive nationalism and imperialism, Mussolini, who was a great admirer of Machiavelli and Sorel, chalked out his programme of expansion and aggrandizement.

Mussolini's Fighting Band. Mussolini established on March 23, 1919, the First Fascist Group in Milan called *Fascio di Combattimento* (the Fighting Band) consisting of extreme nationalists, who were against monarchy and capitalism. The opportunist group changed its attitude after some time as evident from the support it gave to capitalists land-holders and propertied classes.

Formation of National Fascist Party. Conditions in Italy were most congenial for the formation of a Fascist Party with a national programme, and in November 1921 the National Fascist Party was formed. The main objective of the Fascists was to capture power in Italy. After the end of World War I, countries like Italy had to face many serious and nagging problems, and the Fascists in Italy capitalised on the pressing problems of the nation.

Government Lenient to Fascists. Fascists led by Balbo, Grandi and others scoffed at democracy and parliamentary institutions. They decided to destroy the discredited parliamentary institutions and establish their own government. It was indeed strange that the government was unusually lenient and soft, and the army and the police hardly resisted the violent and aggressive activities of Fascists.

Mussolini's March on Rome. Mussolini and his Blackshirts marched on Rome on October 28, 1922, and on the very next day the King of Italy invited Mussolini to become Premier and form a government. Had the government in Italy nipped the Fascist movement in the bud, the Fascists under Mussolini would not scored such a spectacular triumph. Capture of power must have been much easier than what Mussolini had ever imagined. The Fascist revolution was a spectacular success.

Mussolini's Totalitarian Fascist Disctatorship. To begin with Mussolini pretended that he was loyal to the king and was going to form a coalition ministry, and was prepared to co-operate with other parties. But when his position was secure, he brushed aside parliamentarians and non-Fascists and made his dictatorship a reality. Since 1925 he governed by decrees, which set aside constitutional government and gave legal form to his dictatorship. Mussolini and his Fascist supporters remorselessly suppressed all non-Fascist movements, banned all other political parties, butchered people who hindered Fascists and converted Italy into a totalitarian state. In November 1926, when all opposition parties were liquidated, persons who tried to revive the dissolved political parties and conducted propaganda on their behalf were given jail sentences. By clever tactics, Mussolini became all powerful as real head of government, who could rule by issuing decrees. Technically the king continued as head of state with no powers, but all powers, were vested in Premier (Dictator) Mussolini. He treated his ministers as his subordinates, who were responsible to him alone. The Fascist Party, which was a well-knit party, hierarchically organised was under the thumb of Mussolini. This party under Mussolini's absolute control imposed its will and orders on all institutions in Italy in the same way in which the Communist party imposed its iron rule in Stalin's Russia.

Liberty Crushed. Under Mussolini's Fascist dictatorship, the rule of the communes, originally autonomous, was put under the control of a podesta (chief magistrate) nominated by the government in 1922 for a period of five years. In 1925, a bill was passed imposing press censorship. Managers and editors of newspapers, who wanted to assert their independence, were got rid of, and in their places were appointed submissive and spineless persons, who would all the time praise the "great deeds" of the Fascist party. In 1927 a Charter of Labour was drawn up for controlling all forces of production. A bill removing popular rule and representation was passed in 1928. Mussolini's policy was ruthless suppression at home and imperialism abroad. He remained in power during 1922-1943.

Nemesis after Early Imperialist Success. Italy under Mussolini moved on the war path and in 1935 committed aggression on Ethiopia and conquered it with the League of Nations helplessly watching his game of war. Having made common cause with Germany and Japan, Fascist Italy entred the Second World War in 1940, but nemesis overtook her after initial success. In July 1943 Mussolini was deposed and his place was taken by Marshal Badoglio. To complete the degradation of Mussolini, he was imprisoned and Fascism was banned. The Allied armies entered the Italian mainland on September 9, 1943, and Italy unconditionally surrendered. On April 28, 1945, Mussolini while fleeing with his mistress towards Switzerland was caught and shot dead by Italian communists. His corpse was dishonoured by being hung by the heels in Milan.

Salient Features of Fascism

The following are the salient features of Fascism:

1. State an End in Itself.

The Fascist State is regarded as an end in itself and not as a means to an end. It has a will of its own, and it is much more than a more collection of individuals. Fascists treat it as an ethical entity, which inherits ideas and sentiments of people generation after generation. It guarantees internal and external security to the people. It is a living reality connected with the past and the future, and it goes far beyond the limited frontiers of the individual's life. The state should be adored as a spiritual and moral fact. The Fascist motto is: "Everything for the state, nothing against the state; nothing outside the state; beyond the state—nothing." It is the duty of the individual to live in the glorification of the state. "The nation becomes transfigured into a *corpus mysticum,* an unbroken chain of generations, armed with a mission which is realised in the course of the historical process. The duty of the individual is to elevate himself to the heights of national consciousness and to lose completely his identity in it. He has individual rights only in so far as they do not conflict with the needs of the sovereign state." (See *Encyclopaedia of Social Sciences.*)

2. Italy as a Corporate State

Mussolini Converted Italy into a Corporate State. The concept of the Corporate State was based on two ideas: (1) The members of the ruling party (Fascist leaders) only are capable of understanding the problems of the people and the country, and (2) The ordinary citizens are incapable of comprehending the great problems facing the nation and hence they should remain inarticulate. They can understand their problem not as the citizens of Italy, but as men following their own respective professions that is, as farmers, workers, entrepreneurs, lawyers and doctors. A farmer, for instance, can understand the problems of farming and not the problems of the nation.

Economy Controlled under Fascist Ideas. The Corporate State controls the economy of the whole country according to

Fascist ideas. There are state controlled associations of capital and labor and each enjoys monopoly in its own field. No association can follow a line of action which is not approved by the state.

Institutions of Employers and Employees. The Fascist plan of the Corporate State was implemented through the Corporation Act of 1934. The chief institutions of the Corporate State were the following:

(a) *Syndicates:* One syndicate of employers and one of workers for every trade or occupation could be set up in a district. The syndicate of employers must have members employing at least 10% of the workers in the trade in the district, and the syndicate of employees must consist of at least 10% of the workers in the trade in the district.

(b) *Federations:* Employers' Syndicates and employees' syndicates were to form separate federations.

(c) *Confederations.* Federations were to form confederations. There were to be nine confederations: four of employers and four of employees in industry, agriculture, commerce, and credit and insurance; and one confederation of professional men and artists.

(d) *Corporations*: Till the confederation level, employers and employees were to have separate institutions; but at a higher level, that is, of corporation, both the types were to come together. For each trade, there was to be a corporation consisting of representatives of employers and employees. Each corporation was to have a president appointed by the Head of the Government. There were in Italy 22 corporations. Fascists claimed that corporativism gave a new concept of the functions of the state. It was made to appear superior to *laissez faire* and socialism, as it brought about reconciliation between the state and the citizen by reconciling both of them to the corporation. In the corporation, manufacturers and workers resolved their difference with the state standing by to advise and guide them in the process of reconciliation.

(e) *National Council of Corporation*. The most important members of the corporations, that is, about 500 members formed the National Council of Corporations. On page 647 in *Political Philosophies* (1959), C.C. Maxey states: "The corporate state was held up as a paragon, which would give private initiative, ample freedom and at the same time preserve and promote the well-being of all. Another feature of the corporate system, which certainly commended it highly to the Fascists, was that it enabled the state to manage the whole economy as a national autarchy."

3. *Ideals of Superior Class and Superior Nation*. Mussolini spoke in terms of racial superiority, and in this respect, he was like Hitler, though he never reached the fanatical height of Hitler. The Fascists believed that in every country there was a superior class of people, who alone could rule, and similarly, there was a superior nation, whose lead other nations should follow. Just as the ruling class can dominate over all in a nation, in the world the superior nation can dictate terms to the inferior and weak nations. Italians were decidedly superior to Ethiopians, according to Fascists, and it was right for Italy to extirpate the Ethiopians, and annex their country. Italian aggression on Ethiopia in 1935 can thus be explained.

On page 95 in *Today's Isms* (1958), William Ebenstein points out the principal features of Fascism: (1) distrust of reason; (2) denial of basic human equality; (3) code of behaviour based on lies and violence; (4) government by elite; (5) totalitarianism; (6) racialism and imperialism; and (7) opposition to international law and order.

4. *Extreme Nationalism and Militarism*. Fascism is based on extreme nationalism and militarism. Fascists regard the nation as a glorious personality having a will and end of its own.

It is the essential duty of the individual to serve the nation, the supreme arbiter of all Fascism lays great emphasis on the individual's complete and undivided loyalty to his nation through his feeling and actions. In the interest of the national, it is necessary to control the thoughts and sentiments of the people by regulating the press, films and the radio. The nation comes first, and the individual should bend all energies in its service.

5. *Imperialism and War.* Fascism is also based on imperialism and war, and it is dead against international peace and harmony. Lover of peace and advocates of international peace, goodwill and co-operation are ridiculed as cowards. In Fascist thought imperialism is something that is natural, eternal and immutable, and it is preposterous to talk and work for peace. Mussolini scoffed at international peace, which he regarded as a coward's dream. War as a corollary of imperialism is uphold as something glorious. Mussolini said: "War is to man what maternity is to a woman." "War alone brings up to its highest tension all human energy and put the stamp of nobility upon the peoples,. who have the courage to meet it." Mussolini further asserted: "A war for the preservation, expansion or exaltation of a nation may be supremely justifiable, even though it may frustrate the special interest of every lesser group and destroy the lives of the nation's most worthwhile citizens." Under Mussolini's dictatorship, the Italians were made aware that their country was too small for them and therefore they should wage aggressive war for expansion. Mussolini made people believe that Italy was in a permanent state of war.

6. *One Party State Extirpating all Non-Fascists.* Italy under Mussolini became a one-party state. All parties except the Fascist party in the country were ruthlessly suppressed and absolutely no room was left for the very existence of democracy and liberalism. Fascists say that democracy is the worst type of government and it is a "decaying corpse," stupid, corrupt, slow-moving, visionary, impracticable and

inefficient." As essentially men of action and war, Fascists poured ridicule on discussion and consultation and dubbed parliaments as useless talking shops. MacIver says about Mussolini on page 51 in *The Web of Government* (1959): "In one thing he showed consistency throughout his career—his contempt for democracy. Exulting over the decaying corpse of the Goddess of Liberty he proceeded to tear down piece by piece, the parliamentary structure. He nullified and abolished all political parties except 'the' party....He changed his office of premier into that of 'head of the government'....He had his personal army, the Blackshirt Militia, bound exclusively to his service."

As Fascists alone, according the Mussolini, could lead Italy to her goal, it was right and necessary to liquidate all non-Fascists. Conditions in Fascist Italy were topsy-turvy; while in a democracy rulers are responsible to the people, in Italy the people were to be accountable to rulers. Parliamentarianism, liberty, equality, the dignity of the human personality and other features of a democratic form of government were summarily rejected by Fascists. People in Italy had the only "right" of obeying the orders of the Duce or leader or dictator fully and without complaining the least. They were all instruments to be used at the will and pleasure of the Fascist dictator. The Fascist party alone was regarded as the conscience-keeper of the state.

7. *Use of Fear, Violence and Totalitarianism.* A state in which there can be no criticism of government and in which the individual is a mere tool is bound to be authoritarian and totalitarian. The state is omnipotent and all-embracing. The individuals' life belongs to the state, and the individual has to use his life in the service of the state. Fascists struck fear in the minds of the people, who were to obey state orders like faithful slaves. E.K. Aramstedt say on page 51 in *Dictatorship and the Political Police* (1945): "With its back to the wall, Fascism had no alternative but to become thorough-going or totalitarian, and in doing so the technique of control by fear became of vital importance.... Full of fear themselves, they (Fascists) knew how to turn it into violence,

thus causing fear in others. Gradually they developed a technique of injecting fear into the fellow countrymen, which started by making anti-Fascists swallow a jar of castor oil and reached its climax by forcing them to recant or beg for mercy." Violence was freely used to keep people under control. Strikes were ruthlessly broken. In August 1922 after crushing the general strike Mussolini boasted: "After having made use of it (violence) systematically for forty-eight hours, we got results, which we should not have obtained in forty-eight years of sermons and propaganda." To protect the Fascist state and to suppress anti-Fascists, Mussolini the Duce organised his secret police known as VORA (Voluntary Organisation for the Repression of Anti-Fascism).

Though there were differences between fascism on one aside and Nazism and Stalinism on the other, the features of violence, authoritarianism and totalitarianism were common to all of them. All powers was vested in the Fascist party and the Fascist party gave all powers to the Duce. The dictator was responsible to none, but all had to be responsible to him. Fascism became all-embracing in Italy, and all aspects of life of the individual came under the control of the Fascist state. There is nothing valuable outside the scope of the Fascist state. Mussolini loudly proclaimed: "for the Fascists, all is in the state and nothing human or spiritual exists much less has any value outside the state."

8. *Criticism of Socialism.* It is important to note that the Fascists had absolutely no truck with socialism, evolutionary or revolutionary. While socialists underlined the significance of the economic forces in a country and spoke in terms of class war and the materialistic interpretation of history, Fascists criticised the socialist attitude of reducing men to the level of animals, which care only for material things like food and drink. Fascists said that in human life there are precious things beyond the bare physical existence of man. Factors like religion and patriotism play a vital role in human life.

9. *Against Intellectualism and Human Values.* Fascism is diametrically opposed to all human values and feelings.

While all agree that the human mind and intellectual power raise men above animals, Fascists took a firm stand against intellectualism. Fascists wanted absolute obedience from all; all were to behave like faithful dogs to the Duce, who had no use of the intellectual power of the people. In fact, people cannot understand national problems and their only work is "to have faith to obey and to fight." Fascists say that educated people talk unnecessarily and play with knowledge without understanding their own responsibilities. The only force, which Fascism recognised in Italy, was brute force, which they used at all times. It is difficult to say which was more ruthless, Nazism under Hitler, Fascism under Mussolini or Communism under Stalin. Sympathy, pity, love, understanding, regard for others, morality and such other values, which make man a real human being were alien to Fascist thought.

10. *Church Silenced by Compromise and Conciliation.* Fascists in Italy showed the worst type of opportunism. There was a time when Mussolini said that there were two religions, one black and another red, and "two Vaticans were sending forth their encyclicals one in Rome and the other in Moscow," and Italians should be heretics to both. But after 1921 the time-server Mussolini suddenly changed his attitude in favour of the Catholic Church. The practical-minded Duce thought that Vatican-Italian Accord of 1929 was necessary, as the Church, the Fascist rival could be silenced only through compromise and conciliation. To appease the Catholic Church, the Pope's temporal authority over the city of the Vatican was recognised and religious instruction to the children of Catholics was made compulsory in schools. Such a *volte-face* indicated the extreme opportunism of Fascists. Fascists developed "friendship" with Catholics and continued it during the entire rule of Mussolini.

11. *Power as Essence.* Power is the quintessence of Fascism. Absolute power is to be wielded within the absolute state. People are to obey the laws and orders of Fascist leaders

implicitly with unity and discipline. Total obedience of people for national greatness and glorification is the general rule of Fascism.

EVALUATION OF FASCISM

We may briefly refer to the merits and defects of Fascism.

Merits

It is wrong to think that Fascism was an unmixed evil to Italy. it had the following merits:

1. After the end of World War I (1914-18), when Italy was facing numerous problems, it was Fascism that rescued her from demoralisation.

2. Before Fascists came to power, leaders of Wetsern democracies showed scant respect for Italy, which they felt, was not on a par with them. Under Mussolini, Italy began to command respect in the comity of nations.

3. Mussolini and other Fascist leaders working under him galvanised and vitalised the Italian nation. Italians became proud and conscious of the fact that they belonged to the land of Julius Caesar and Emperor Augustus, who ruled over a might empire in ancient times.

4. Mussolini raised great hopes and expectations among Italians, who were happy to se their country ranked among the most powerful in the world.

5. Fascists gave good government to Italy. Finance was property organised and production was increased. Public services functioned well, and there was national discipline. People lived in security in their home and where they worked. Mussolini claimed that the Fascist Government gave the people what they most needed: roads, bridges drains punctual trains and well managed industries.

Defects

The following are the main drawbacks of Fascism:

1. *War and Destruction*: Fascism is based on aggressive nationalism, imperialism and war. Nationalism developed by Fascists is perverted, and it is the younger brother of imperialism. Fascist Italy was guilty of committing aggression on Ethiopia and making a mockery of the principles of the League of nations. Italy in collaboration with Germany and Japan brought unprecedented devastation and sorrow to the world.

2. *Sacrifice of Individual Freedom*. Fascism converts the individual into a tool of the state. The individual's liberty is sacrificed at the altar of the state, and all aspects of his life are brought under state control. The individual has no rights in the Fascist state.

3. *Ruthless Dictatorship*. Fascism has contempt for democracy and all that is allied to it. It is ruthless in its methods, and is entirely alien to human compassion, sympathy and understanding. Fascism becomes the basis of dictatorship of the worst type. In Italy, many non-Fascists, who criticised Fascism were got rid of. In 1924, Matteotti, a member of the Italian Parliament, was assassinated under mysterious circumstances. The same was the fate of Count Balbo in Africa.

4. *Invited Nemesis*. Mussolini was shortsighted and lacked true wisdom. Though he seemed to have solved the problems of Italy, it was only for short time. In the long run, Fascism failed miserably. Mussolini invited nemesis to himself and to his country. Italy had to pay a heavy price morally and materially for Mussolini's misdeeds.

BOOKS FOR FURTHER STUDY

1. Agarwal, Bhushan and Bhagwan, *Principles of Political Science*—1971, Ramchand & Co., Delhi.
2. Aramstedt, E. K., *Dictatorship and Political Science*—1945.
3. Asirvatham, Eddy, *Political Theory*—1968, Upper India Publishing House, Lucknow.

4. Burns, E. M., *Ideal in Conflict*—1960.

5. Coker, F. W., *Recent Political Thought*—1966, The World Press, Calcutta.

6. Ebenstein, William, *Political Thought in Perspective*—1957.

7. Ebenstein, William, *Today's Isms*—1958.

8. Joad, C. E. M., *Introduction to Modern Political Theory*.

9. MacIver, R. M., *The Web of Government*—1959.

10. Maxey, C. C., *Political Philosophies*—1959.

11. Roucek, J. S. and Others, *Introduction to Political Science*—1954.

12. Singh, Sukhbir, *A History of Political Thought*, Vol. II—1974, Rastogi & Co., Meerut.

Nationalism and Internationalism

Disgruntled nationalities are sources of endless tension and misunderstanding, and a sure menace to peace and security. In certain states, neither the government nor the nationalities are happy. The attitude of the one is an eyesore to the other, and the rulers will never receive the loyalty and co-operation of the ruled. Such nationalities are easily provoked to rebel and riot. The suppressed nationalities in the mighty empires of the 19th century were vexed problems not only to the respective empires but also to the whole world. In fact one of the causes of two World Wars was the problem of the disgruntled and suppressed minorities. The Balkan volcano of highly discontented nationalities, which erupted every now and then was one of the real causes of World War I. The dissatisfaction of German minorities in the newly created nation states of Europe on the basis of self-determination was fully exploited by Hitler, who let loose his war machine in the midst of the small states and triggered the second World War. The numerous national movements, rebellions and wars in the 19th and 20th centuries in Europe, Asia and Africa were the manifestations of the dissatisfaction and anger of oppressed nationalities.

Nationalism Peace and Freedom

Nationalism emerged in Britain, France, the USA and other democratic countries spontaneously. In these countries, the individual's personality was fully recognised, and the individual felt the national urge in an atmosphere of complete peace and liberty of thought and action.

Nationalism Militarism and Totalitarianism

In Germany, Italy, Soviet Russia, Communist China and other totalitarian countries, nationalism arose on the basis of a militant and aggressive spirit. In such countries nationalism is completely divorced from the methods of peace and freedom. These totalitarian states under war-mongering dictatorship provoked the individual to develop under artificial stimulation an extremely aggressive type of nationalism, which is diametrically opposed to peaceful co-existence.

In Italy, under Benito Mussolini "fascist nationalism, rejected parliamentarianism and democracy, which were characteristics of nineteenth century Italian nationalism; it repudiated peace and harmony and prepared the national for combat." (See J.S. Roucek and Others, *Introduction to Political Science*—1954, p. 604.)

In Hitlerite Germany, nationalism in its extreme form was built on Nazis. Based on the false racial theory of Nordic superiority and on ruthless militarism and aggressive imperialism, nationalism in Germany was worked up artificially to fever pitch. It was such nationalism that pushed the world into the complete cataclysm of World War II.

In the 20th century, in Soviet Russia, a communist totalitarian state, nationalism was built as an antithesis to liberalism and parliamentarianism. Slavophilism, Marxism and totalitarianism are the features of Russian nationalism. Communist China has also whipped up artificially aggressive nationalism under leader like Mao Tes-tung.

Meaning of Internationalism

Just as individuals have rights, national also have rights. Similarly, nations like individuals in society have to co-operate with one anther for collective good. Sometimes individuals have to dilute their own rights for the larger good of society. So also, nations may have to water down or even surrender their rights for the common good of the world at large. The principles governing relationship between nations are recognised by nations are their own good as well as the good of the whole world. In the course of a long time, nations came to recognize the rights of each other and evolved principles of mutual co-operation and understanding for the maintenance of peace and general progress of mankind. These principles are called internationalism. *The Random House Dictionary* gives briefly the meaning of internationalism. "(1) the principle of co-operation among nations for the promotion of their common good, sometimes as contrasted with nationalism, or devotion to the interests of a particular nation. (2) international character, relations, co-operation or control." Internationalism can co-exist with nationalism. The two should not form an antithesis, if nations understand one another and have wholesome respect for the rights of one another. Nations may have to adjust their relationship with each other for the promotion of internationalism. A nation, which believes in peaceful co-existence of various nations, international peace and brotherhood of man works for the promotion of goodwill and understanding among nations.

Perverted Nationalism Harmful to Internationalism: Perverted nationalism, which is based on false national ego, selfishness, militarism and imperialism is harmful to internationalism. As it is the enemy of internationalism, it cannot make compromise with principles of peace, co-operation and understanding among nations. It divides the world and brings sorrow and suffering to mankind. Hitler and Mussolini generated perverted nationalism in their respective countries. They wrought widespread havoc and destruction before inviting annihilation to themselves.

Evaluation of Nationalism

Whether nationalism is good or bad, blessing or curse depends upon the way in which people, who claim to be nationalists implement their principles. The type of nationalism practiced by Nazis in Germany, and Fascists in Italy and militarists in Japan is certainly a curse. It is a kind of mania. Healthy nationalism is a blessing to mankind, as it is wedded to peace and freedom, and is ready to make concessions to internationalism. We may briefly summarize here the advantages of wholesome nationalism and the disadvantages of perverted nationalism. Sometimes it is difficult to say whether the nationalism in a particular state is morbid or healthy.

Advantages of Healthy Nationalism. The following advantages of healthy nationalism may be enumerated:

1. *Evokes the Greatest Virtues.* Healthy nationalism is based on the highest type of patriotism and it has an ennobling effect on the human mind. It evokes the greatest virtues of the human beings, who become ready to serve their nation selflessly to make it great and glorious. There is no sacrifice which noble patriots and nationalists will not do for their nation. Amar Nandi says on page 83 in *An Introduction to Political Science*—1955: "The history of freedom movement in every land is replete with instances of men and women sacrificing their lives at the altar of national salvation. The stories of some of these martyrs will remain an enduring source of inspiration to mankind."

2. *Beneficial to the World.* Nationalists are ready to work hard to make their nation great. When every nation makes tremendous progress, the world itself rapidly progresses and becomes a happier and better place to live in. Thus nationalism becomes beneficial to the whole world.

3. *Preserves National Cultures and Values.* Every nation has its own culture and values. Nationalists jealously guard their own culture and the values attached to it. Thus in the entire world a variety of cultures is preserved and different values are cherished.

4. *Curb on Imperialism.* Another great advantage is that healthy nationalism is an antidote to imperialism, and consequently reduces the chances of the outbreak of a world war. Nationalism breeds legitimate pride and self-respect in a country; it makes no compromise with slavery and foreign domination. The nationalists in America, Italy, Germany, India, and other countries created national pride and prepared

their countries for full nationhood. In this process they fostered independence and curbed imperialism.

5. *Unifies People.* Nationalism can mobilize and unify people as nothing else can. Among forces of unity, nationalism has the greatest pulling power.

Disadvantages of Perverted Nationalism

The following disadvantages of perverted nationalism may be enumerated:

1. *Wedded to Imperialism.* Perverted nationalism is based on false national pride and ego. The perverted nationalist feels that his nation is always right and the nations criticizing it are always wrong. Evil nationalism is surcharged with ego and selfishness. Rabindranath Tagore, who regarded nationalism as the "organised self-interest of a whole people", criticised it in the strongest possible terms. Aggressive nationalism known as "wolf-pack nationalism" is an antithesis to peaceful nationalism or "sheep flock nationalism." A state overrun by perverted nationalism tries to extend its territory and dominate over other nations, which are militarily weak. Thus it develops imperialism. It is difficult to satisfy fully the appetite of the aggressive nationalist and imperialist.

2. *Based on Militarism.* Perverted nationalism develops militarism. When half a dozen nation states racing for more power and territory try to implement their heavy armament programmes for making their respective nations great and glorious, the international atmosphere gets vitiated and peace is disturbed. Militant nationalism becomes imperialism, which leads to international rivalry; and wars.

3. *Enmity and Intolerance.* Evil type of nationalism sows the seeds of enmity and intolerance everywhere. As the dominant nationality within a state ill-treats the minorities, the latter angrily react against the discrimination and intolerance. This breeds enmity and hatred within a state. Fascist nationalist

in Italy and Nazi nationalists in Germany did much to produce hatred and ill will.

4. *Detrimental to World Peace.* Perverted nationalism not only disturbs peace within the state, but throughout the world. It breeds contempt for peace-loving people and nations. As nationalism becomes more and more aggressive and imperialist, seeds of a world war are sowed. Aggressive and soulless nationalism stands for naked force, and it can easily make man a brute utterly devoid of any decency and finer feelings. It teaches strong nationals the technique of bullying over weak nationals and grabbing their territory and wealth. This was exactly what happened during the inter-war period (1919-39), when Germany and Italy launched their careers of aggression after establishing ruthless totalitarianism. Fanatics in both these countries blindly worshipped the nation state and did great harm to the entire world community.

5. *Great Sufferings to Humanity:* Perverted nationalism is the mother of numerous ills in the world. Going hand in hand with imperialism, aggressive nationalism in the ultimate analysis subjects the whole of humanity to intolerable sufferings. It was perverted nationalism, which was behind both the World Wars, which brought death and destruction on an incredibly large scale all over the world. Perverted nationalists blinded by power hunger and false pride ignore the true welfare of people all over the world. The promotion of the welfare of the people of the whole world had a set-back owing to the disease type of nationalism developed by Germans, Italians, Russians, Americans, British, Japanese and other peoples.

6. *Perverted National States Morally and Materially Inadequate:* Perverted nation states expose not only their victims but themselves to complete annihilation in the modern world of science in which inter-continental missiles cut across national boundaries over thousands of miles. Amar Nandi says on page 53 in *An Introduction to Political*

Science (1955): "How the bellicose nationalism of Japan scattered sorrow and devastation over wide areas in the world and finally made Japan herself a victim of atomic attack, and led to the occupation of the country by foreign forces is fresh in the memory of people all over the world." While the maniacs in power in an excessively aggressive nation state take delight in admiring their own power and greatness, they are not aware that national frontiers, which are jealously guarded are meaningless before the onslaughts of missiles, which can be hurled at an incredibly terrific speed. Unless aggressive nationalism is leashed and nationals are made to follow a civilised code of behaviour, humanity has no hope. All the trouble starts with the sin or vice of perverted nationalism. The perverted national state in the modern world context is frightfully inadequate morally and materially. The nation state cannot save itself. It can only be saved by international harmony and understanding.

Nationalism in India

India under British Rule: After the collapse of the Mughal Empire and the Maratha power, it was easy for the British to conquer the whole of India, which they did by 1857. Till August 14, 1947, India was under British rule. The next day India became a full-fledged nation state.

Opinion of Western Writers Whether India is a Nation: Several Western writers do not see anything good in India and do not miss any opportunity to run down India unfairly. They have expressed the view that India is not a nation, but a loose group of castes creeds and communities. The same writers have also commented that India did not deserve independence. Winston Churchill had made several derogatory remarks about India, and if all these remarks had been correct, India would have lost her independence and her democratic institutions would have gone to doges by now.

They think nationalism can never strike roots in India, because Indians are in a state of political slumber and are utterly oblivious to the nationalist forces, which welded Germans, Italians and other European nationalities into full-fledged nations. It is further argued that Indians do not belong to a common race, do not speak a common language and do not profess a common religion. Indians constitute a mass of heterogeneous groups, which can never be woven into the fabric of a nation in the vast sub-continent. It is concluded that India is still in the medieval age, and is no more than a mere geographical expression.

Arguments that India is a Nation. The following arguments can be advanced to debunk the jaundiced view and show that India is a nation:

1. *National Movement.* Indians were able to launch a great national movement under dynamic leaders like Dadabhai Naoroji, Pherozeshah Mehta, Lala Lajpat Rai, Lokamanya Tilak, Bipin Chandra Pal, C.R. Das, Mahatma Gandhi, Motilal Nehru, Jawaharlal Nehru, Subhash Chandra Bose,Vallabhbhai Patel, Maulana Abul Kalam Azad and others. The Indian National Congress, which was established in 1885, was able to build up a mass based and rouse national consciousness.

2. *Impossible for British to Continue Imperialism.* The British tried to crush the national movement, but they failed because it was able to evoke the co-operation of all the sections of Indian society Mahatma Gandhi, the "leader of leaders", called upon the British to give *Poorna Swaraj;* but when they refused, he launched the Quit India Movement in August 1942. The British retaliated and tried to suppress the movement by imprisoning most of the great national leaders including Mahatma Gandhi. The British firmly but wrongly believed that with leaders in jail, leaderless India could be kept in bondage. But for the first time the British rulers were made to realize that even without their great leaders at the helm, Indians as patriots and nationalists would continue to fight against British imperialists. The Quit India Movement, in which Mahatma Gandhi had asked the people "To Do or Die", shook the British Empire in India to its foundations, and the British were compelled to draw the conclusion that

continuing their rule in India would ultimately result in losing India and all the British assets in India along with India's friendship and goodwill. It was clear that national awakening had made India a British liability. Within 5 years of the Quit India Movement, the British granted independence to India. If Indians had not developed nationalism to fever pitch, the British would not have left India.

3. *Good Examples of National Consciousness.* Several good examples can be given to show national consciousness in India. As stated above, it was the high tide of national consciousness displayed during the Quit India Movement in 1942, which drove out the British. Five years later, the teeming millions of India were mad with joy on their first Independence Day (August 15, 1947), when they became politically conscious that the long night of British imperialism and India's bondage under it came to an end. If nationalism had not emerged, people would find no difference between slavery and independence. It was genuine national consciousness which was behind the expression of extraordinary and spontaneous joy on that day. On January 30,1948, when Mahatma Gandhi was shot dead by Nathuram Godse, India as a nation was in deep mourning, as it lost its greatest national leader. It is significant to note here that the people of India regarded the Mahatma as the Father of the Nation. In October 1962, the whole of India was roused to angrily react, when the news spread that the Chinese had committed aggression on India. The rich and the poor, the young and the old, the literate and the illiterate, men and women, people from all political parties rallied round the national flag and expressed their readiness to extend their greatest cooperation to throw out the aggressors, who had attacked their nation. On May 27, 1964, India as a nation felt a rude shock, when Prime Minister Jawaharlal Nehru, who had played a very great role to win national independence passed away. In August-September 1965, when Pakistan committed aggression, India rose as a nation to throw out and punish the aggressors. When Prime Minister

Lal Bahadur Shastri appealed for help to fight against Pakistan, the entire sub-continent rose as one man to render service and to contribute generously to the war fund. Even poor farmers and workers donated their meagre savings and women gave their jewels. Again on January 11, 1966, when Shastriji died at Tashkent in Soviet Russia after a heart attack, the whole of India as a nation was in deep mourning. In 1947, when more than seven million refugees from Bangla Desh poured into India as a result of President Yahya Khan's genocide and his country Pakistan again attacked India, the whole of India as a nation expressed its iron determination to punish the aggressors. It is nothing but calumny to say that Indians do not form a nation and that they are dormant and quite indifferent to what is happening in their country and in the world.

Serious Drawbacks in Indian Nationalism

However, Indians should be aware of the serious drawbacks in their nationalism and of the need to cover a vast distance before reaching the level of nationalism in Western countries. In this connection Indians should try to set their own house in order to eliminate the following dangers to national unity.

1. *Communalism.* Communalism is one of the greatest dangers to Indian nationalism. Communal quarrels and riots which erupt from time to time in the various parts of the country have engendered avoidable ill feelings and destruction of property.

2. *Caste Consciousness.* India is a democratic state, but Indian society is not democratic, as caste distinctions go against the principle of equality. Even during elections casts differences come to the surface and candidates secretly appeal to vote for them on the basis of caste. Caste makes people narrow-minded and incapable of developing the higher loyalty to the nation.

3. *Linguistic Chauvinism.* Linguistic chauvinism has assumed dangerous proportions in recent years. Linguistic fanaticism

raised its ugly head immediately after the release of the States Reorganisation Commission (SRC) Report in 1955. Linguistic lunacy still continues, and at times it results in disturbances and riots. Before independence, English and Hindi unified Indians. But conditions have changed for the worse particularly since 1955. Large sections of population are against Hindi or English, and this has prevented the country from developing a common language, which can be called national. Loyalty to the regional language has secured an upper hand at the cost of loyalty to a common language. Unfortunately leaders have badly handled the language problem, and done immense damage to national unity.

4. *Regionalism.* Regionalism is another dark spot in the body politic of India. People in the various regions of India have been misled by selfish and short-sighted local leaders to develop loyalty to the region at the expense of loyalty to the nation. To many people, the region is everything, and nation is nothing. Owing to this morbid and myopic attitude, fissiparous tendencies have been strengthened and nationalities have been weakened.

5. *Various Types of Disputes.* Centre-state and inter-state disputes, border disputes and river water disputes have also spelt much harm to national unification.

Remedial Measurers

Remedial Measures at the highest level will have to be adopted to counteract fissiparous tendencies and strengthen national unification.

1. The top-ranking leaders should by their sincerity set good examples to the people in developing centripetal tendencies. Neither by their acts nor by their words the leaders should betray any fissiparous symptoms.

2. Periodical meetings of central and state leaders should be held and steps should be taken to strengthen national unification.

3. True secularism should be practiced and encouraged, and religious tolerance increasingly shown.

4. People should extend full co-operation to their leaders in fighting against the menace of regionalism, communalism and casteism, and in developing national politics in the place of village politics, regional politics, communal politics and caste politics.

These steps can be taken only if there is a real change in the minds and the hearts of the people.

Books for Further Study

1. Agarwal, N.N., *Soviet Nationalities Policy.*

2. Asirvatham, Eddy, *Political Theory*—1957.